THE RAVEN CONSPIRACY
CODE NAME: ICARUS

A Novel by Julian Jay Savarin

Also from JULIAN JAY SAVARIN
And available from Caliber Books

Waiters on the Dance
Beyond the Outer Mirr
The Archives of Haven
Water Hole
Wolf Run
Naja
The Quiraing List
Villiger
Windshear
The Queensland File
Lynx
Gunship
Hammerhead
MacAllister's Run
MacAllister's Task
A Cold Rain in Berlin
Romeo Summer
Winter and the General
A Hot Day in May
Hunter's Rain
Summer of the Eagle
Seasons of Change
The Other Side of Eden
Sunset and the Major
Arena
Red Gunship
Trophy
Pale Flyer
Target Down!
Horsemen in the Shadows
Starfire
The Raven Conspiracy – Code Name: Icarus

THE RAVEN CONSPIRACY - CODE NAME: ICARUS

Copyright 2026 Eagle One Media, Inc.
Original Copyright 2010 Julian Jay Savarin
All Rights Reserved.

No part of this book may be copied or retransmitted without the express written permission of the publisher and copyright holder. Limited use of excerpts may be used for journalistic or review purposes. Any similarities to individuals either living or dead is purely coincidental and unintentional except where fair use laws apply.

Caliber Books is an imprint of Caliber Comics.
For further information visit the Caliber Comics website:
www.calibercomics.com

During World War II, many small units operated unsung, carrying out extremely dangerous missions behind enemy lines, or missions which by their very nature, were extremely hazardous, irrespective. Some of this work was so secret, that even to this day, the existence of some of these units remains unacknowledged.

Raven Squadron might have been one such. Did it exist? No records remain to prove it. But those who survived and those who created it, know. And that, might be dangerous knowledge...

PROLOGUE

Munich, Germany, September 1931. 1000 hours, local.
The woman, in her early twenties, was screaming. It was a long keening, sobbing scream that pierced the nerve ends, far beyond the edge of hysteria.

"*Oh God, no! Please don't take my babies! Please, please, please...*"

The infant twins were a bare month old, their own screams mingling with those of their mother. The young woman, who had taken the children while the mother was being restrained by two heavy-set, ungentle men in fear-inducing uniforms, looked at her with eyes that displayed no pity. Dressed in civilian clothes, but incongruously wearing heavy jackboots beneath her knee-length skirt, the kidnapper would have been unexpectedly attractive, but for the malign poison of the ideology she embraced without question. Without this distortion, it would have been an angelic face, framed by dark wavy hair that was swept back and clipped by a simple brooch from which fell her rich tresses. Instead, she was the embodiment of pure evil.

Two other men, also in civilian clothes, stood in a corner of the room, watching it all with expressionless faces. One wore schoolmasterish glasses.

"These children are the future," the one without glasses said to the mother. He spoke in a harsh voice which lacked all emotion.

These children are abominations, the man with him thought. His eyes were chilling behind his glasses. *I should have them, and the mother, killed.*

He was destined to become the second most powerful man in

Germany.

The struggling, screaming mother turned her tearful, imploring nightmare eyes upon the man who had spoken.

"*Please!*" she begged. "*Think of me! Please don't take my babies!*"

"*For the last time!*" He snarled. "*No!*"

She would never see her children again.

Outside, the dark-haired woman hands the babies over to a priest in a waiting car. The car immediately shoots off. The woman follows with the guards in a second car. A third car, big and ominous, with the man in glasses and the cold-eyed man as passengers, trailed behind.

A few days later, the distraught young mother supposedly killed herself.

Two days after that, the men who had restrained her were themselves dead; each by a single shot to the head.

Galen Private Archives, New York. July, 2006. 1400, local.

Ellen Haines picked up the phone at the first ring. "Ellen Haines."

"Hi, Ellen..."

Her eyes lit up. "Martha!" she exclaimed with pleasure. Then the bright mood vanished. "Something wrong?"

"No, child. Just that old fool acting up again."

Ellen's eyes chilled over.

"What's he want?"

"Too see you."

Her lips tightened. "Why?"

"If I knew that, I'd be tellin' you. Seems important. As I said, he's acting up."

"I'm not being summoned. I'm not coming."

"I'll tell him."

Outskirts of Macon, Georgia, USA. July, 2006.

The big, colonnaded ante-bellum mansion showed its years, like a flawed beauty caught by time, and seemingly faded. Yet, it was in a good state of repair. It's presence had not been dimmed by the years,

THE RAVEN CONSPIRACY – CODE NAME: ICARUS

but despite its continuing use as a home, there was something of the decline about it, as if a long-gone era having hung on for dear life, was finally about to give up the ghost.

In the Southern warmth of the July day, its huge and well-kept garden was a riot of blooms; and like an island on a vast green sea of that pristine lawn, was a recliner beneath a parasol. In the recliner, was an old man well past his eightieth birthday, all in white, with a straw hat upon his head. He appeared to be dozing, but was not. A small table was next to the recliner.

"*Emma-Mae!*" he suddenly yelled in an unexpectedly powerful voice.

From somewhere within the building, an answering female voice could be heard. Eventually, a small but elegant woman, perhaps in her seventies but looking younger, came into the garden. The faded beauty of the house seemed mirrored in her, as if she were herself an indelible part of it. Her hair, tied in a bun, was less grey than would have been expected. There was still abundant evidence of the natural red of her hair.

She smiled fondly as she came up to the old man. "What is it now, Leroy?"

"My grandchild. I want her here. She coming?"

"But, Leroy...she's in New York. She works there, as you know."

"She's not turned into a Yankee yet. I want to see her. She'll come."

"Joshua Leroy Haines...for more of your arguments?" She always called him Leroy, except during moments of emphasis. "You and that child have argued for more times than you've had good words for each other."

"Differences of opinion."

"If that's what you call it."

"Now, Emma-Mae, don't you go giving me an argument. I want to see her!"

"All the way from New York so you two can have another little war?"

"Martha called her yet? You called her? Call her again," he insisted. "She'll come. She's our grandchild. I ought to know something about how she'll behave."

"You never can tell with people...even family. I don't see why it's so important all of a sudden. I'll call her if Martha has not yet...but it does not mean she'll come."

"She'll come."

His wife sighed, giving up. "Alright." As she turned to go, she paused, and gave him a searching look. Then she moved closer to the recliner, gazing down at him with a sudden anxiety. "Are you alright, Leroy?"

"Of course I am alright. Why shouldn't I be?"

"The experience of years," she said, and began to return to the house.

"And tell Martha to bring me my julep," he called after her.

She did not turn round; but there was an oddly pre-occupied look in her eyes.

In the house, she found their black helper in the kitchen. "What's he want this time?" Martha asked.

"He wants me to call Ellen."

"Again?"

"You called her?"

"I did."

"And?"

"She ain't coming. I've not told him."

Emma-Mae Haines sighed. "Now he wants me to call her, to ask her to come down."

"Don't see why," Martha said. "They'll just tear at each other. Like always."

"I think I know why."

Something in her voice made Martha look at her sharply. "Miss Emma, you don't think..."

"I don't want to think about it."

"Do you mind if I say something?"

"Why not? In all your years with us, you've always said whatever you pleased."

"You never fired me."

Emma-Mae smiled, showing some of the beauty that had once broken the heart of many a disappointed suitor.

"I would not dare. And what would we do without you?"

"Get someone else."

"Never. She would not be able to put us in our place."

Martha grinned.

"And what," Emma-Mae went on, "what did you want to tell me?"

"You've been living in this big old house since you married the colonel. Children gone, grandchildren gone. Why don't you..."

"No, Martha. I know what you're going to say. This is our home. We stay here until..." she stopped, killing the rest of the sentence. "Oh," she continued. "He wants his julep." She went out.

"Yes, ma'am," Martha said quietly to herself.

"Hey, you old fool," Martha said, interrupting Haines in a catnap. "Your julep."

Haines brightened. "Ahh. Bless you, Martha," he said as she put down the tray with its tall glass that would not be out of place in a bar. "Real Georgia julep, and in man-sized quantity. The right amount of cognac, and of peach brandy. No one makes it like you. No one." He'd been saying that to her for years.

"No one will put up with you, you mean."

"That too," he agreed with remarkable candor. "So...you fixin' to die off on me, Joshua Haines?"

"What gives you that idea?" Eyes that seemed far younger than their years looked up at her. They did not waver.

"Miss Emma's looking worried."

"She worries too much."

Martha gave him a skeptical look. "Hmm," she said, not believing a word.

"You called my granddaughter yet?"

"Been busy," Martha lied. "But Miss Emma will."

"If she doesn't, you must. It is very important. I must see her."

"One of us will call," Martha said, not promising much.

"Tell me, Martha..." Haines said, changing tack suddenly— "...do...do you hate us for what we've done?"

"What kind of a question is that?"

The young-old eyes still did not waver. "One that I would like you to answer."

"Do you mean you? Your family? Or white folks in general?"

"All of the above."

"No," she said, after a long pause. "To do that, I would have to hate myself. And that...ain't good."

She turned, and left him to it.

Haines stared after her. "Profound. Very profound, and I think I understand. Reality," he continued when she had gone back into the house. "Reality is catching up. I could have done with that in 1941. Hating oneself..."

He took a sip of his mint julep, sighed with pleasure, and put it down. Then he lay back in the recliner.

Galen Private Archives, New York, two days later. 1400 local.

Ellen Haines picked up her phone, just as before, at the first ring. "Ellen..."

"It's me."

"Martha! I'll say one thing, your timing keeping is good. It's exactly 2 p.m."

"That's me. Keeper of time."

"Martha the philosopher."

"Martha the maid telling you to come on down here."

Ellen paused, a slight frown creasing her forehead. "So it's serious?"

"If you call driving your grandma and me crazy...you can say that. The old fool's giving us no peace. So please come down, Ellen. He's got something on his mind, and he is not letting go. There's only one thing worse than a baby that won't stop yelling till it gets its way—that's a mean old man who won't stop yelling till he gets his way. I swear I'll strangle him and end up in jail. Even these days, I don't think they'd be kind to a black woman killing an old white senator."

Ellen gave a soft chuckle. "Alright, Martha. To keep you out of jail."

"Thank you, Ellen. I'm sorry to trouble..."

"For you, Martha, no trouble. You've been a mom to me since my mom died."

Martha went quiet.

"It's true, Martha," Ellen said into the silence. "I owe you plenty."

"I didn't do much."

"You gave me courage. From where I'm sitting, that's plenty. I'll see you in two days."

"Okay."

Ellen was as good as her word. Two days later, Martha picked her up at the airport. "Hey, Mom," Ellen greeted softly as they hugged each other like mother and daughter.

"Now don't you go saying that in the house. He will not like it."

"I won't. I remember the last time. Eight years…not so long ago."

Seeing her eyes grow cold, Martha said as they walked to where the car was parked, "I know that look. No war."

"I come in peace."

When they arrived at the mansion, Emma-Mae hugged her granddaughter no less warmly. "You look more beautiful each time I see you, Ellen…" she said, stepping back slightly to study her grandchild. "…and I get a little older…"

"You'll never look old to me, Grandma."

"And you know the right things to say."

"Only telling the truth. Where is he?"

"His usual place at this time of day, julep in hand."

"Some things never change."

"Ellen…"

"Don't worry, Grandma. I've already promised Martha no war. I'd better get this over with."

"Will you be staying a little…" The words faded, but the plea and the hope, were unmistakable.

"That depends."

Ellen went out into the garden, and found Haines at his usual spot. A mobile handset was on the small table.

"So you came," he said, squeezing a button to raise the back of the recliner, which did so with a low hum. His eyes were neutral.

She stopped a short distance from him. "Not because of you." Her voice held little warmth.

"I guess Martha persuaded you." It was said without apparent rancor.

Ellen did not respond. Instead, she asked, "Why did you ask me here? I had to take special time off. We're busy."

He squinted at her. "How do you like the Galen?"

"You ask me now? I've been there for..." She paused. "Did you have something to do with my getting that job? They don't know I'm Senator Haines' granddaughter, so I hope not."

"I had nothing to do with it. Your intelligence had everything to do with it."

She gave him a speculative look that said she was not sure she believed him. "So tell me...why am I here?"

"Your hostility has not diminished."

"I promised Grandma no war." She deliberately said nothing about Martha. "I'll stick to that promise if you tell me why you called me down here; then I'll be away as quick as I can."

He took a deliberate swallow of his julep. "Damn. But Martha makes this good..."

"*Senator!*" She never called him Grandpa; not since she was fifteen.

Haines fished into a pocket and took out a small bunch of keys with just three on the ring—a big, old-fashioned example about five inches long, a smaller version of the same, and the third was much smaller and could have belonged to anything.

He thrust out the hand with the keys. "Take these."

She stared at the hand. "Your study keys. I've never been allowed in there. Not since..."

"Now I'm giving them to you. Take them!"

After some hesitation, she took the keys from him.

"The big one, as you know," he said to her, "is for the door. The second is for my roll top. It opens the top, as well as the left and right cabinets on either side of my chair. They won't unlock until you first open the roll top. Open the left cabinet. You'll find a valise in there. I got that during my time in France, during the war. Used to be a radio inside. Now there's something else in its place. The small key will open the snap locks. Don't open the valise here."

She stared at him. "Why shouldn't I open it here if you're giving it to me?"

"It would not be a good idea."

"Why?"

"You'll know soon enough." Now the eyes stared at her, as if from a great distance. "I should warn you. That valise is dangerous. To you, to me, to many other people. You can leave it, if you like..."

"You call me all the way down here to tell me of something you want me to take, then you say I can *leave* it?"

"I'm giving you a choice. I owe you that."

"You *owe* me? What *is* in that damned valise, Senator?"

"Look at it, leave it in there for tonight. Your Grandma does not know of its existence. You can't take it on a normal flight back to New York. You can leave early in the morning before she comes out of her room. Keep the keys until then. Take the small one with you, and leave the others with Martha."

She kept staring at him. "What is in that valise?" she repeated. "Political dirt on people you don't like?"

"Hah!" he barked. "If only." He paused. "Your destiny. Maybe."

Ellen made her way to the study she had been barred from entering since that terrible day in her fifteenth year. She stared at the door that had been off limits to her.

"My destiny," she muttered as she put the key into the lock. "Playing games, Senator? You knew that would make me curious."

The lock turned smoothly and she entered, shutting the big door softly behind her. She stood there for some moments, staring about the room that held terrible memories.

She had rushed into the room that day, surprising Haines in the act of locking the left-hand cabinet of the roll top desk.

"*Grandpa!*" she had wailed, going to him for comfort. "*Mom's dead!*"

His reaction had been as shocking, as it had been unexpected.

"*So what?*" he had yelled at her with a brutal savagery. "*How dare you blunder in here without knocking? You are never to come into this study again! You hear?*" He had walked swiftly to her and smacked her across the face. "*Now get out!*" He had snarled.

Ellen raised a hand to the cheek as she remembered. It felt hot.

"Thank you for the memory, Senator," she said in a low voice, "and today, you send me in here. Why?"

She fought back the tears the memory had brought, and went to the big old desk. She first opened the roll top as instructed then lowering herself to one knee, opened the left-hand cabinet.

Shiny with use but in perfect condition, the leather valise gleamed at her.

In the garden, Haines had picked up the handset to make a call.

"Lowell Johnson."

"Lowell," Haines said. "Leroy Haines."

"Senator!" Johnson spoke with undisguised pleasure. "Damn, but you sound like a young man. Younger than me!"

They both laughed.

"The mind is still young," Haines said, "but I think the old flesh is finally giving up the ghost."

"Not you, Senator. You'll see most of us gone before that happens. Can I be of service?"

"Need a favor. Can you spare one of your jets?"

"Senator, without you, there would have been no Johnson Bizjets. Of course I can spare you one. Name your requirement."

"I may need it for an open-ended time, with an absolutely trustworthy crew."

"You've got it. Type of plane?"

"The smallest will do."

"I've got a brand new four-passenger Cessna jet, ready to roll. When do you need..."

"Tomorrow morning."

"No problem. Where to? Europe to revisit old battlefields?" Johnson suggested, joking.

"Not for me, Lowell. My granddaughter. It goes where she asks."

Johnson digested this for some moments. "Got it," he said. "Need security?"

"No. This is to be low key. She'll have unobtrusive protection."

"I...see," Johnson said, not seeing at all. "She'll be with you in the morning."

"We'll be ready."

"And Lowell, I'll cover all expenses."

"Senator," Johnson began, "you saved my business and never took a cent in return. Let me do this."

"Alright, Lowell," Haines said after a pause. "Thank you."

Haines put down the phone just as Ellen came back into the garden. "Have you seen it?" he said to her as she reached him.

"Yes."

He nodded. "Good. You've got your flight back to New York. Private jet in the morning. One of Lowell Johnson's. Martha can drive you to the field. That way, you don't have to subject the valise to security scanners. Lowell's people will handle all formalities. You've got the jet for as long as you need it."

"*What?*"

"You'll understand when you open the valise. Do you have a secure room at the Galen to which you only, have access?"

Eyes narrowed, she said, "Yes."

"Put it in there."

"But..."

"You'll understand everything...in time. You will make your own decisions, based upon what you will learn. You'll find a nigra magazine in the valise..." Haines paused, noting her expression at his use of the word. "I'm too old for you to try and change me, girl," he said, then went on, "There is an article on a boy—I don't use the term racially. Anyone below seventy is a boy to me. He's scarcely older than you. Try and find him. His name is Tad Duchamps II. When you have read the article you'll know why you must find him."

"You're asking me to make contact with a *black* man? That's a first."

"You are entitled to your opinions of me," Haines said, eyes staring at her, "but you're intelligent enough not to allow preconceptions to affect your judgement. Some of us lack that skill."

"An *apology*? After all these years?"

"No. Too late for me."

"I think I prefer that. I'll go see Martha about tomorrow."

"And trust no one."

"Not even this...Tad Duchamps?"

"You should be able to."

She said nothing, turned away, and returned to the house.

"Guess you won't be saying goodbye in the morning," Haines said to himself, watching her go.

He took another swallow of his mint julep, sighed with pleasure, and put it down. Then he lowered the back of the recliner.

After a while, an opaque look came into his eyes as they began to stare into a vast distance.

ICARUS

"I suppose, it could be said it all began with a boy who wanted to fly high; but that would not be the complete truth of it. It is perhaps more accurate to say he was there at the beginning..."

From the Journals of Joshua Leroy Haines

CHAPTER ONE

100 miles from Royal Air Force Shawbridge, Cambridgeshire, England. July, 1941.

The train gasped steam into the warmth of the day as it waited for its passengers to board for their cross-country journey eastwards. Tad Duchamps, kit bag slung from a shoulder with one hand, moved along the corridor towards a still-empty compartment. He had received some curious stares from soldiers and airmen in the occupied compartments, and from those loitering in the corridors, but no one had said anything to him. He had no doubt that their minds were full of questions about him. But he was so excited by the prospect of what lay ahead, this mattered little to him.

Not for the first time, he thought of the RAF-blue uniform he wore. It was not the uniform of his country; for his own country had done its very best to ensure he would never realize his dream; but the dream denied him by his country, had at last become a reality. He now wore the wings of the RAF.

He reached the compartment, and opened the door. As he did so, another airman hurried up. On the man's sleeves were three chevrons topped by a crown. Tucked into the left epaulette of his blue serge battledress, was a forage cap. He too, carried a kit bag.

"That's luck!" the newcomer said. "Still empty." He glanced at the single, thin blue ring on the cuffs of Tad Duchamps' best blue. "Share?" Pause. "Sir?"

"Sure," Duchamps replied.

The other stared in surprise. "You a *yank*?"

Duchamps nodded.

"I've heard a few yanks were over here, but never seen one. Might be some on this train; but never expected to see one like you, in pilot's uniform. No offence."

"None taken."

He glanced past Duchamps. "Better get in fast, man. Or we'll lose this. People looking for a place. *In*...and close the door."

He rushed in ahead of Duchamps who followed with a tiny smile, closing the door behind him.

"They might still look in," the man with the chevrons said, "but if we're still in luck, they'll go on."

Duchamps dumped his bag, and removed his peaked cap as he sat down, placing it next to him. He began to open his tunic. He looked at his new companion, who was already lounging opposite, legs stretched out. He had noted the pilot's wings, and the decoration beneath.

"That medal..." he began, as he removed the tunic and folded it neatly inside out; to then place it on his cap. "Distinguished Flying Medal?"

The other nodded. "Yes."

"You must be good."

"I am." It did not sound like a boast. Then Fernando added with surprising deprecation, "They give these things out if you stand in a NAAFI queue long enough."

Not certain of how to take this response, Duchamps said, "Er...sure. Were you in the Battle?" he added.

"No. Got to the Mother Country too late for that." He sounded disappointed. "I wondered about the accent. Where from?"

"Trinidad." The other grinned. "Land of rum and coca cola."

"So how many kills?" Duchamps leaned forward, a picture of eagerness. "Not many. Five."

"*Five!*" Duchamps did not try to hide how impressed he was. "Fighters?"

"Three fighters, two bombers..."

Duchamp's eyes widened in awe. "*Three* fighters...! Were they...good?"

"I was better. Those 'super Aryans' over there are not so super when a bullet or cannon shell hits. They die just like the rest of us." A coldness had come into the Trinidadian's voice.

"You hate them?"

"I hate what they stand for. That's why I'm here. Imagine what would happen to people like you and me, if they won."

Duchamps gave a bitter little laugh. "I know some people back home who would join them if they won." He held out his hand. "Tad Duchamps."

The other reached forward to shake hands. "Jamie Fernando."

"*Spanish?*"

Fernando, whose gene pool included indentured servants from India, slaves from Africa, Amerindians, and Spanish conquistadores, laughed. "Yeah, man...via India, the Amazon, and Africa. I'm Spanish like you're French."

His was proud of his inherited, straight black hair, which he'd had cut in a manner that left two short wings on either side of a central parting, and which he tended to pass his hand through on occasion. The wings bounced back when he did that.

Duchamps smiled. "Well, I come via a Louisiana pirate, and an African slave. Although the family say we've got some Cherokee blood in there somewhere. Where I come from, blood doesn't count. Color is what matters."

"So you're from the Deep South?"

"You said it. Savannah, Georgia."

"Then what are you doing in that uniform?"

"I wanted to wear Army Air Force chocolate and pinks, but some of the white folks in the military think we black folks are only good for digging latrines. I went to Moton Field in Alabama to get my civilian training. There's a black college there that tries to train as many black pilots as possible. It's in a place called Tuskegee.

"There's a military field nearby, and some folks are trying to start a program for black military pilots. But they're getting hard resistance from the white guys with the say so. Seems black folk just can't cut it to be pilots." Duchamp's voice was full of sarcasm. "And they'll go to the devil himself to prove they're right. I didn't want to wait around while they convinced themselves.

"I heard that the British wanted all the pilots they could get, and that all kinds of people were joining up to fly, many going from the States via Canada. I decided to do it. I thought the British would not be so stupid to say no, if a guy could really fly.

"My family got me some money, and I headed for Canada. When I got there, it was a different world. People spoke to me like a human being, not as if I was some animal to be kicked. If a white girl looked or smiled at me, I could smile back without looking over my shoulder to see where the lynching party was coming from. It was like coming into the light, from a world of darkness..."

Fernando gave a slight cough. "There's a little bit of that here too. Nothing that bad, of course. But some people see people like you and me as 'darkies'. I think they've been watching too many Tarzan flicks."

Both men began to giggle, then burst into roars of laughter. When it had subsided, Duchamps said, "You're crazy, man."

"Of course I am. There's a war on, and I'm in it. Well? Go on..."

"I got through training, made it to fighters..." Duchamps pale brown eyes, inherited from his pirate ancestor, looked inwards at a pleasing memory. "The day I got my wings, I remember thinking of those lying bastards in the military who wanted to make sure there would be no black pilots if they could help it. It felt real good getting those wings. I wished they had been my country's; but my country cheated on me. I just hope the guys at Tuskegee make it, and prove those bastards all wrong."

"If they're like you," Fernando said quietly, "they will."

"Even if they do, the white folks will keep them segregated."

"I tell you, man," Fernando said, "death knows no segregation and up there where you want to be, the bullets and cannon shells don't give a damn where you're from, or what color you're wearing. The holes they make will be the same."

The train had begun to move

Fernando glanced at the corridor. "Well, Tad Duchamps from Savannah, Georgia, looks like we were lucky. People found seats, so let's make ourselves comfortable. It's about two hours to go on this steam job." He removed his battledress blouse and taking a leaf out of Duchamps' book, folded it inside-out, intending to use it as a rudimentary pillow. "I hear they took an old steam loco that used to haul freight, and tagged it to some passenger wagons."

"We're freight," Duchamps said with a grin. "War freight."

"Whatever we are, I'm off to sleep. Oh shit."

"What?"

"The corridor."

Duchamps looked. A white officer in US Army Air Force uniform was staring at them. Because both had removed their tunic and blouse, no badges of rank or wings, could be seen. Duchamps had not put the thin rings of his rank on his shirt epaulettes.

The officer, a second lieutenant, opened the door. "I need this compartment." Fernando looked at him speculatively, but did not move.

Feeling he was in territory where the lynch mob mentality held no sway, Duchamps gave a bright smile. "Georgia!"

The officer stared at him with a frown. "You from Georgia, boy?" The familiar insult did not deter Duchamps. "Yes."

"Yes, *what?* And what are you doing in that uniform? And stand up when an officer speaks to you!"

Fernando had had enough. "What do you want him to do first...sir?"

The officer turned his baleful glare upon Fernando. "And where do you come from?"

"Not Georgia. That's for sure. Don't think I'd like it there."

The officer glared at him some more, before turning back to Duchamps. "If you're really from Georgia, boy, you're in big trouble. I need that compartment!"

"We heard you the first time," Fernando said. "But you're welcome to share with us. Sorry...no segregated places available."

The officer rounded on him. "Are you British?"

"In a manner of speaking."

"Don't they show respect for rank in the RAF?"

"That depends..."

"I'm not standing here debating with you. Both of you...*out!*" They stared at him, and did not move.

"Unless you want to stand there for the next two hours," Fernando said, "you've going to have a problem." He unfolded his blouson, until the wings and the decoration, were prominent.

The officer stared at them in astonishment. Even so, there was a stubborn refusal in his eyes as if somehow, what he was looking at was not real.

"*Three* fighters, and two bombers," Duchamps informed his rude compatriot, rubbing it in. "An ace. I've got none, but I aim to catch up." He unfolded his own tunic to display his rank, and wings. "As Jamie Fernando just said...you can share with us, or stand outside. You're giving no one any orders."

The officer gave Duchamps a poisonous look. "No nigger talks to Leroy Haines like that."

"Wrong country, Leroy Haines. You should have left the lynch rope at home. As a fellow officer, I'm still offering you to share our compartment."

"I'm 'fellow' nothing to you, boy. And I share nothing with you!" Haines walked away, leaving the door open.

"Thanks for closing the door!" Fernando shouted after him. "I think he's on the side of the Jerries," he added drily as Duchamps shut the door again. "The man's a donkey's backside."

Duchamps gave a sigh that carried generations of pain with it. "I met some Canadians on the way over on the trooper;" he said, after a while. "Great guys. I hope I see some of them again. But I hope Leroy Haines is not headed where I am."

"That," Fernando said, "would be shit."

Fernando was twenty-one years old. Duchamps, twenty.

Haines was striding along the thumping, rocking corridor, seething with anger, and feeling humiliated. This made his sense of outrage even worse.

"Goddam niggers!" he muttered to himself. "Don't know their goddam place!"

He crossed into another carriage. He had gone just a few steps when a strong hand reached out, seemingly from nowhere, and hauled him into a compartment that was empty, but for the man in civilian clothes who had dragged him in.

"Where the hell have you been, mister?" the American voice demanded. "And why are you in uniform? The United States is not yet officially at war with Germany. You're on your way to active duty with a Royal Air Force unit in your goddamned *uniform?* Didn't they tell you *anything?*"

Confused by the verbal barrage, Haines was at a loss for words. "I...I..." The man pointed to a suitcase on one of the seats.

"Yours. There's a second civilian suit in there. Change into it. Then put all the contents of that case you're carrying into it. Leave the uniform and the case. I'll attend to them." He drew all the curtains.

"I...I went to the compartment. There were a couple of niggers in there. I was told I'd be met. I did not expect niggers..."

"You have been met. *I'm* the one you're supposed to meet. You went to the wrong goddamned carriage!"

Haines opened his mouth, then closed it without saying anything.

"If you want to live long, mister, *listen* to what you're told. A mistake like that in the wrong place could cost you your life. Remember that in the future. There will be others in civilian clothes joining the unit—Poles, French, Czechs, Danes, Americans, and more. Go with their group. Not the uniformed ones. Do you understand?"

"Yes."

"Now change out of that uniform." Haines did as he was told.

The man took the uniform, folded it neatly, and put it into Haines' old case. He then went to the door, and opened it slightly. "You will not be seeing me again."

He went out, closing the door quietly behind him on the stunned Haines. The train puffed its way towards Shawbridge.

It was the slowing down of the train that roused Fernando.

"Hey! Georgia! I think we're getting close, man." He glanced at his RAF-issue, aircrew watch. "Yep. Two hours dead." He yawned, then stretched.

But Duchamps, keyed up, was already preparing himself and putting his tunic back on. Duchamps had inherited other characteristics from his pirate ancestor. He had a finely-chiseled nose and his hair, when cut short to a particular length, lay flat upon his scalp. He always kept it trimmed that way.

THE RAVEN CONSPIRACY – CODE NAME: ICARUS

He was taller than Fernando, with a deceptively slight, but muscled body. By comparison, Fernando was compact, almost stocky, with a slow grin that belied the dangerous fighter he was in the air.

The train was definitely slowing to a stop.

"Looks like we're there alright," Duchamps said, peering through the window. "There's a small station coming up." He got to his feet, and went into the corridor to peer out. "Yep," he said as he returned. "Air Force vehicles waiting. No sign of that nice lieutenant from Georgia. Guess he found a seat somewhere, among some human beings."

They laughed.

"Wonder if everyone on this train is getting off here," he went on.

"We'll soon know," Fernando said. "Got your kit?"

"Got my kit."

"Well, let's go see what trouble we've got ourselves into." They got off the train and saw some civilians getting off.

"We've got civvies too," Fernando observed.

Duchamps was looking about him, when an RAF sergeant came up to them. He saluted Duchamps, who returned a salute that was half-RAF, half-USAAF. The sergeant gave his effort a curious, tolerant appraisal, then consulted a clipboard, sliding a pencil from its holder.

"Pilot Officer Duchamps?"

"That's me."

The sergeant ticked the name, glanced at Fernando, consulted the clipboard again. "Flight Sergeant Fernando?"

"It's me."

The sergeant ticked the name. "Right, gentlemen. If you'll follow me to your transport."

As they picked up their bags to follow, they could see other NCOs moving through the passengers who had left the train, doing the same.

Something made Duchamps glance round. Just as he did so, he thought he saw a civilian turn quickly away. He frowned.

"Not everyone got off," Fernando was saying. "I think I just saw that lieutenant."

"*What?* Shit. Where?" Fernando took a quick look around. "I don't see him."

"He's with the civilians."

"In *civvies?* You sure, man? He was in uniform when we saw him."

"He sure was. Now, he's in civilian clothes. Or...I'm seeing things."

"Well don't go seeing flies on the canopy up there. Bad for the health. That's an old joke," Fernando added.

"I know."

"I hope you're wrong about that bastard."

"I don't think I am."

"Shit."

"Did you see wings on that uniform?" Duchamps asked.

"No."

"Same here."

"So...what do you think?"

"I think wherever we're going, it's to some place special."

"Well, they need fighter pilots. If they need fighter pilots, I'm happy."

The sergeant was suddenly with them. "Careless talk, gentlemen," he cautioned. "Careless talk."

"Sorry, Sarge," Fernando said.

"Don't apologies to me. Just be glad I'm not the CO. It's very easy to find yourself on the next train out of here."

The sergeant walked on.

"We've been told," Duchamps said. He wasn't smiling.

"We have," Fernando agreed, taking the warning to heart.

Whatever the unit was, they knew, it would be like nothing they had each individually experienced before.

The realization made each retreat into his own thoughts as they went towards the waiting transport vehicles, single-decker Leyland coaches in RAF blue.

RAF Shawbridge was indeed a special place. Even its command structure was special. It had two commanding officers—one British, one American—both of whom wore RAF uniform. Both were pilots, and both wore RAF wings. Both had similar rank. There were no special shoulder patches to overtly identify the American.

The unit was ostensibly a basic training base. Nothing was further from the truth. An extremely specialized combined operations establishment, it was enclosed within a high perimeter fence which was well away from its buildings and asphalt runways, and unobtrusively well-guarded. The interested observer would never get close enough to glean information of any use. There was open ground beyond the perimeter fence to the nearest main road, a good five miles away. A single access road branched from it to the main gate. Squads of personnel on routine "training" exercises within this outside area, were in fact armed guards pretending to be recruits; for despite openly playing its role as a training unit, its commanders were well aware that there were many ways of gleaning intelligence through casual observation, and by other means.

The legend at the main gate proclaimed it to be No. 32 General Training and Maintenance Unit (GTMU). An authentic RAF Station insignia, specially designed for the purpose, adorned the legend. At its center was a raven with golden eyes on a sky blue background, snatching a scroll from a green field beneath. The motto was a single word: "*Knowledge*". Whether the other 31 units existed at all, was debatable.

Operational flights from the station always commenced the first part of their journey by heading in a direction that had nothing to do with their ultimate destination. They always returned from the "wrong" direction. There were diversion airfields, specially allocated for use by unit aircraft too damaged to make it back, or for a decoying, deliberately planned diversion.

The access road skirted a stream for a mile or so. The stream itself meandered its way through a small copse to the north, a good three miles from the perimeter. It was bordered by high shrubbery which at that time of the year, was speckled with brightly colored wild flowers.

The vehicles, loaded with their passengers, rumbled in convoy towards the guarded main gate. In the one carrying Duchamps and Fernando, no one spoke. All were looking out at the wide, virtually empty landscape; all clearly with many questions on their minds; all keeping their thoughts to themselves.

These thoughts were suddenly interrupted by a flurry of

animation. Someone was pointing at a pair of dots, flitting low across the wide expanse of green.

"*Jerries?*" another asked in a tight voice. It was both a question, and a yell of alarm.

"Do you hear any guns, sir?" the sergeant who had escorted Duchamps and Fernando asked. There was a pointed edge to his voice.

Duchamps and Fernando, who were sitting together, looked at each other with straight faces.

"Er...er...no," the questioner replied.

"Can't be Jerries, then, can they? We need to brush up on our aircraft recognition, don't we, sir?"

The gentle manner in which he had spoken made the censure worse. Silence greeted his remark.

By now, the shapes were clearly recognizable as a pair of Hurricanes in tight formation, their engines roaring in a powerful crescendo as they hurtled towards the convoy so low, it appeared they were certain to hit. Some of those aboard actually seemed to be readying themselves for hasty flight.

Then with a deafening scream of Merlins at full chat, the Hurricanes swept above the convoy, banked steeply left in formation and rapidly disappeared, still keeping low.

"*Wow!*" an American voice exclaimed. "Who the hell were those guys? I thought they were gonna hit!"

Excited chatter in several languages indicated that many others had thought so too.

Duchamps and Fernando glanced around the bus interestedly, but remained silent...

"They gave you plenty of room," the sergeant said, deadpan.

"So who were they, Sarge?"

"Your welcoming committee."

"I've never been welcomed like that before. Usually, people run the other way."

Sporadic laughter greeted this.

"Alright, sirs," the sergeant said. "Show's over. Let's settle down."

The station beyond the main gate was a revelation. Built upon the grounds of a former priory, most of the original buildings had still been in reasonable shape when construction of the unit had begun. Restoration was considered more economical than building everything up from scratch. As a result, most accommodation, offices and even kitchens, were housed within the original buildings. There was even a fully repaired chapel. But for the runways, the camouflaged hangars dotted about the place, the military equipment, the aircraft, Shawbridge would have looked almost like an ordinary, ecclesiastical village. A place of prayer had been morphed into a place of war. It seemed wrong, yet at the same time, had a strange congruence.

The 11th century priory had had a checked career down the centuries. It had once belonged to warrior monks, subsequently turfed out and the land appropriated as property of the Crown at the time, to be given over as a private home to a court favorite whose family had used it for generations; until they themselves had fallen out of favor. Then it had become a school up until the first World War, when it served as a military hospital. It was then closed for just under two decades, before being taken over to be turned into 32 GMTU.

There were small clusters of woodland and the stream, doubling back upon itself, entered through a low culvert beneath the perimeter fence from the north, curved westwards through the "village" to form itself into a large pond, stepped itself into a low waterfall of a few feet, before letting itself out again 300 meters from the waterfall, through another culvert. A sentry post with a powerful searchlight was sited at its entrance, and at its exit. A wide, short causeway bridged the pond to end in a graveled path that crossed a vast lawn, to the entrance of the main building. The unit took its name from the priory. It was, without doubt, a beautiful setting.

The convoy came to a halt at the main gate. Armed RAF police boarded each coach, their job to check everyone's ID thoroughly before letting it through.

"They must think we're Germans," someone with a Newcastle accent quipped from the back of Duchamps' coach.

The RAF policeman stared coldly at the culprit. "Are you with ENSA...sir? Come to give us a show?"

"Who...what?"

"Oh. My mistake, sir. I thought you were a comedian."

Fernando glanced at Duchamps, nodding in approval. "That was good," he whispered.

"I'm glad you approve, Flight Sergeant," the policeman, a sergeant from Yorkshire, barked without looking round.

Fernando's eyes opened wide for a brief moment. "How did he..." he mouthed at Duchamps.

"If you're wondering how I knew it were you, Flight," the SP barked on, handing back the ID he had been rigorously inspecting to the person to whom it belonged, "we know everything in this back of beyond. Just so you know, gentlemen,"

It sounded like a warning.

At last, the policeman was satisfied. He got off the coach, and waved it on.

The others were soon in trail.

"Bloody snoop," Fernando muttered, low enough for the sergeant at the front to feign ignorance.

"Will you look at this place!" Duchamps exclaimed softly as the vista began to unfold. "*This* is an RAF base?"

Fernando was grinning. "We've got a cushy number, man. This is a holiday camp."

Their sheepdog sergeant had risen to his feet and stood in the aisle, facing his charges. "In case you're all wondering, gentlemen," he began loudly above the noise of the coach, "whether you've come to a *holiday camp...*" He did not look in Fernando's direction. "...forget it. This will not be a holiday."

That too, sounded like a warning.

"The coaches will go to separate briefings," he continued. "The first and second coaches, with the aircrew, will be stopping soon. You, gentlemen, are the lucky ones going to the CO's briefing. That is all."

He stopped speaking as if a switch had been flicked, turned, and regained his seat, despite the tentative raising of one or two hands. It had not been meant to be a question-and-answer session.

The sergeant was right. He had barely settled in his seat when the two coaches stopped before a classic building that would not have been out of place in Mayfair.

He was on his feet again. "Right, gentlemen! Leave your kit, and follow me." He got off the coach without a backwards glance, and marched towards the entrance.

"Guess we do as he says," Duchamps said to Fernando. "Either that, or get barked to death."

"Or something worse," a voice said behind them as they left their seats.

They looked into smiling blue eyes, beneath gleaming blond hair. "Peter Farley-Wyatt," he announced in a public school accent, introducing himself. "PW for short, or Pew, if you prefer...but not blind." He grinned as they shook hands while the other passengers squeezed past to get out. On his cuffs, was the slightly broader ring of a Flying Officer.

"I'll take Pew," Fernando said, straight-faced. "Fernando. James, or Jamie."

"Righto, James."

Duchamps shook the proffered hand. "Duchamps. Tad..."

"For?"

"Thaddeus. Blame my mom."

"Won't blame her, old boy. Good name..."

"Come on, ladies!" Came the sergeant's voice from beyond the coach. "Don't keep the COs waiting!"

"Did he say COs?" Farley-Wyatt asked.

"What I heard," Duchamps said.

Fernando grinned. "Perhaps they think we need two to keep us under control."

"He sounds just like my old drill instructor," Pew said.

"I had a Scottish DI," Fernando said. "He was not human."

"My Canadian DI was a MacDonald..." Duchamps began.

"Scottish!" Fernando and Pew said together. They nodded sagely at each other. "Same mother! They all have the same mother, wherever they come from..."

The sergeant was at the coach. "You ladies can have your knitting party later. Now *move!*"

They moved.

* * *

With its highly polished floor, and lofty ceiling, the vast briefing room could have been the ballroom of a stately home. In it many incarnations, it had indeed been one.

Now, sixty RAF-issue chairs, arranged midway in neat rows of five with a central aisle, were dwarfed by its generosity of space.

They faced a low dais with a plain table upon it, at one end of the room. Two chairs were placed a little to the back, on either side of the table. To the left of the table was a high and wide, closed door.

"Take your seats, gentlemen!" the sergeant barked. His voice echoed. "And try to remain silent!"

Sixty chairs were soon occupied. An expectant hush fell upon the room. The sheepdog sergeant stood to once side, alert eyes scanning like a teacher hunting out possible for mischief-makers. No one gave him an excuse.

A minute or so later, he bawled, "*'tenn'hahn!*" His voice turning upwards, to end in a hoarse scream.

As if on cue, the wide door opened and two wing commanders entered, as sixty chairs rumbled as one, and sixty pairs of feet boomed to attention. They sixty-first, the sergeant's, outdid them all with a slam that would have caused the polished floor to warp in pain if could feel.

The two officers were tall men, one slim, the other solidly built. Dark hair peeped from beneath both peaked caps. Each had a row of the same decorations beneath his wings: DSO, DFC, AFC.

The slim one had a bar to his DSO, in effect, two DSOs.

"At ease, gentlemen," he said, in English accents. "Please be seated." There was a laid-back air about him, as if the world in general should be looked upon with weary amusement. "And Sarn't Morris..."

"*Sahr...!*"

"No need to bawl them out..."

"*Sahr!*"

The wing commander gave the sergeant a tolerant glance. "Welcome to Royal Air Force Shawbridge, gentlemen," he continued to his audience as sixty seats were regained. "My name is Hamilton and next to me, is Wing Commander Murchison.

"We are the joint commanders of 32 GMTU. The more observant

among you will already have noticed that this is a somewhat unusual establishment. The less observant...we'll wait for you to wake up."

He paused as smiles broke out on many faces.

"We are housed within some rather classic buildings, in beautiful surroundings," he went on. "Treat them as you would your own homes...on second thoughts, perhaps not." There were a few subdued chuckles. "We have what is virtually a little town, with all amenities necessary for the effective administration of a fully self-contained unit...from a comprehensively equipped gymnasium—we expect our personnel to be fit—to a full-grown NAAFI store and canteen-cum-tea-shop, and every other section you would expect on a standard Royal Air Force station, plus a few more. There are also three mobile NAAFI units. These vans do rounds at regular intervals, and visit every nook and cranny on the station. You won't feel deprived."

Hamilton added that with a dry smile.

"We depart slightly from normal custom," he continued. "in our messing arrangements. The Sergeants' Mess has become the NCO Mess, for *all* NCOs, irrespective of rank. The Airmen's Mess remains as normal, without the junior NCOs. The Officers' Mess has become the Aircrew Mess. This means aircrew of *any* rank. There are specific reasons for this, which we won't go into here. There are, of course, Waafs on the station..."

A cheer greeted this.

Hamilton took no offence. "I thought that might put a few smiles on faces. However, as with Royal Air Force custom, the Waaf quarters are strictly out of bounds..."

"Shame!" came some voices.

"Sorry, gentlemen, but we do not deviate from that rule. Female officers are housed within the Aircrew Mess...and, before you cheer, *their* quarters are also strictly out of bounds. They have their own separate wing in the Mess."

Groans all round.

"However," Hamilton continued in the same tolerant manner, "all other areas within each Mess, are shared. This place may have had ecclesiastical beginnings, but we are not a convent..."

"Thank God for that!" someone said.

"He obviously heard your prayer," Hamilton said, looking directly at the speaker, a Frenchman called La Roche.

There was a round of laughter, some of it directed at La Roche.

"Thank you, gentlemen..." Hamilton interrupted, then waited for the laughter to subside. It did so quickly. "One other point about the NAAFI—it is of course open to all ranks, including the canteen—which is more of a restaurant—and the tea shop. Now that you've had your fun, to the reasons why you are here. Being sent to these salubrious surroundings has its price and sometimes, this may be very high."

He paused deliberately, to allow that to sink in. Expressions became very serious as everyone was suddenly closely attentive.

"I won't beat about the bush," Hamilton went on. "Each of you was selected because your original units considered you to be the best of the bunch. Your confidential files were minutely scrutinized. Each of you possesses qualities which will be of valuable use to us. What we are doing here will not make the news. It cannot. And what you will be asked to do will be done without overt acknowledgement. If you die on a mission, it will go unrecorded in the outside world. Any decorations you may receive will not be, and cannot be, gazetted. If you choose to remain here, you are ghosts. If after what you have so far heard you decide this is not for you, no shame will be attached to you. However, you will not speak of having been here, nor of anything you may have seen during your short stay. The penalties for breaking this rule will be severe...and that, is an understatement. I trust I have your undivided attention."

Hamilton's expression had gone from that of the tolerant joker, to that of an unforgiving commander. Everyone took note of that change for future reference. Here was a man who would have no tolerance for those who broke the rules of the unit.

"More than ever before," Hamilton said, "you must be able to rely upon each other; totally. Failure to do so *will* result in the loss of life...yours, or that of the person relying upon you. I cannot stress this sufficiently. There will be occasions when the outcome will be out of your hands; but for all other occasions, you will be held responsible. If anyone has any further doubts after we are finished here, see Sergeant Morris. You will be returned to your former unit with all speed. We will never have seen you, and you will never have seen us."

He paused again, eyes raking the sixty faces before him. "I have respect for a person who knows this may be too much and owns up to it; than the person who is beset by doubts carrying on regardless until at a later date, these doubts cost a life, or the failure of a mission. Such a person would be better off not returning alive. It is not courage to soldier on, when you know you cannot give of your best. It is courage to accept it. It is also perfectly normal to be afraid. Someone with a healthy dose of the survival instinct is more likely to complete a mission alive, than someone who does not. A dead fool is no use to man, or God. I therefore ask again...anyone here with any doubts?" His gaze tracked among them. "This is your chance to speak up. *No one*—and I include myself—will think the less of you for it."

No one spoke. All looked back at him without wavering.

He gave a short nod of satisfaction. "Good show." He glanced at his companion. "Anything to add, Bob?"

Murchison shook his head slowly, eyes on the aircrew before him.

"As you can see," Hamilton went on to his new intake, "the wing commander is a man of few words. That can be a good thing, or a bad thing. It depends on whether you annoy him. Take my advice. Don't. Thank you, gentlemen. Sarn't Morris will take it from here and get you settled in." He paused. "The following will please remain— Messrs Farley-Wyatt, La Roche, Fernando, Duchamps, Lucek, Graves, van Hoon, Levin..." He continued until twelve names had been called. "The rest of you please follow Sarn't Morris. Thank you."

They all rose to their feet.

After Morris had led the others out, Hamilton said, "Take those worried looks off your faces...unless you're all guilty of something," he quipped in passing. "Gentlemen, you are to form the nucleus of what will be known as Raven Squadron. There will be no squadron number and record of your activities—if set down at all—will be accessible to but a very few. Your eventual numbers will be as many, or as little as necessary. You will operate a variety of aircraft. You will operate almost exclusively, within and over, enemy territory." He noted the sudden changes in their expressions. "You still have an opportunity to say no...but this is your last chance. And bear in mind what I said about having the courage to do so."

He stopped, waiting.

No one spoke.

He nodded again. "Very well, gentlemen. You have just signed what you may perhaps one day come to think of as the devil's pact. From now on, everything you do and say must be done in the light of what I have told you. If you go off the station, consider yourselves surrounded by invisible walls inhabited by countless ears, all interested in listening to what you have to say. Keeping mum is not just a saying; It is an article of faith. It is an unbreakable rule.

"You will talk to no one about any mission you be may assigned, beyond those actually involved in that particular mission. That includes those in this room with you at this moment. That includes myself, and Wing Commander Murchison, if neither of us is specifically involved." He looked at the surprise on their faces. "I believe you are now beginning to understand." He turned to Murchison. "Call them in, Bob."

Murchison went to the door, and opened it, standing back for whoever it was to enter.

"Some people with whom you will be working," Hamilton was saying, when three people came into the room: two men, and a very young woman. There were gasps of astonishment as they all rose to their feet.

Tad Duchamps stared almost transfixed at the woman, instantly smitten without realizing it. Helle Andersen, just eighteen was, to Duchamps, a vision of beauty he dared not consider would ever want to be anywhere near him. Yet, in the classic dream of the hopelessly struck, he also dared to hope. He watched in awe as she went to one of the chairs on the dais, and sat down

The second person to enter dragged his uplifted spirits as swiftly back down. It was, he felt, an act of cruelty by a malevolent fate; for the person who entered was none other than the second lieutenant from Georgia, still in civilian clothes. The third person was the one who caused the loudest gasps.

A major, in Luftwaffe uniform.

"Yes," Hamilton said. "He *is* German, the uniform is genuine and he is indeed, a major in the Luftwaffe. He is also a member of that highly endangered species: the tiny German resistance movement. We know him as Karl-Gustav Stroeme. Whether this is his real name is immaterial. Apart from being an exceptional fighter pilot, Major Stroeme has other skills you will soon get to know."

They stared at the enemy uniform, at the blond hair showing beneath the high sweep of the peaked cap, the pale blue eyes; the perfect epitome of Hitler's aryan *Übermensch*.

"Those of you having difficulty assimilating the fact that the major may have shot down some of our own, should consider this— *we* have shot down many of his comrades. Yet...he is here among us...to work with, *and* for us, at no small risk to himself, and his family and friends back home in Germany. Jerry would make short work of them, if he but suspected the truth; and not in a very pleasant way. The major's own fate if found out, needs no explanation. Consider him a bona fide member of Raven Squadron. He is among the ghosts."

Hamilton turned briefly, towards the young woman, who stood up, and came forward.

"Let me introduce Miss Helle Andersen," he said. "Miss Andersen has just passed her eighteenth birthday; but do not allow her extreme youth to fool you. She is a member of the Danish underground, and has been fighting Jerry longer than many of you have. According to reports, she is a fierce fighter. She also has a remarkable aptitude for languages among which...is German. Andersen may, or may not be, her real name. She too, is a member of Raven Squadron. And last, but not least..."

Hamilton turned to the second lieutenant from Georgia.

"...our third new member of Raven Squadron...Second Lieutenant Leroy Haines, USAAF. Mr. Haines is also good with languages. In his case, French is the strongest, but he also has an extremely good capability in German. Enough to comprehensively fool a native, under certain circumstances. He is in civilian clothes because most of the time, that will be his operational 'uniform'."

Tad Duchamps and Jaime Fernando were looking at Haines with a wariness they would have reserved for a psychotic dog. If asked why, they would not have been able to explain it.

Hamilton had missed neither Duchamps first look at Helle

Andersen, nor of the looks both he and Fernando had given Haines; nor for that matter, Haines' own undisguised expression when he had seen Duchamps among the Raven Squadron pilots.

"Mr. Duchamps," Hamilton now said.

Duchamps focused on the wing commander. "Sir?"

"I am most impressed by you, Mr. Duchamps. Hard not to be. Anyone who has managed to overcome the considerable obstacles deliberately placed in your path to prevent you from achieving your goal, deserves respect. The manner in which you did not lose sight of that goal, and succeeded in achieving it in a way sufficiently impressive to get you here, is to be strongly commended. It is excellent to see His Majesty's wings upon your chest. You deserve them."

"Thank you, sir!"

Duchamps felt the chest in question expand. He wished his parents could have been there to hear Hamilton's words. In their absence, it gave him great satisfaction that Haines was there to witness the praise from a white man, to whom Haines was very much a subordinate.

Not in Georgia now, boy, he mentally said to Haines. *Go suck a lemon.*

Hamilton's voice broke into that pleasurable thought. "Mr. Duchamps, as of this moment, you are improperly dressed."

Duchamps was stunned. "*Sir?*"

But Hamilton was smiling. "It would seem that your former CO has a high regard for you. He recommended your promotion to Flying Officer. As soon as you find the opportunity, rectify that improper uniform. There is a tailor on the station."

Duchamps grinned his astonished pleasure. "Yes *sir!*" Both Pew and Fernando smacked his shoulder,

"Well done, that man!" Pew said.

The other pilots congratulated him unreservedly. "Flight Sergeant Fernando," Hamilton interrupted.

Fernando looked at the wing commander, wondering what was coming next.

"Sir?"

"You, I'm afraid, are also improperly dressed. It would seem that *your* former CO appears to think that you are fit to be commissioned."

"*Me*, sir?"

"You, sir. And don't sound so shocked, man. Being an officer is not that bad. As you can't be sent off to learn to become an officer, you'll have to make do with raiding the stores to find yourself the proper badge of rank, Pilot Officer Fernando. Congratulations."

"Er...yes, sir. Thank you, sir." Fernando looked stunned.

Firm footsteps were heard approaching from the main entrance.

"Sarn't Morris on his way back," Hamilton said. "He will get you settled in. Make most of the time. Tomorrow, your new life begins. Thank you, gentlemen."

He stepped off the dais and came towards them, to shake hands with each.

As did Murchison, Helle Andersen, and Stroeme.

Haines came too, but managed to avoid shaking hands with both Duchamps and Fernando.

Both Hamilton and Murchison saw it, as did Helle Andersen who had given Duchamps a wide smile when they had shaken hands.

After the pilots had gone, Hamilton said to Murchison, "Bob, I believe you want to have words with Second Lieutenant Haines."

"Sure do," Murchison said in a voice that should have warned Haines. "Very well. I'll leave you to it. Helle, Karl, if you please."

After they too had gone, Murchison turned hard eyes upon Haines. "What's your problem, mister?"

"I don't follow, sir."

"In a monkey's ass you don't!" Murchison snapped.

"Permission to speak freely, sir!"

"Speak!"

"Where I come from," Haines began, "we don't abide by, or mix with nigras...except to have them work for us. They have their place, and know it. Coming from the North sir, you don't understand..."

"Permission rescinded!"

"But sir...!"

"*I've heard enough, damn you!*" Murchison shouted. "Let me tell you something, mister...sure I come from the North, but I have Southern blood in me! I come from a family that once owned slaves. The difference between us, mister, is that I don't consider it something to be proud of. You want to refight the Civil War, wait till you're back home! So get this into your skull. In *this* outfit, there is *no* room for any of your good ol' Southern ways. You're *not* down South now. You're across the goddamn ocean! So you leave your crap where it belongs! The people who sent you here did so because they believe you may be of some worth to us. God knows why; but if you are ever responsible, because of your attitude, for a fouled-up mission or worse, a single death...then mister, I'll hunt you down for as long as it takes. *You got that loud and clear, mister?"*

Haines stared back at him, clearly outraged, but smart enough not to object.

"*Have you got that?*" A fuming Murchison barked, emphasizing each word.

His voice echoed round the vast room "Yes, *sir!*"

"Now get the hell out of my sight!"

Murchison stood there alone when Haines had left, waiting for his anger to subside.

"Sweet Jesus!" he said. "Why that bastard?"

Outskirts of Macon, Georgia, USA. July, 2006.
"But you got it all wrong, you goddamned Yankee idiot!" Haines shouted, cackling. "All goddamned wrong! You looked in all the wrong places. Dumb idiot!"

In the kitchen, Martha and Ellen were chatting. Both heard the noise in the garden.

"What's up with that old fool now?" Martha asked rhetorically.

"Is it always like that?" Ellen asked.

"Getting worse. He's losing it fast, if you ask me."

Ellen said nothing to that. Neither of them went to check on Haines. "Mom..." she began quietly.

"Honey, I told you not to call me that in here."

"He's in the garden, and Grandma's upstairs in her room. We can talk normally. I'm not flying back to New York tonight."

Martha beamed. "Ooh...I hoped you would stay."

"I'm leaving early in the morning, and you're driving me to Lowell Johnson's airfield...if you don't mind."

"Of course I don't mind, child." But Martha was surprised. "You're going by private jet?"

"Something the Senator fixed."

Martha's eyes were questioning. "Why?"

"I don't know myself."

"You be careful, Ellen. I don't trust that old man."

"Neither do I."

Early the next morning, Ellen went into her grandmother's bedroom to kiss the barely awake Emma-Mae goodbye. She then went into Haines' study to pick up the valise, locked the room, and hurried down to the waiting car.

Martha was already at the wheel, and had the engine running.

She stared at the valise as Ellen put it behind the seats. "He *gave* you his old radio from the war?"

"You know about this?" Ellen asked in surprise as she got in.

"Only seen it once. Way back. Never seen it again...till right now. Why would he give it to you?"

"I'm asking myself the same question," Ellen replied, saying nothing about what was now supposed to be in there. She handed the astonished Martha the two remaining keys. "He said I should leave these with you."

"Hm," Martha said, taking the keys and putting them into a pocket of the jeans she wore. She put the car into gear. "Remember what I said yesterday. Just you be careful, child."

"Yes, Mom," Ellen said. They smiled at each other.

The journey to Johnson Bizjets took half an hour. When they arrived, the car was directed to the waiting Cessna, whose engines were already spooled up. They gave off a barely perceptible whine.

Martha stopped the car close by.

She stared at the spanking new jet as they climbed out. "My. That's a pretty little bird."

"It looks good," Ellen agreed.

A big man with greyish hair, in a suit, descended from the aircraft and came towards them.

"Ellen. Martha. Haven't seen you two for a while. Not since you took off for New York, Ellen."

"Hi, Mr. Johnson," Ellen said as they shook hands.

"Mr. Johnson," Martha greeted as Johnson also shook hands with her.

"Your plane awaits," Johnson said with a grin to them. "Mike Nolan and Mary Adams are your crew. Mary's the captain. They'll take good care of you." Johnson was looking at them both.

"I'm not going," Martha said.

"Oh. I see. Well..." He looked at Ellen. "Whenever you're ready."

"I'm ready." Ellen gave Martha a warm hug. "'bye, Mom," she whispered, low enough so that Johnson could not hear.

"You take care," Martha said in a normal voice, eyes suspiciously moist.

"I will."

With a slight wave, Ellen went to the aircraft and climbed in. She did not look back.

"Beautiful girl," Johnson said, watching as the staired exit raised itself to fit neatly into the aircraft's body.

"You talking about your plane?"

"Same, dry Martha," Johnson said with a smile. "But this time, I'm talking about our Southern beauty, Ellen Haines."

They watched as the jet taxied to its allocated runway where it paused at the threshold. Then the engines swelled to a soft roar and the little jet scuttled rapidly down the runway to pull steeply into the air.

"Always a pleasure to watch Mary take off," Johnson remarked. "Clean every time."

Martha watched as the jet grew rapidly smaller, and said nothing.

Aboard the aircraft, after first ensuring that the pilots were fully occupied, Ellen opened the valise. The first thing she saw was the magazine that was primarily aimed at a black readership. It was a year old.

She took it out slowly, and shut the valise. It did not take long to find the article which opened with a two-page spread, one of which was a picture of a man in jet fighter pilot's gear, standing by his F-15.

"He looks good," she commented.

Captain Tad Duchamps II (30), the caption proclaimed.

THE RAVEN CONSPIRACY – CODE NAME: ICARUS

Former Air Force pilot Tad Duchamps II, the article began, and grandson of one of Georgia's most famous sons, Tad Duchamps, WWII hero and air ace, is on a quest: to unravel the truth behind the mysterious shooting of his grandfather in France, several years ago. His grandfather it appears once belonged to a squadron no one seems to have heard of...until now. It was called Raven Squadron. He was never on the squadron he is supposed to have served with. Even this small amount of knowledge is shrouded in mystery. Tad is convinced that there are people who are determined to ensure he never finds out more. He has deliberately resigned his commission—so ending a highly promising career—to devote his time to finding out the truth...

Ellen stopped reading. She had to, because her hands were shaking violently. When they had at last stopped, she closed the magazine and placed it back in the valise.

Then she sat back in the comfortable seat, feeling a deep sense of foreboding as the Cessna winged her towards New York.

CHAPTER TWO

Thirty miles out from Teterboro airport, New Jersey. July 2006.
The Cessna captain, Mary Adams, left the flight deck of the small twin-jet to go into the passenger cabin.

Ellen was dozing on one of the four sumptuously upholstered seats, her left leg propped against the locked valise. She had deliberately chosen to sit back towards the cockpit, so that the pilots could not see what she was doing, should one of them decide to glance back.

She opened her eyes as Mary Adams approached.

"Hope I'm not disturbing..." the pilot began.

"No. No. I was just dozing lightly."

"How's the flight, Miss Haines?"

"Wonderful. So smooth, it feels as if we're not moving."

Mary Adams smiled. "Well we are, or I'd be worried. I love this plane. Very sweet to fly. We're a few minutes from Teterboro..." she began to add.

"*Already?*" Ellen peered out of her window. "That was quick."

"We flew high. We've been in our descent for a while. So fasten...oh, I see you've done so."

"Never took it off."

"You don't seem like someone who's afraid to fly."

"I'm not. I just thought if I fell asleep, I might as well keep it on, in case we landed while I was still out."

Mary Adams smiled again. "Wise decision. A helicopter will be waiting to take you wherever you want to go."

"A helicopter? Whose idea was that? My grandfather's?"

"I don't know. My boss has arranged it all."

Perhaps her boss had arranged it, Ellen thought; but she saw the hand of her grandfather behind it.

"I'll go to my office," she said. "There's a landing pad on the roof of the building."

"Then that's perfect. We're at your disposal for as long as you want. We'll be staying at Teterboro. It's convenient, and we can make sure the plane is secure."

"It will be fine at the airport, won't it?"

"Yes. But we have instructions. Here..." She handed Ellen a card. "Just call me when you want the jet prepared."

Ellen took the card with the embossed golden wings. "Thank you. I will. But I'm not sure..."

"No problem. We can wait for as long as you wish. The helicopter is also available when you want to come to the airport. It's part of the service."

"Thank you," Ellen said again, not really sure what else to say. The Cessna began to bank to the left.

"Time to get back to *my* office," Mary Adams said. "Looks like we're preparing for the landing." With a parting smile, she returned to the flight deck.

Ellen stared at the valise. She wondered what could be so important and dangerous to drive her grandfather to using his connections to arrange putting a private jet and a helicopter at her disposal.

"I should just dump this in a strong room, and forget all about it," she told herself.

But she knew she would not. She had already decided that one of the first things she would do when she got to her office, was to try and make contact with Tad Duchamps.

RAF Shawbridge, July 1941.

As the coach had driven them towards the Aircrew Mess, the nucleus of Raven Squadron had properly introduced themselves to each other. Tad Duchamps found that he liked them all. Each had his own peculiarities, and to Duchamps, that made them all the more interesting. A world very different from the segregated one he had left was opening up to him. Georgia and its pain were drifting further and further way, the sole beacon of memory worth preserving being that of his family.

As he now looked about him, he began to spot the strategically sited, well-camouflaged anti-aircraft gun emplacements, there for the defense of the station. There were many.

Others had spotted them too.

"More guns than a battleship," Fernando commented. "And a lot more guns than on my old station."

"We must be important," someone said.

"We're not," Farley-Wyatt remarked in sober tones. "This place is."

"Whatever we are," Josip Duczek began in his heavily-accented English, "this place makes up for it. Look at those buildings! They remind me a little of some mansions in my country."

Already a pilot with the Czech air force he had escaped, walking almost all the way across occupied Europe to southern France where he had been taken over the Pyrenees to safety, by an escape organization run by a Frenchman whose codename was Jock.

"Then you'll be right at home," Brig Levin said to him. "Say, Tad," he went on, "what's it like to be a Flying Officer?"

"Now I'll be able to see the ring without squinting."

Their laughter rang through the coach. Even the sheepdog Sergeant Morris, sitting away from them up front, permitted himself a secret smile.

"And you, Jamie, old son," Farley-Wyatt said to Fernando who was sitting across the aisle, "an officer and gentleman to boot."

"Don't know about the 'gentleman' bit. I'm a Trinidadian ruffian, man."

More laughter echoed as the coach came to a halt before the Mess. Duchamps looked out, and frowned. "Goddamn."

"What, old boy?" asked Pew Farley-Wyatt from the seat behind him.

Fernando had peered across to where Duchamps was looking. A small group in civvies was standing next to another coach. "That bastard," he said.

"What bastard?" Pew enquired.

"Haines," Duchamps replied without enthusiasm. "What's wrong with him?"

"Everything," Fernando replied for Duchamps. "He'd better keep out of my way. Trini ruffians have a way of dealing with people like that."

"Steady, old son. You can't whack a fellow officer, no matter what the provocation..."

"I did not hear that, gentlemen!" came Morris' stern admonishment.

"You did not hear that, Sarge," said Pew.

They filed off the vehicle, taking their kit with them.

Duchamps moved a little way from the coach to stare up at the classic, ancient building that would be his new home.

"Damn," he said in admiration. "That is some Mess. With its own stream too. If you could see me now, Ma and Pa. Living high with the white folks."

"Don't fly too high, boy," a hostile voice said next to him. "You might get too near the sun. Remember what happened to the last one who tried."

Duchamps snapped his head round, but Haines was already walking away.

Duchamps watched him as the fellow Georgian increased distance, feeling a powerful rage of centuries welling within his heart.

"I swear to God," he remarked softly, voice tight with the anger he felt.

"Swear to what, old son?"

Almost guiltily, Duchamps turned to see Pew Farley-Wyatt smiling at him. "Talking to yourself," Pew continued. "Not good. Not good at all. The station doc might think you're a candidate for the funny farm if you're not careful."

"Didn't you see him?"

"See who, whom, what?"

"Haines."

"Nary a sign. Was he here?"

"Yes." Duchamps looked around, but Haines was nowhere to be

seen.

Pew gave Duchamps a sideways look. "And the problem?"

"Haines is from Georgia. Like me."

"Someone from home. Good show..."

"Not quite, Pew. Where I come from, people like Haines hate people like me."

"Ah. That sort."

"Yes."

"Not good." The words carried a wealth of meaning. "Come on, old boy. Forget Haines. He's not a pilot and thus, not really one of us...which can only be to the good. Now let's go see where they've decided to billet us in this monstrous pile."

"Monstrous? It's fantastic."

"My little joke. This place was once a priory—monastery—monstrous... Ah, bad joke."

"Yes."

"You could be more appreciative."

Tad Duchamps grinned. After Haines' little slice of malevolence, Pew was like a breath of fresh air.

"The wing commander calls us ghosts," he said to Pew as they walked towards the Mess. "Any real ones in there?"

"We do have our haunted houses in old Blighty...or so some people insist. Never met a ghost meself. As for here...you never know. We might find a few monks patrolling the corridors..."

"I'd prefer not to," Duchamps said with feeling.

"What? Big, bold fighter pilot frightened of ghosts? They're probably scared of us, if they exist."

"Big bold fighter pilot wants his hair to stay flat on his head."

Pew grinned at him. "And talking of hair raising...I saw that look you gave the comely Miss Andersen. Must say she appeared to reciprocate. Warm smile, if I ever saw one."

"I just...looked at her."

"We *all* looked at her. She looked *through* us, but looked at you. And as for that smile..."

"She's just a kid."

"Says the old man of what...nineteen?"

"Twenty."

"On bad luck. *Really* old, that. Besides, according to the wingco, she's been teaching Jerry a thing or two about fighting. Face-to-face, old son. Not like us in the vaulting blue. God knows what she's seen. And speaking of angels, what do I spy?" Pew was looking at someone just entering the Mess. It was Helle Andersen. "Perhaps you'll see her at dinner. Lucky sod."

But by the time they had themselves entered, Helle Andersen was gone. Duchamps had the feeling It would be a while before he would see her again.

The converted Mess was so big, there were more bedrooms than people to occupy them. Duchamps walked into his, and was impressed. Not overly spacious yet at the same time, giving him plenty of room. Its high ceiling had been retained; and though the bedrooms had been constructed to give more sleeping quarters per square foot, the original décor from its time as a family home, had been renovated. The only incongruities were the standard issue bed, and furniture. A single large window looked down upon the lawn from the third story.

Duchamps liked what he saw. "Luxury!" he exclaimed in a happy whisper.

The bed was freshly made, with neatly tucked sheets. The room was spotless. He put down his kit then sat on the bed, testing it for softness.

"Not soft, not hard. Perfect."

He got to his feet, and began to unpack. He was nearly done, when a knock sounded.

"It's open."

Farley-Wyatt opened the door and poked his head through. "Am I interrupting?"

"Nope. Come on in."

Pew entered. "Well? How do you like it? You've got the end room too. You lucky, lucky sod."

"It beats home." Duchamps began putting his stuff away.

Pew nodded, then leaned against a wall and watched him work. "If I say so meself, quite an impressive pile. All the Ravens are on this floor. I'm two doors down. Jamie's next to me. You've got Brig Levin as your next door neighbor." He peered around. "This room's bigger than mine. We are indeed the lucky one." He said this without rancor.

"Must be my pretty face."

Pew grinned. "I wouldn't go that far, old son."

"Thanks, Pew," Duchamps remarked drily.

"We-el, perhaps there's a little someone who thinks it's pretty..."

"In my dreams."

"Dreams can come true..." Pew warbled.

"That," Duchamps said with feeling, "is not singing."

"And a hard man to boot," Pew said.

There was another knock on the door. "Step right in," Pew called.

Fernando pushed the door open, entered, and looked around. "It's bigger."

"My very words," Pew said in triumph.

Fernando looked at Duchamps. "The wingco loves you."

"Er..." Pew said, "...I think that may be someone else."

"Who do you mean?" Fernando enquired with sharp interest.

Pew tapped at his nose. "Know what the wingco said. Mum's the word."

"Don't mind him," Duchamps said to Fernando. "It's that Limey mind of his."

"Don't call me Limey," Pew said cheerfully. "It rhymes with scurvy. Ugh!"

"I'm getting worried about you, Pew."

"You're late. My parents were worried about me the day I was born."

"And the man's an officer," Fernando commented in fake wonder.

"Of course," Pew said. "All officers are mad. And that includes you two." He gave them his widest grin.

A third knock came and Levin entered. "If there's a party, I want in. Hey. This place is..."

"Big," Duchamps said. "I know. Those two beat you to it."

"Why you lucky..."

"Pew beat you to that."

Levin made a quick reconnaissance of the room. "Perhaps they're planning to give you command of the first bunch of Ravens."

"That would be crazy. I have the least experience. Jamie here is already an ace. Josip has been fighting since they took his country. Karol shot down three when they marched into Poland. Pew's got two and... What did you call it, Pew?"

"A probable. The bugger ducked into cloud trailing a nice black tail headed by a bonfire. But never saw him actually explode, or hit...the bloody sod."

"There you go. Like I said. It would be crazy to give me command. I wouldn't give it to me."

"And I don't want it," Fernando said. "Nor me," from Pew.

"Same here," Levin added. "So who?"

"I do like mysteries," Pew said. "I know," he went on with a mad brightness in his eyes. "They'll give it to our tame Hun. As a major, that makes equivalent to Squadron Leader, and senior to all of us..."

"Even for you, man," Fernando said, "that's a mad idea."

"You firing on all cylinders there, Pew?" Levin asked looking at him as if certain Farley-Wyatt's brain had gone awol. "The guy's a full-blown Luftwaffe pilot!"

"*Our* Luftwaffe pilot," Pew corrected.

"And how does he command the Ravens when he's busy flying for the enemy?"

"That is a hitch," Pew admitted. "Oh well. Back to the drawing board." The fourth knock of the day sounded on the door.

"Never knew I was so popular," Duchamps said, looking at the door. "It's open."

They all stared when this new visitor entered.

"I hear there's a party going on," Stroeme announced into their astonishment.

"Er..." Pew began, and stopped.

"Well..." Levin started to say.

"Sir...er," Duchamps said. "Major Stroeme, er..."

Fernando said nothing, looking steadily at the German.

Stroeme gave an unexpectedly pleasant smile. "I can see you're all having problems deciding how to address me. Karl will do. And by the looks on your faces, I can see exactly the same expressions on the faces of my Bf-109 squadron colleagues if an officer in RAF uniform walked into the *Fliegerhorst*."

"And is that likely to happen?" Pew asked, being the first to recover.

"Most unlikely...unless as a prisoner of war."

"But would they have someone...er...like you..." Leven began.

"You mean someone in the RAF working for them. I doubt it...although anything can happen, of course. But there will be special troops—Germans pretending to be RAF—or any other members of the Allied military..."

"Like they did with Poland," Fernando said, still looking steadily at Stroeme.

"Poland was a different matter but essentially, yes."

"Your English is very good," Pew said. "Excellent, in fact. Better than most people around here."

Stroeme gave another of his smiles. "Cambridge." They stared at him.

"You've been to university *here?*" Levin asked. "You're kidding."

"I was a student over here before the war."

A silence fell. The incongruity of a man in genuine Luftwaffe uniform, and a genuine "enemy" pilot in the Mess, talking calmly to them was bizarre. It was something beyond anything any of them had experienced, or expected to experience during their wartime careers.

"I am not here," Stroeme was saying into their silence, "to talk about my student days. I have spoken with the wing commander, and he has authorized me to say what I am about to. The missions you will fly, will be dangerous. You will be deep inside enemy territory for most of the time. If you are shot down, you must try to escape. This is important for all of you. Raven Squadron does not exist, and must never be known to exist."

Stroeme looked at Fernando and Duchamps. "I have to say this. You two especially, must not allow yourselves to fall into the hands of the Gestapo if unfortunately, you are shot down. I think you understand me."

Duchamps nodded slowly, lips tightening. "Jim Crow in Germany, huh?"

"Worse, and it's national policy." Stroeme turned to Levin. "You are Jewish, Mr. Levin?"

"Does it matter?"

"No need to be so...forthright, Mr. Levin. It does not matter to me, but to most others over there..."

"My father is Jewish. My mother's not. There's not the usual 'evidence' in my pants to show it."

Stroeme gave his briefest of smiles. "I like the wit...but they won't make the distinction. So like Jamie and Tad, be extra careful."

"What about you, Major?" Fernando asked. "Why are you doing what you do?"

"Spoken like the ferocious fighter pilot. You shoot straight, Mr. Fernando."

"So they tell me."

Stroeme looked at each in turn. "Why do I do it? It's a fair question. There are those of us who believe the Nazis will bring terrible destruction upon our country. We believed that very early; but there are very, very few of us. Some brave people speak out. You will not have heard of them—Niemoller, Bonhoffer, Adenauer, Brandt, and several more. Then there is the Scholl family. The daughter is no older than you are, but she is a force to be reckoned with. She is very brave, but perhaps a little reckless. But what she says is right..."

"Do you know her personally?" Pew asked.

"Not personally...no. It would be dangerous for both of us...but I have met with people who are close friends. I believe in what she is doing; but her courage will perhaps cost her her life. She and her brother picked this up from their father. Time will tell how long they have. After this is all over, if some of these people have not been killed by then, we will need them to rebuild. My own feeling is that many will get themselves killed. If we are here by this time next year, or the next, ask me then.

"The attack to the east into Russia last month," Stroeme continued, "is an insanity we saw coming. The Russians will take terrible revenge when they recover. Eventually, my country will be destroyed, and its name tarnished for a very long time. That is inevitable. I believe the scale of the destruction will be even worse than any of us who can think ahead can imagine. Germany will have to be rebuilt, and regain its honor. I don't know how long that will take. But it must be done. I hope that is an answer to your question."

They remained silent for long moments, then Fernando held out a hand. "Major, I don't know what I would have done in your place. It sounds like my idea of hell."

Stroeme shook the hand. "It is hell. And thank you."

Levin offered his. "You're one gutsy bastard, Major."

"I don't know about the gutsy...but I can be a right bastard when the need arises." Stroeme gave them an infectious grin.

They all shook hands with him.

"I hope we never run into to you in the air," Pew said.

"If that happened," Fernando said, "would you fight us?"

Stroeme appeared to pause for thought. "The aircraft you will fly normally in the area will have normal RAF markings. This is, after all, supposed to be a training unit. But the ones you will fly on operations, will have no unit markings, no number, no letters. Just a low-visibility RAF roundel. If I see such an aircraft, I'll know."

"Would you attack?"

"If I am with members of my squadron, I will have to. If I did not attack, they would find that strange, and become suspicious. I have never failed to go into the attack. I would have to fight the Ravens, to protect our secret. You must defend yourselves well if that ever happens. We must hope it never will."

"How will we know it's you?"

"My 109 is very distinctive. The tail is Cambridge blue."

Levin stared at him. "How did you get that past Fat Herman's boys?"

Stroeme actually chuckled. "*Ach ja*," he said, briefly lapsing into German. "*Armer, fetter Hermann*. He hates Spitfires."

"So he should!" Pew said, grinning. "We aim to give him a lot of headaches."

"He has them already," Stroeme said. "As for how I managed it, I simply said it was to upset the *Tommis*. They like that."

"Rubbing our noses in it, you mean," Fernando said.

"Exactly."

"Do you know who our welcoming committee was?" Levin asked. "I thought they were going to hit our bus."

"We had plenty of clearance," was Stroeme's surprising response.

"'*We*'?" Fernando exclaimed.

Stroeme seemed amused. "Yes. The wing commander and I."

"*You* can fly the Hurri?" Pew asked in surprise.

"Of course," Stroeme replied as if this were an everyday occurrence. "And the wing commander can fly the 109. There are many...unexpected things about this unit, as you will all discover during your time here. Well, gentlemen," he continued into their astonishment, "thank you for your time. I must be going."

"Over there?" Duchamps, still assimilating the revelations, asked. "Or shouldn't we ask?"

"You should not."

"Understood."

"One last thing, Major..."

"Yes?"

Duchamps hesitated. "Miss...er..."

Stroeme's eyes showed clearly, he knew what was coming. "...Andersen."

"Er...yes. Will she be at dinner?"

Just then, they heard the sound of an aircraft taking off.

"I am afraid not. What you're hearing is her aircraft leaving."

"Oh." Duchamps felt as if the sun had gone behind a cloud.

"Ah," Stroeme said with a tiny smile. "I almost forgot." He fished into a breast pocket, and took out a small, white envelope. "For you, I think." He handed it to an astonished Duchamps, who took it reverently. "And I think you know where it comes from."

"Thank you, Major! Thank you!"

The sun had returned in a blaze of glory. Duchamps put the envelope into his own breast pocket. He had no intention of reading what was in it, in front of the others.

"And now, gentleman. I really must go. It is an honor to serve with the Ravens."

"The Royal Air Force does not salute with hats off," Pew said, "But I think we can make an exception today. Gentlemen! Atten*tion!*"

They drew to attention, and saluted Stroeme.

Unexpectedly moved, Stroeme swallowed. "An honor," he repeated softly. He returned the salute, and went out.

As the door shut behind Stroeme, they lowered their hands

slowly.

"I never thought I'd say that about the Hun," Pew said. "But there goes a singular gentleman."

"Amen," Duchamps seconded. "We can't even imagine what it must be like for him...knowing that one slip and his family, his friends, and he himself, will get the chop."

"How the hell does he sleep at night?" Levin wondered.

"Probably like a baby," Fernando said with remarkable insight. "When you're in that kind of danger, it's stupid to dull your senses with worry. Makes it worse, man."

"I dare say Jamie is right," Pew said.

"Of course I'm right, man."

They were all still looking at the door.

Inevitably, it was Pew who broke the silence. "I really do hope we never meet him in the air. I'd hate to have to kill him."

"Or he kills us," Fernando said.

"There is that." Pew admitted.

"If things are already coming apart over there," Levin began, "perhaps it will all be over sooner than we think."

"Longer than we think," Pew said. "My father was in the first shindig. Now, he's something at the War Office. When I told him I was joining up, he said, 'During our time, we all thought it would end by Christmas. We waited for many, hard Christmases. This one won't be any different, and could last longer'." He paused. "Old Pater was right. This will get a lot worse before it gets better. It's going to be a long haul, the work of Karl's resistance chums notwithstanding. Brave as they are, they will have minimal impact. Karl is certainly right when he says his country will be destroyed. The Hun will have to be pounded mercilessly, before he will get weak enough to force him to stop."

Fernando was staring at him. "Man, I've never heard you so serious."

"It's a serious business," Pew said. Then he slipped his customary mantle back on as he turned to Duchamps. "So, bold pilot...what's in that billet doux from the lady we all know about?"

"You expect me to read it while you guys are here?"

"One did hope."

Levin grabbed Pew by a shoulder. "Come on, Pew. Give the guy some space. Leave him to his...what did you call it?"

"Billet doux."

"Whatever. Come on, guys. Know when it's time to leave."

As they went out, Fernando turned briefly to give Duchamps a thumbs up.

Duchamps waited long after the door was shut, just to make certain no one was going to sneakily pop in to surprise him.

At last, he took out the envelope, opened it, and extracted the single, small sheet of paper. He took his time flipping the single fold open.

I hope we will meet again, he read. It was signed, *Helle*.

He felt an unimaginable lifting of his spirits, this was beyond anything he had dared hope for.

"One day," he said to himself, "I will marry that woman." It was said with absolute certainty. Then he paused. "If we live through this, where would we go? Not back home to Georgia. That's for sure." He paused again. "I'm kidding myself."

With great deliberation, he began to tear up the note. Then he paused once more, just before the first rip had reached the message she had written. The jagged line of the tear in the paper had stopped just above "hope".

He refolded the note, and put it back into the pocket beneath his wings. "The future has no horizon," he said. "Anything can happen."

In the rooms along the corridor where the nucleus of Raven Squadron was housed, were eight officers (now including Fernando) and four SNCOs, among whom were two warrant officers. Stroeme was quartered in another part of the Mess, with Hamilton and Murchison.

Soon after Stroeme had returned to his room, Hamilton entered, removing his cap to place it upon a small writing desk.

"How did it go?" Hamilton enquired.

"I think they were left in no doubt about what they're getting into."

"Did you tell them we were at Cambridge together?"

Stroeme shook his head. "I gave them enough for one day." A faint smile flitted across his features. "The story about my blue tail shook them up enough...as well as our welcome party. I think they were also a bit stunned by my Hurricane exploits." Then he sighed, "They are so young, Richard."

"We're not much older. We just look it."

"This war does make old men of the young," Stroeme agreed. He was 26, Hamilton 24.

"We'll be a lot older before this is over."

"The way we look, perhaps...but we may not be given the years to catch up."

Hamilton nodded. "It's a roulette. So what do you think, Karl?" he went on. "Will they be up to it?"

"I am sure they will be. They remind me a little of my own squadron. Keen, serious, making little jokes, but steady. I recognize the type. Duchamps even reminds me of our newest and youngest, Jürgen Fritz. We call him Fritzi. The sad thing is, he's a dedicated Nazi and would be shocked to hear me compare him to a black man. Our youth have been polluted." Stroeme paused. "All in all, it's been an interesting Sunday."

"That it has. All set for the return trip?"

Stroeme nodded. "And tomorrow morning, I shall once again be the *Herr Major*." He studied Hamilton's thoughtful expression. "What's on your mind?"

"Haines. We might have trouble with him."

"Ah yes. Haines. He has more in common with my fellow countrymen than I have."

"Someone, somewhere, with a lot of weight, must have a high opinion of him. The recommendations are so powerful, I can't give a believable reason to wash him out." Hamilton spoke with a distinct lack of enthusiasm. "I heartily wish he hadn't been landed on my doorstep."

"Then let us hope he does not do any damage before we find out exactly why they sent him."

"Be extra careful over there, Karl. Even your Knight's Cross won't serve as any protection if they ever take it into their heads to come after you."

"Don't worry. I have no wish to grace one of Himmler's meat hooks.

Occupied France, Sunday, July 1941. 1700 hours local.
The open *Kübelwagen* sped along the Normandy countryside. It was some time yet before sunset, but the light was exceptional and predicted the spectacular sundown to come.

There were just two people in the speeding vehicle—SS *Standartenführer* Heinrich Bock, resplendent in his intimidating black uniform and his driver, SS *Scharführer* Marius Löringer.

Bock lounged in the rear seat, the ominous prow of this death's head black cap at a rakish angle upon his head. His expression bore the arrogance of the conqueror. When the vehicle sped uncaringly through the single thoroughfare of a village, he did not even look at the people, secure in the knowledge that not one would dare attack the black *Kübelwagen* with the SS runes on the doors.

"Tell me, Marius," Bock began to the driver. "Do you ever feel that one day these people would wish to attack us?" When it was just the two of them, Bock always addressed Löringer by his first name.

This never ceased to please the driver, who felt privileged that someone as important as the SS colonel would design to speak to him in such familiar terms.

Löringer, who was just into his twenty-second year, laughed harshly. "They are our allies now!"

"Yes indeed. Defeated enemies, now subservient allies."

"Nothing can defeat us, *Standartenführer*." In this SS unit, the *Herr* before the rank was never used. "Nothing. And anyway, the French should not hate us for being here. They should hate the Jews for forcing us to come."

"Good point, Marius. Good point."

Löringer grew a little taller in his seat. Praise from the Colonel! He drove just a little faster as they passed the open gate of a farm. A dog ran from the field to chase the vehicle, but misjudged the distance. Löringer did not swerve and the military car slammed the animal into the air. The dog gave a dying yelp before hitting the ground with a sickening thump.

"Should I have swerved, sir?" he asked.

"Don't be ridiculous, Marius. What for?"

Löringer grinned as they sped on.

Ten kilometers later, in open country with an exceptional view of the sea, Bock said, "And here we are, Marius. The usual spot, if you please."

"Yes, *Standartenführer*."

Löringer again felt a sense of pride. The Colonel even said "please" to him! No SS officer as far as he knew, even spoke to non-commissioned subordinates in such a manner and certainly, none of such high rank.

He turned off the road and onto the open field with the familiarity of several visits. He drove to the far edge of the field and stopped near the natural barrier of a line of trees. Just beyond them was a small open space that gave an uninterrupted view of the water, which stretched to the far horizon. There were no ships upon it, and no aircraft crossed the sky above them. There were no fortifications in the area.

"Hard to believe it eh, Marius?" Bock said as the driver came round to open the door for him. "You'd never think there was a war on."

"Which is why you like this place, sir?"

"Indeed," Bock said as he climbed out. He looked about him in satisfaction. "Moments of peace, Marius. Moments of peace. Well...let's get things set up. It should be a spectacular sunset. I want to have everything ready."

Working together, the two men took some things from the vehicle and carried them to the small clearing, 100 meters above the surface of the water. There, they set about erecting what later turned out to be an artist's easel, and a folding stool. There was a full set of brushes; oils, and all the necessary accessories Bock would need; and finally, a small hamper with food and drink. The SS colonel kept a fully loaded MP40 submachine gun with him, with four spare magazines, plus his sidearm.

Bock also carried a small portfolio about 15x15 inches in size, and about 4 centimeters thick. This was cross-secured by strong twine.

THE RAVEN CONSPIRACY – CODE NAME: ICARUS

Bock opened it carefully and pulled out two sheets. One was blank; the other, a finished painting. Bock passed this to the astonished Löringer, who took it open-mouthed.

"For you, Marius," Bock said. "For your uncomplaining service, and something to remind you of this amazing landscape when the war is over. I doubt this place will look the same by the time the war is over, and we have won. I put the finishing touches to it last night. I have also signed it."

"No one will believe me!" Löringer breathed, holding the painting out in admiration. "This should be in a gallery, *Standartenführer!*"

"Nonsense, Marius. My daubs are nothing of the sort. But thank you. And now, I must get some work done before the light goes."

"Thank *you*, sir!" Löringer, beside himself with pleasure, exclaimed. "The same time as usual, sir?"

"Yes. Two hours. No more. We don't want to get back in the dark. Our French allies may feel brave enough to try something." Bock gave a raucous laugh of derision.

Löringer heartily joined in, then holding the painting in one hand as he snapped to attention, shot out the other in a stiff salute. "*Heil Hitler!*"

Bock responded with a languid, Himmler-style wave. "Heil Hitler."

Löringer turned smartly around, to head back to the vehicle.

"Brave enough," Bock heard him repeat as he went, breaking out into contemptuous laughter.

Bock waited until he heard the vehicle start and Löringer had driven the 900 meters back to the road, before removing his cap and settling down to commence work on the coming sunset.

All about him, the world was eerily quiet.

He looked seawards, then glanced up at the sky. The water was devoid of any shipping, as far as the eye could see; and above his head, the bowl of the sky was empty.

"It's as if everyone is having a tea break," he said to himself.

He gave a tiny smile, and began to work.

Precisely one hour later, Bock did something that would have astonished Marius Löringer even more.

The SS colonel got to his feet and threw his palette away from him, watching neutrally as it trailed an arc of paint as it flew. He then kicked the stool over, and roughly shoved the easel so that it toppled untidily, sending the barely started painting spinning wildly away.

He first kicked the hamper, causing it to spill its remaining contents, then trampled on both hamper and food. He looked at his pristine cap, then trampled on that as well. He picked up the MP40, pointed south, and emptied the magazine in a sweeping arc. Spent casings sprayed about his feet. He reloaded, but did not fire again.

He picked up the portfolio which had been re-bound, then picking up the remaining full magazines, set off at a run in a north-easterly direction.

Marius Löringer was as punctual as ever, and almost to the second.

He stared in shocked dismay at the wreckage where his colonel should have been waiting.

"*Oh my God!*" he whispered. "They've taken him! I've been warning him for weeks about this!"

He ran back to his vehicle to make a radio call to his HQ. The person on duty—a *Scharführer* like himself, answered.

"*Franz!*" he shouted. "They've taken him! There are spent shells on the ground! Tell *Hauptsturmführer* Grenzl!"

"Calm down, Marius! Who's been taken?"

"The *Standartenführer!*"

A shocked silence followed, then, "Where are you?"

Löringer told him.

"I'll see to it. It will take some time before anyone gets to you. Wait there!"

"Where do you think I'm going to go?"

Transmission was cut.

Löringer clipped the radio handset back into its holder and looked morosely about him. "I'm in the shit."

Hauptsturmführer Norbert Grenzl was a thickset man with the face of a bully, and mean reptilian eyes that were more than a little crazy. What he lacked in inherent intelligence, he more than made up for in voracious ambition, and cold-blooded cruelty. In his mind, he was already enjoying the things he would do to the French people responsible, if Bock had indeed been abducted, or killed. It was worth a promotion; at the very least.

A man of humble beginnings with a future that had been going nowhere until the advent of Hitler his fellow Austrian, he had grasped the Nazi ideal tightly with both hands and without a single shred of doubt, or regret. He now belonged to a special detachment of the *Totenkopf* SS, a *Sonderkommando*, or killer unit. This particular unit had already blooded itself during the invasion of France, by casually murdering dozens of surrendering British and Canadian soldiers of the Expeditionary Force, and defeated French soldiers. They were now tasked with the protection of a highly secret unit, to which the missing SS colonel belonged.

Grenzl had obtained permission to lead the search and arrived in SS-runed steel helmet, at the head of what seemed like several companies of SS in halftracks, at the spot where a very worried Löringer had been waiting for nearly an hour. In reality, Bock had brought 100 heavily-armed men hungry for blood, in twelve halftracks. Ten of those were 251/1a *Schützenpanzer* and carried 10 fully equipped troops each, with two others up front—a driver and commander.

The other two were 251/2 *Schützenpanzer*. These particular halftracks carried an 80mm mortar and a six-man team each, plus driver and commander. All were fully equipped with a radio suite; and all carried a mounted, heavy caliber machine gun.

They fanned out with a well-honed choreography as they rumbled into the field. When they had stopped, two opened their rear batwing doors, and twenty black-clad *Totenkopf* spread out, moving swiftly to strategic positions.

Grenzl climbed out of the front of the leading halftrack.

There was plenty of light still left in the day for Löringer to clearly see the expression on Grenzl's face, as the SS captain bore down upon him. The sun was about to produce as glorious a sunset as the colonel had expected; but a glorious sunset was not the first thing on Löringer's mind.

If he frightens me, Löringer thought with apprehension, *what will he do the French if he catches them?*

Löringer was not worried about the fate of any French individual unfortunate enough to be caught in Grenzl's net. He was worried about his own future. Driving for the sometimes informal colonel had been a dream duty. As a sergeant of the SS, he was no shrinking violet. His comrades knew him as a seriously hard man who could give more than a good account of himself in a fight, with or without weapons, which was why Bock had chosen him as his personal driver. It therefore said much for Grenzl's infamous reputation, that the incident now shot a bolt of fear through Löringer.

Grenzl stopped directly in front of Löringer, planted his gleaming jackbooted legs apart, hand on sidearm, and stared at the unfortunate sergeant with his merciless, crazy eyes.

"Show me!"

Löringer took him to the small clearing. Grenzl stared at the scene of the apparent struggle and firefight. He said nothing, looking at everything, cold eyes emotionless.

It was during this time that Löringer noticed that the portfolio was missing. Why would the abductors take it? He wondered. He glanced towards the sheer drop. Perhaps they had thrown it over the edge. They would not be interested in an SS colonel's paintings. They had left the one he had started on.

Though the anomaly raised a mild question in his mind, he said nothing about it. With the sharp instincts of soldiers everywhere for avoiding the minefields of military life, he offered nothing unless he was specifically asked.

Grenzl had finished his scrutiny of the scene. "Pray to your grandmother that we find the *Standartenführer* alive and well," he said, "or being sent to the Eastern Front to join the rest of the Division will be the least of your problems! *Hirschmann! Garschang! Möll!*" He barked before Löringer could say anything, even if he had wanted to. "Here! *Move!*"

"*Jawohl, Hauptsturmführer!*" Their voices chorused.

The three SS men came running.

"Pick everything up," Grenzl ordered, "and put them in your halftrack! Be quick about it."

"Including the spent cases?" Möll asked.

"Of course, Möll!" Grenzl snapped with impatience. "Everything means everything! We need to know how long he was able to resist."

"Looks like he managed to empty a magazine," Hirschmann, who was picking up the casings suggested. He pointed to the discarded magazine. "That means just a few seconds. He seems to have been firing south or south-eastwards...though to the main field. So they must have come out of the trees over there and fast enough to take him by surprise. But he still reacted quickly enough to get off a long burst. Wonder if he got any of them. No blood around here."

"We'll get anyone he missed," Grenzl snarled. He stared at Hirschmann. "Why did you say south?"

"The trailing pattern of the casings, sir. They're streaming from south to north as he moved forward; then stopped here. The greater number of casings are here...so he was pointing south, or southeast."

"Of course," Grenzl said, as if he knew that all the time. "What are you, Hirschmann? A policeman?"

Hirschmann, an *Oberscharführer* and at 25 a little older than many of his comrades for the rank, said, "I was, sir, before I joined the SS."

"What branch?"

"Criminal Investigation."

"I didn't know that."

"It's in my records, sir."

"Why aren't you with the Gestapo?"

"I prefer this."

Hirschmann's response pleased Grenzl, but he did not show it.

"Alright. Now hurry! Get this done!" He turned his reptile's eyes upon Löringer. "You, *Scharführer*, will drive me!"

"Yes, *Hauptsturmführer*."

Bock had been making his way through woodland for about 20 minutes after he had left, when he found the stream he had been looking for. At the spot where he had chosen to stop, was a fallen tree whose upper trunk was partially submerged.

He had been in the gloom of the woods for less than five minutes, when a voice from somewhere behind him said in French-accented English, "I need a pee."

Bock did not move. "Use that tree over there," he responded in perfect English.

"Come!" the voice went on urgently. "Transport is waiting. We must get you to where you must be before it is fully dark. As you know, you Germans do not permit us to travel during hours of darkness." This was said with biting humor.

Five armed men appeared out of the trees.

"I wonder why," Bock said.

They did not disarm him; nor did they introduce themselves, or even shake hands.

"We must hurry," the man who had spoken said.

Clutching his portfolio, and with the man walking just behind him, Bock followed the others through the trees.

Back at the field by the cliffs, Grenzl was in the passenger side of the *Kübelwagen*, standing. The entire group was about to start the search, when the radio squawked. "Siegfried One, Siegfried Two." Hirschmann's vehicle.

Instead of grabbing the handset himself, Grenzl chose to thrust a hand at Löringer who was sitting at the wheel. Löringer passed him the handset

"What!" Grenzl barked.

"*Brigadeführer* Forst, sir."

Grenzl swallowed. "Put him through," he said quickly.

"Grenzl!" the sharp voice of SS Brigadier General Helmut Forst sounded with ominous portent in his ear.

Grenzl actually stood to attention. "*Brigadeführer* Forst! An honor..."

"Cut the shit, Grenzl! Have I heard correctly? *Standartenführer* Bock is *missing?*"

"Yes, sir..."

"*Find him!* He is doing extremely important work for the Reich. He *must* be found. So you find him, Grenzl. Do whatever is necessary to catch the people responsible. That is a direct order. I will ensure you have full co-operation from any unit you may need...without exception. Succeed, and you will reap a generous reward. Fail, and..."

The general ended the conversation with chilling suddenness. There had been little need for him to continue. Grenzl knew exactly what was meant.

The SS captain snapped the handset back into its cradle. He looked down at Löringer, eyes merciless.

"Start praying," he said coldly.

He raised a hand to his waiting troops, then chopped it forwards. The vehicles began to move in a rolling thunder of engines.

They went south, sticking to the roads.

Macon, Georgia. July 2006.

Leroy Haines eased himself up just long enough to take a long sip of his mint julep, before laying back down on the recliner in his garden.

"Big mistake you made there, Grenzl, boy. *Big* mistake. You sure as hell paid for it."

CHAPTER THREE

Galen Private Archives, New York. July 2006.
"The Ivory Chronicle?" Ellen Haines enquired into the phone. The year-old magazine was lying open on her desk, at the editorial page.

"Yes. May I ask who is calling?"

"I'm Martha Thomas," Ellen lied, silently begging Martha's forgiveness, even though Thomas was not Martha's surname. "Can I speak with the editor, please?"

"This is she," the person said.

"Oh!" Ellen exclaimed, as if surprised. "I didn't think I'd get straight through."

The woman chuckled. "We're a small magazine. We're all accessible to our readers. If you don't mind my saying so, you sound like a Southern sister."

"I am," Ellen said in feigned surprise, and doing an excellent impression of Martha. It was something she had perfected, with Martha's collusion. "How did you guess?"

The woman at the other end gave a soft laugh. "It pours out of the phone."

"I'm sorry..."

"Don't be. Be proud of it. So...how can I help?"

"Well. I came across an old issue of the magazine—about a year old. There's an article in there that interested me. I'm taking 20th century history, particularly concerning the two World Wars. I wondered if you knew how I could make contact with Tad Duchamps.

I thought what he had to say was very interesting..."

There was a long silence. "Hello?"

There was still silence.

"I guess you're going to hang up on me, so I'd better..."

"Who are you?" the editor demanded suddenly.

"Why...Martha. Martha Thomas."

"And why do you want to contact Mr. Duchamps, Miss Martha Thomas?"

"Look. I'm...I'm sorry if I have said something to upset you. I just want to talk with the grandson of one of our heroes. That's all. I can't find the story anywhere else, so I thought I'd try you. But if you think I was wrong to call you, I guess I'll have to see if I can try someplace else..."

"Perhaps I am the one who should apologize, Miss Thomas. But your bringing up that old story shook me. You obviously don't know what happened."

Ellen paused. "What happened?"

"We had to pull the story from all issues that were not yet sold."

Genuinely astonished, Ellen said, "*What?*"

"That was no fake," the editor remarked drily. "You sound shocked."

"I am!"

"Perhaps I was too suspicious. Well, Miss Thomas, I don't know how you will get hold of Mr. Duchamps. But after we printed his story, we got a lot of funny calls...and I don't mean humor."

"You were *threatened?*"

"That's a way of putting it. My advice to you is to forget all about that story...but as you sound like someone who will go your own way, I can give you a number that may or may not be working. We tried to call him after the article was pulled. He never returned the calls. That was a year ago. Whatever is behind that story, I don't think it's something a history student should get into..."

"Especially a woman?"

"I did not say that. I'm all for strong women, particularly smart ones. I don't think going after this is smart. Still want that number?"

"I do."

"It's your funeral...which I hope it won't be in reality."

"Are you trying to scare me?"

"That would be a good start." But she gave Ellen the number.

"Thank you," Ellen said.

"Don't thank me. You might hate me one day, for giving it to you."

As soon as they had hung up, Ellen called the New York number. It rang several times before an answering machine came on.

"You've got me," the voice said. "Leave your number, and I'll be right back."

"The way you got back to the magazine?" Ellen said in her real voice, and slammed the phone down.

In his New York loft apartment, Duchamps stared at the answering machine.

"That sounds like one pissed lady. Not from the magazine. So who?"

He shrugged, and went back to what he'd been doing: trying unsuccessfully to hack into a military archive. It was just one of an unbroken string of failures.

After half an hour of more failure, the phone rang again. He did not even turn to look at it. The answering machine clicked on.

"If you're there, Duchamps, pick up the damned phone. If you're not, wait for my next call when you get this. I might be able to help you with your problem..."

He grabbed the phone. "Speak."

"So you're not hiding in some cave, after all."

"I don't hide. Who the hell are you?"

"An angel from on high."

"Alright, joker. You've got two seconds..."

"Then you'll hang up? I doubt it. Banging your head against a wall is painful. Stopping is a relief."

"And you know the secret of this relief?"

"I might."

"I'm waiting."

"From what little I do know, I'm certain you don't expect me to tell you anything on your phone. This is probably a conference call.

You never know who we may be talking to."

"You're smart."

"I know. Although someone I just spoke with might not think so."

"Say I buy this..."

"You're buying it already."

"Alright, smart lady. Where do we meet?"

"Teterboro. I'll be wearing a pilot's uniform."

"You're a *pilot?*"

"I thought that would get your attention."

"There are a lot of pilots hanging around out there."

"Way it goes."

"So how do I find you?"

"Be there. I'll find you."

"When?"

"You've got one hour to get there."

"But..."

He was talking to the tone.

"Is this a setup?" he asked aloud, as he put the phone back down. But he began to get ready. He stared at the computer. "I wasn't getting anywhere, anyway."

Ellen took the helicopter back to Teterboro. Mary Adams was surprised to see her. "Are we flying? Mike's not here. I was just doing a general inspection, or I'd be gone as well. You've got to give us warning, Miss Haines..."

"First, call me Ellen. Second, we're not flying, but I need you to do something for me."

Mary Adams looked at her with curiosity. "As long as it's not illegal," she said as a joke.

"They haven't made that illegal as yet."

"Give it time. So? How can I help?"

"I'm expecting someone to arrive in about 30 minutes, perhaps earlier. I told him I'd be in pilot's uniform."

"You want to borrow my *uniform?*"

"No, no. I want you to pretend to be me..."

"Miss Haines...Ellen, I think..."

"Please, Mary. This is really important. It's all to do with the reason you're flying me."

"I...see. No. I don't see."

"Trust me."

"Hah. Good thing you're not a man. Okay. What do I do?"

Ellen took the magazine out of the shoulder bag she carried, and opened it at the article page. "Look out for him," she said, showing Mary Adams the photograph of Tad Duchamps. "You won't miss him."

Mary Adams' eyes lit up. "I certainly won't. A fighter jock, and a looker. I envy him that Eagle."

"You wanted to fly one of those?"

"You bet."

"What happened?"

"A man. I was in. I had an affair. He was married—but separated. Then wifey decided she wanted him back. She threatened a stink. Bang would have gone his career. He sacrificed me. I left."

"Sorry."

"Nothing for you to be sorry about." Mary Adams patted the Cessna. "But I've got this sweet baby, and none of the military crap." She gave the F-15 a wistful look. "Even so, I would have liked to have got one of those. Alright, Ellen, I'll go find your fighter jock and restrain my antipathy. Where will you be?"

"In the plane."

"Okay."

"If you feel that way about men, how do you get on with Mike?"

"Mike's a sweetie. He does what I tell him." Mary Adams smiled. "Joke. He's a fine pilot. We're like brother and sister without the fighting. Now I'd better go find your jock."

"One more thing..."

Mary Adams paused.

"There may be people...watching him. I don't know for sure."

"But just in case?"

Ellen nodded.

"And here I was thinking I was just flying a little rich girl around. This could be interesting, after all."

"I'm not rich."

THE RAVEN CONSPIRACY – CODE NAME: ICARUS

"Someone is."

RAF Shawbridge, 0001 hours. Sunday, July 1941.

The Westland Lysander was a unique beast. Originally intended to be a virtual maid of all work—army co-operation, night fighter, ground attack, and others—it excelled in one thing that no one at the time expected: as a clandestine taxi and equipment supplier. As a fighter, it was a non-starter and such squadrons entering combat were virtually wiped out by the fierce 109s. It was an extremely handicapped David versus an overwhelming Goliath.

But the Lysander reigned supreme in its unexpected niche; the only aircraft capable of doing the job it was really meant for—a perfect jewel in the perfect place, at the perfect time.

It was not a small aircraft. With a wingspan of exactly fifty feet, a height of fourteen and a half and a length thirteen and a half, it was no midget. It was also one of the few aircraft of the time to have fully automatically deployable leading edge slats and trailing edge flaps, enabling it to carry out extreme maneuvers at extremely low altitudes and speeds. The pilot, with many other things on his mind, could simply let them do their thing while he got on with the serious business of keeping himself and his passenger alive.

The irony was the Lysander's nemesis, the Bf 109, had exactly the same kind of aerodynamic aids. But Lysanders had been known to kill 09s. In the right set of circumstances, it was no lamb to the slaughter. There were many variants and the Raven Squadron Lysanders had a more powerful engine, plus a pair of 20mm cannon, mounted on the spats of the sturdy, fixed main gear. They also had modified carburetion systems that minimized the tendency for the engine to cut out during hard maneuvering; an Achilles heel that Raven Squadron did not need. Of all the Special Duties Lysander III aircraft used by other units, the Raven Squadron III SDs were the only ones thus modified in 1941.

In general, the aircraft had become a clandestine taxi for the very good reason that metaphorically speaking, it could land and take off on a sixpence. A stretch of turf no longer than a football pitch was its playground. Its powerful single engine could lift it off the deck in the kind of climb that would have other aircraft sinking or stalling rapidly back to mother earth.

It was an agent's dream; a lifeline, and it required exceptional pilots to master its idiosyncrasies, and to fly it properly. It required edge-of-the-cliff nerves to take it safely into enemy territory, alone, at nap-of-the-earth altitude, and safely back again.

At night.

Richard Hamilton was an exceptional fighter pilot. He was also an exceptional Lizzie pilot.

Stroeme, in full Luftwaffe uniform, walked in the gloom to where the silhouette of the two-seat Lysander stood. The aircraft's all-black paintwork made it almost invisible. With its huge strutted, gull-like wing, it was a specter in the night.

"Taxi, sir?" a voice enquired softly.

Stroeme almost jumped. "My God!" he whispered. "Richard! What are you doing here?"

"I'm your driver."

"*You?* I thought Sergeant Jones was taking me. You can't risk going over. You're needed here. If anything should go wrong and you're caught..."

"*You* worry about not getting caught, and I'll worry about me. Hop in."

Stroeme gave Hamilton an anxious look that could not be seen in the gloom; but his body language telegraphed plainly enough.

"It is very strange, Richard, that you are doing this. You have never done it before."

"Let's just say I want to deliver you safe and sound. Now do hop in. Time's rushing by. We don't want to be late for your reception committee. They won't wait if we're late."

"Alright." It was a reluctant acceptance.

Stroeme went to the left side of the aircraft to climb up the fixed ladder and into the rear cockpit. He strapped himself in, stowed his cap, and put on the flying helmet that was already there. He plugged into the intercom as Hamilton climbed into the front.

Hamilton swiftly went through his pre-flight-checks, and started the big radial, Bristol Mercury.

Presently, Stroeme heard him say, "Ghost Two-Four."

"Ghost Two-Four," the tower responded. "Clear taxi and take off. Runway Three-One. Good luck."

"Ghost Two-Four. Roger."

The Lizzie began to taxi.

"Whenever I see this aircraft," Stroeme said, "I think of a big moth."

"It's meant to have seagull wings." Hamilton said.

"To me, it will always be a moth. And the night is its territory."

"I have to agree on the night part."

They taxied to the allocated runway, then Hamilton eased the throttle forward. The Lysander surged along the tarmac and in mere seconds, it seemed, was lifting off the ground. It banked steely left, heading inland and within moments, vanished into the night.

Just over an hour later, still in British airspace, it was approaching an airfield on the south east coast. Hamilton made a single radio call.

"Ghost Two-Four."

"Roger, Ghost Two-Four," came the immediate response. "Clear to land. Wind zero."

The Lysander came straight in, landed smoothly, and taxied to the end of the runway. A fuel bowser with attendant ground crew was waiting. Ambient lighting had been deliberately kept to just sufficient levels to enable them to work safely.

They moved swiftly and with barely any noise, to top up the fuel in the aircraft.

The Lizzie would need no more until it returned.

Hamilton and Stroeme did not leave their cockpits. No one spoke. Within the semi-gloom, the ground crew moved in eerie choreography.

Then one of them raised a hand, giving the thumbs up.

All clear. Time to go.

"Ghost Two-Four," the tower announced. "Clear take-off."

"Ghost Two-Four," Hamilton acknowledged.

Hamilton waited until the bowser and crew were safely out of the way, then started the engine. He turned the Lysander round to the reciprocal, eased the throttle forward almost before he was fully lined up, and sent the Lizzie hurtling down the runway.

Seconds later, it climbed steeply into the night to head east, and towards occupied France. Soon, it was over water and at barely 100 feet, made for the northern coast of Normandy. Within the aircraft, neither man spoke.

South of their route, places like Abbeville and Fécamp were having a night of it. The vivid flashes in the distance were proof of that. Bombers were pounding the fighter airfields and night fighters prowled, waiting for any German counterparts that managed to get off. Jamming aircraft would also be making life difficult for the radar operators. The activity succeeded in keeping any enemy interest away from the solitary Lysander.

According to information supplied by Stroeme and independently confirmed by a local resistance group and agents in the area, there were no flak batteries for at least 20 miles from where Hamilton would make his landfall. Similar information had also given him a gap in any possible E-boat patrols that night. He hoped they would all be occupied by the raids.

There was no guarantee that the information had not already been overtaken by events which could change from day to day, or hour to hour. A flak battery could have appeared where previously there were none. Or a patrol.

Ten miles out, he made a shallow turn towards Fécamp, keeping extremely low.

In the event, nothing disturbed the Lysander's stealthy flight.

About a mile from the coast, Hamilton made a tight turn to the left, heading north towards the far end of the Fécamp cliffs, edging closer to the coast as he did so. At the last moment, he banked steeply right. This took him on a course that would thread him through a ravine. There was enough of a wan moon to enable him to see clearly. He was in the right place. He was still within the region of the Abbeville Bf109 nest, but far away enough not to worry unduly. The Abbeville Boys had enough on their plate this night.

He throttled back gently. The Lysander almost seemed to understand that it needed to be quieter as the drone of its engine decreased to what seemed like a whisper. The aircraft appeared to float above a stream that glistened in the moonlight.

"Won't be time for goodbyes," Hamilton said. "Look after yourself out there, Karl."

"I'm good at doing that," Stroeme said. "Watch out for nightfighters on the way back."

"I most certainly will."

They said nothing more until five minutes later, Hamilton spotted three weak lights in arrowhead formation to the left. He eased the aircraft round until the three lights were directly ahead. He prepared for the landing. The slats and flaps deployed automatically, leaving him free to concentrate on getting down. Clear space would commence just past the red tip of the arrowhead of lights.

He swept over them, and brought the Lysander down to a perfect landing. He stopped with plenty of space to spare.

"Thanks for the taxi," Stroeme said as he quickly snapped open his harness, removed the helmet, and put on his cap.

"Any time," Hamilton said.

Stroeme climbed rapidly out of the aircraft, to be met by two men. No one spoke.

Hamilton was already taxying to as far as the clearing would allow, and turned the aircraft round.

Stroeme paused.

"No time to watch," one of the men said in urgently whispered in English. "We've got to go. She's waiting."

"Yes, of course."

Stroeme quickly followed the men as Hamilton took off, steeply pulling the Lysander upwards, to clear a screen of trees.

Stroeme and the two men arrived a few minutes later at a small, open-backed truck, hidden in some woods.

"Get in!" one of them urged. "The front."

The man climbed in behind the wheel as Stroeme got in next to him. The second man heaved himself into the back.

The truck was moving almost before the one in the back had settled down, pulling onto a narrow, unpaved road. After about ten kilometers of fast driving along winding back roads with blacked-out headlights, it stopped at a junction.

"Okay," the driver said. Stroeme got out.

The truck was again moving as soon as he had shut the door. He watched as it disappeared round a bend, then looked about him.

Two pinpricks of light blinked from the shelter of some trees, then a car emerged slowly like a night animal leaving its lair, to come towards him. The low-slung Citroen pulled up next to him. A young woman was at the wheel.

Stroeme smiled, and got in next to her. "Missed me?" He asked in English.

"Of course," she said, and leaned over to give him a quick kiss.

"Any excitement?" he went on as the car began to move.

"I'm not sure. Something's happened. When I drove here, the roads were quiet. No patrols. But I've heard from Jean—he was one of the men who signaled your plane—that there are now some patrols about. It's all very sudden. We may meet one on the way back."

"I'll handle it if we do," Stroeme said.

She nodded, but said nothing further as they headed eastwards.

Hamilton had turned back to sea after takeoff, then turned north in the direction of Boulogne, but he was not going anywhere near the town.

He turned again towards land and five minutes later brought the Lysander down in another clearing, again guided by the familiar three pinpoints of light in arrowhead formation. This landing spot was a mere five kilometers from where had had dropped off Stroeme.

He had barely stopped, engine running, when a bare-headed man hurried towards the aircraft. As the man got closer, he recognized the SS uniform. The man was clutching something. The new passenger went round the back to get to the ladder, then climbed in. None of the people holding the indicator lights came close.

The red light marking the tip of the arrow was the ID for the night.

If this were an ambush, Hamilton began to think; then he killed the thought.

The clearing was big enough to allow takeoff without turning round. Hamilton had the Lysander moving within moments of his SS passenger strapping himself in.

Neither man spoke.

* * *

They were just five kilometers from their destination, when they saw the faint lights of the roadblock.

"Too much to expect a clear run," she said.

"I'll handle it," Stroeme repeated.

She slowed down as they approached. It was not a matter of choice. A halftrack as directly across the road, its mounted machine gun swiveled to point at them. Soldiers lined each side of the road. One was standing in their path, hand raised in an unmistakable command.

She stopped.

The soldier came round to her side, and shone his torch in her face, before moving its beam to Stroeme. There was a sharp intake of breath.

The man snapped to attention. "*Herr Major!*"

Recognizing the voice, Stroeme was astonished. "*Feldwebel Krähnen?*" He climbed out. "What the devil are you and your men doing out here? Who gave the orders?"

Seeing who it was the soldiers, though all now at attention, had lowered their weapons. Even the one on the halftrack had lowered the machine gun, to follow the exchange with interest.

"Well, sir..." Krähnen began awkwardly. He stopped.

"Well, Sergeant?"

"It...it was the SS, sir..."

"*What?* Since when do the SS give orders to Luftwaffe troops?"

"Since they lost one of their colonels, sir."

Soft titters from the other soldiers followed this.

"*Quiet!*" Stroeme barked. The titters died as if cut off.

"Explain to me, Sergeant," Stroeme ordered.

"*Standartenführer* Bock, we were told, is missing. The SS believe he was kidnapped by a Resistance group, but they don't know which."

"If this Resistance 'group'—whoever they are, and if they exist at all—have kidnapped an SS colonel, they must be mad. It is not a good idea for them to provoke the SS."

"Well, sir, the SS think they have and they're going crazy—the SS, that is. Earlier in the evening, their overall commanding officer in the area, a *Brigadeführer*, came to the airfield. He demanded..."

"*Demanded?*"

"What I heard, sir. He demanded some troops to help with the search. The Commandant had no choice. Berlin orders. What I heard. I hear they've even got *Wehrmacht* and *Kriegsmarine* troops as well. The search is very wide. We're all under the command of an SS captain called Grenzl."

"I see," Stroeme said. "I'll talk with the Commandant in the morning. See if we can get you and your men out of this."

"Thank you, sir!" Krähnen sounded relieved.

"Now can we move on, please?"

"Of course, *Herr Major!*" The sergeant responded. "Bremer!" he called to the machine gunner. "Get Lehrbach to move that thing!"

"Right away, Sergeant!"

Within moments, the halftrack was moving out of the way.

"Thank you, Sergeant," Stroeme said.

"Sir!" Krähnen saluted.

Stroeme casually returned the salute, and got back into the car. "Drive away very calmly," he said in a low voice to his companion.

"I'm not foolish," she hissed back.

The soldiers watched as the Citroen went on its way.

"Wish I had something like that in my bed," one of them said.

"When you're a fighter pilot with many kills, and a major with the Knight's Cross, perhaps you'll get one."

"Do you have to spoil a dream, Sarge?"

"I'm a sergeant. That's my job."

The halftrack moved back into position, again blocking the road.

"Think he'll get us out of this, Sarge?" another asked.

"Major Stroeme is a good sort. Not like some officers I know. If anyone can do it, he can."

"I'd like to provoke the SS," a third soldier announced with venom. "Getting us to stand out here like a bunch of pricks."

"Keep your thoughts to yourself, Loehm," the sergeant said; "even if we think the same thing." He paused. "No need to mention the major and his lady unless we're asked about it. We tell the SS nothing. None of their damned business what the major does in his private time." He looked at each in turn. "Are we agreed?"

"Agreed," they all confirmed one by one.

There was no love lost between them and the SS.

"Did you get most of what went on back there?" Stroeme asked.

"I understand enough German," she replied. "My mother's family comes from Alsace, as you know. Why would they kidnap an SS colonel?" she added.

"Who knows?" Stroeme said. "Whatever the reasons, the SS will react violently. This could be a very dangerous thing for whichever group did it. You don't want the SS to start killing innocent people. They don't need much of an excuse as it is."

"I'll try and see what I can find out."

"And I'll see what the Commandant knows about this, if the SS have even bothered to tell him. But you be careful."

"I should be saying that to you," she said.

"I'll be fine."

They arrived at their destination—a big, wood-beamed cottage with a large garden overlooking the ocean—without running into further roadblocks. The cottage was well away from other buildings, and not in an area with troops.

She parked the car in its garage at the back. They got out, and entered via a back door. Familiar with the place, they did not put on any lights. There was sufficient light by the ghostly moon to give illumination, even within the building. They went upstairs to the main bedroom.

"After all this," she said, "we're both a little tense. I know what will relax us."

She began to remove her clothes. The pale light of the moon coming through the windows gave a silky sheen to her body. She glanced at him and even in the weak light, could clearly see his expression from across the room.

"I don't know why you like this so much," she said. "I've got a peasant's body."

"You've got a great body," he corrected.

"A Rubens, you mean."

"I mean perfect...and perfect for what we are about to do. Rubens would probably look upon you as emaciated, but he would still fall on his knees before you."

"Then let's show him what he missed," she said.

Hamilton made it safely back to the south east coastal airfield.

"Ghost Two-Four," he called.

"Welcome back, Ghost Two-Four. Clear to land."

"Roger."

Hamilton did a straight run in, and landed on the same runway he had used previously. He again came to a stop at its end. The fuel bowser and crew were already waiting. There was another vehicle too.

A big official-looking car. Two men in suits were standing next to it.

Hamilton remained in his cockpit as without a word, his SS passenger got out and went over to the waiting men. One shook hands with him. The other took the package that the SS officer handed over.

Then all three got into the car, and it moved swiftly away.

When the aircraft had taken on sufficient fuel, the bowser moved away. Hamilton again received the thumbs up from one of the ground crew.

He nodded at the man, then began to turn the Lysander round until he was facing in the direction of his takeoff run.

"Ghost Two-Four," he heard in his helmet. "Clear takeoff."

He eased the throttle forward, letting the speed build. Slats and flaps automatically deploying, he lifted the Lysander steeply into the air and headed back to Shawbridge.

When he'd landed, he was met by Murchison.

"How'd it go? Murchison asked.

"Piece of cake."

Outskirts of Macon, Georgia. July 2006.

"But it wasn't a piece of cake, was it? Not what came after." Lying eyes closed on the recliner, Haines was mumbling to himself.

"Now you want cake?" Martha had come to check on him, and had caught just a part of what he'd said.

Haines opened his eyes. "Wha...what?" He seemed unsure of where he was.

"Cake," Martha said. "You asked for cake."

"Did I? I don't remember."

Martha shook her head in resignation, and turned to go...

"Did I tell you about Helle?"

"Hell? You mean where you're going to?" she said as she went back to the house.

"Guess I didn't," Haines said to himself, either ignoring Martha's comment, or having genuinely not heard her response. "Guess I did not," he repeated. "I never did tell anyone about Helle."

Occupied France. Monday, July 1941. 0730 hours. Local.

There were two surprises waiting for Stroeme at his squadron airfield: one a mixed blessing, the other decidedly unpleasant.

The Citroen pulled up before the main gate.

Guarded by two machine gun nests manned by two Luftwaffe ground defense soldiers in each, plus another six fully armed men spread out behind, the closed, iron-barred gate. Beyond them was a parked halftrack. Its machine gun was also manned.

Some of the guards were familiar with the Citroen. They smiled at it; but the respectful smiles were really meant for the woman behind the wheel.

"Your admiration society," Stroeme told her.

"They'd still shoot me if they thought I was Resistance."

"That would depend."

"On?"

"Whether you really were Resistance."

They smiled at each other, enjoying a private joke. "Better join your men before they drool all over my car."

"I'll see you when I can, Marie, Comptesse du Vaillon."

"Oui, Monsieur," she acknowledged in the spirit of things.

The soldiers drew to attention and saluted as Stroeme climbed out. The ones in the machine gun nests did not, but they too smiled at the Citroen.

Stroeme returned their salutes with a single casual movement towards his cap, then patted the car.

Marie gave him a slight nod, then turned the car round to drive back down the road.

As he made for the small pedestrian gate to the right, Stroeme saw one of the squadron staff cars—an open-topped *Kübelwagen*—approaching. It stopped and his deputy, Hans Dasinger, a captain, got out.

"So, *Hauptmann* Dasinger," Stroeme said with a smile, "any excitement to ruin the wonderful weekend I just enjoyed?"

Dasinger returned the smile, gave a jokey salute, and glanced in the direction the Citroen had gone. "I can imagine the kind of weekend. As for excitement... Abbeville, Fécamp, and points south have received calling cards from the *Tommis*, but nothing's come our way. No one was sent up, although Fritzi wanted to go."

"He would. He's keen."

"Keen to die early, if he's not careful," Dasinger said with ghoulish humor.

"What I like about you, Hans, is your sense of humor. The *Tommis* would appreciate it."

"Says the man who went to Cambridge. Which reminds me. Get in. Something to show you."

"I'm intrigued," Stroeme said as he got into the passenger seat. The car set off for the squadron flight line.

Stroeme stared when they got there, and slowly climbed out of the car.

Dasinger got out, a huge grin pasted upon his face as he looked at Stroeme, who was staring at the neat line of the squadron's Bf-109s, with each pilot standing next to his aircraft.

Every single one now sported a blue tail.

"Their idea," Dasinger said. "They wanted to express their respect for you. Fritzi suggested it, and they all took it up. They wanted to get it done before you got back, so the weekend was spent having the tails repainted. The squadron is now unofficially called the Cambridge Boys." Dasinger gave another grin. "Why should Abbeville have all the glory? They thought the *Tommis* will now have a hard time working out which one is you. It's their way of using themselves to protect you. Mine and yours are next to each other..." He pointed to two aircraft without pilots. "Well? What do you think?"

Stroeme's mouth opened slightly, then closed again. His feelings were in turmoil. He felt a solidarity with the men who had so honored him. At the same time, he felt a loyalty to what he was doing against Nazism; and finally, he felt a horror at the thought of members of Raven Squadron coming up against several blue tails, when they expected only one.

I'll have to get a warning through to them, was his first coherent thought. "I'm...I'm moved," he said to Dasinger.

"So you should be. Come on. Let's tell them."

As they walked towards the line of aircraft, the pilots left their mounts and approached in a gaggle, big smiles upon their faces, like children awaiting approval.

"So, *Herr Major?* What do you think...?"

"*Cambridge Boys* in your honor. Do you like the idea...?"

"Fritzi came up with this madness..."

"And we agreed..."

The chorus of eager comment came from sixteen voices.

"Gentlemen..." Stroeme began when the excited voices had fallen expectantly silent, "...I approve." There was nothing else he could have said.

A shout of glee went up from Stroeme's pilots.

"From now on," Fritzi yelled, "we are the Cambridge Boys! *Staffel* Stroeme! Look, *Herr Major*," he continued, "at what else we've done. The left side of the nose."

From his position, Stroeme could only see the right side of the aircraft. Led by the eager Fritzi and followed by Dasinger, he went round to inspect the left flank of his own aircraft, the nearest.

The others remained in a loose group, smiles still pasted upon their faces.

Stroeme came to a halt, and stared at the black, elaborate Gothic double S, just beneath the forward edge of the windscreen.

"The Abbeville Boys have got one," Fritzi remarked, "but the *Staffel* Stroeme have got two!" His eager eyes looked at Stroeme. "Well, sir?"

Stroeme thought it looked too much like the SS symbol for his liking, but kept his thoughts to himself.

"Impressive," he said to Fritzi, who looked enormously pleased.

"I knew you would like it, *Herr Major!* Now when the *Tommis* meet us up there, they'll remember us!"

They certainly will, Stroeme thought, meaning something entirely different from what Fritzi meant.

"They certainly will," he said.

RAF Shawbridge flight line, Monday, July 1941. 0630 hours local.

Hamilton was holding court. Four gleaming, Mark IIc Hurricanes, four 20mm cannons each protruding from their wings, stood in a neat row behind him. Before him, were three of the four pilots who would be flying them—Duchamps, Fernando, and Pew.

"Now that you've had breakfast, gentlemen," he said, "let us hope you won't be bringing any of it up. Wing Commander Murchison will be giving you a sharp introduction to the Welsh mountains. We do not have to teach you how to fly, or none of you would be here. However, we're going to teach you how to use the Hurri in ways you never thought possible. Low-flying is just one such. Pay close attention to the wing commander. What he teaches you *will* help you to live longer. When he's finished, he'll take you on a dress rehearsal later. You'll be told what, when you return from this first flight. Don't hit any mountains. That is all, gentlemen. To your aircraft."

Occupied France, Monday, July 1941. 0756 hours, local.

"And now that I've taken away the enjoyment of your weekend..."

"Why do you say that?" Stroeme asked.

They were on their way to unit headquarters.

Dasinger gave him a sideways glance. "There's a tightness about the corners of your eyes. You're not pleased about something."

"You can't blame yourself for that. The Cambridge Boys idea is good for morale. I'm not so sure about that Gothic double S. The *Tommis* will come hunting. Bad enough rubbing their noses in it with the Cambridge tails. They will see that double S as an SS symbol, not as Fritzi's attempt to go one up on the Abbeville bunch. Once they've identified us, they *will* come hunting. It's a challenge they won't refuse. Fritzi might die sooner than he expects. That thought is not a good one."

"Then why didn't you order it removed? They would have done so without question."

"You were in command in my absence. Why did you not stop them?"

Dasinger gave that some thought. "For the same reason that perhaps, you let it stay."

"Which is?"

"Prudence," Dasinger replied. "We're a special Luftwaffe detachment," he continued, "autonomous, but with specific orders to defend the airspace in this area. The area happens to house a secret SS establishment, about which we know nothing; and about which we will continue to know nothing. The overall commander in the area is an SS general. This airfield is Luftwaffe territory, and the SS are not allowed in, unless by invitation. Although the Commandant holds authority for this detachment, he can be overridden in certain circumstances, by that SS general, which is what happened last night. That double S might actually work for us. That's why I left it on. What's your excuse?"

"Marie and I ran into a roadblock, manned by Krähnen and some of our troops, last night."

"Ah. So he told you."

"Yes."

Dasinger shook his head in disgust. "The SS lose one of their damned colonels, and we have to supply troops to help them find him."

"I promised Krähnen I'd try to get them relieved of that duty."

"Well, you're about to get the chance. But I would not hold out much hope."

"What do you mean?"

They were approaching the headquarters building, a commandeered Louis XIV mansion.

Dasinger pointed to a long black car parked virtually at the entrance. It carried an SS pennant. Two SS guards in black uniforms were standing next to it.

"The general," he said, "plus a nasty-looking customer. Gestapo. They're inside reminding the Commandant of his true position in the pecking order. I don't think he's putting up much of a fight. An *Oberst* does not outrank a *Brigadeführer*, much as we'd like it."

"They're not Waffen-SS. That rank means nothing to me."

"In this instance, it should," Dasinger warned. "I would not display your antipathy too openly. Wrong timing."

Stroeme stared at the SS car as they pulled up next to it. "They're bright and early."

"Best time to catch your fish...in this case, unsettle a Luftwaffe Commandant. Anyway, he asked for you."

Stroeme looked at him. "The general? The Gestapo man...?"

"The Commandant. I'll wait out here."

Stroeme gave his deputy an understanding smile, and climbed out.

The two SS men snapped to attention, shot out their right arms, and almost screamed, "*Heil Hitler!*"

Stroeme waved a hand to his cap.

The SS men—both NCOs—glared at him, on the edge of insubordination. He ignored them, and went in.

Two Luftwaffe troops inside came to attention. "*Herr Major*," they said together. They shot poisonous glances at the SS men outside.

Stroeme nodded at them with a faint smile, and walked along a wide polished hall before turning right into a short corridor. At the end of this was the former salon which was now the Commandant's office. Two further Luftwaffe guards were on sentry duty at the wide, high double door.

They came to attention. "*Herr Major*," they greeted.

"Gentlemen."

One of them coughed softly. "He's got...company, sir." It was clear what he thought of the "company".

"Yes. I know."

Stroeme knocked on the door, and one of the men opened it. He went through into the vast room.

The door closed softly behind him.

THE RAVEN CONSPIRACY – CODE NAME: ICARUS

The Luftwaffe colonel, Harald Feldbruck, was sitting at a large, inlaid desk. To his left in one of the classic chairs belonging to the original owners of the house, was the black-uniformed figure of the SS general with severely cut, faintly greying dark hair. His dark eyes were cold as he looked at Stroeme.

To Feldbruck's right, was the ominous figure of the Gestapo man in a white suit. Stout, with a round face topped by a shaven head, his pebble glasses framed pebble eyes which, if anything, displayed even less life than the SS general's.

Stroeme looked at his superior, came smartly to attention and saluted. "Sir."

The SS general, Forst, was staring at him. "Don't you salute superior officers, *Herr Major?*"

"I just did," Stroeme replied. "I saluted the commander of this unit when I entered the room. The salute includes all in the room with him."

Forst gave him a baleful stare, but was unable to counter. It did not please him. The Gestapo man studied Stroeme with interest.

Feldbruck cleared his throat. "Yes. Well. At ease, Karl. Take a seat."

Stroeme removed his cap, and took a chair that placed him directly in front of the desk.

"This is *Brigadeführer* Forst," Feldbruck went on, "commanding the SS contingent in the area. And this, is *Herr* Schelberg of the Gestapo. There is, I'm afraid, an extremely serious security threat to the establishment whose airspace we have been commanded to defend."

Feigning ignorance, Stroeme waited.

"It would appear," Feldbruch continued, "that some time yesterday, *Standartenführer* Bock went missing. It is strongly suspected that perhaps an opportunist Resistance group may be responsible."

"If I may, sir."

"Go ahead."

"Are there Resistance groups in this area? We have never had evidence of this..."

"Lack of evidence, *Herr Major*," the Gestapo man said in a soft voice that was tinged with a warmth that somehow made it more chilling, "is not a lack of existence. No possibility must be overlooked. *Standartenführer* Bock is a very important man, vital to the Reich. All effort will be made to find him. If a Resistance group have taken him..." Schelberg paused. "...they will regret it."

"I am not here to argue with the SS," Stroeme said, "or the Gestapo, about the details of the *Standartenführer's* disappearance. I am here to fly fighters..."

"Can you fly a Storch, Major Stroeme?" the Gestapo man asked suddenly.

"Yes, of course," Stroeme replied, wondering about the question. "We have four on the unit for liaison, observation, and communication purposes. I have not flown one for a very long time; but we've got four Storch pilots on unit strength..."

"Would you do me the honor of flying me, Major? I would like to do an aerial search."

Stroeme stared at the Gestapo man. "With all due respect, I am a squadron commander, not a..."

"It would not be for long, Major," Forst interrupted. It sounded like a threat.

Stroeme glanced at his colonel, then turned to Forst. "With the greatest respect, *Brigadeführer*, the operational requirements of this unit are vested in the Colonel. I am responsible to him, and he in turn to *Reichsmarschall* Göring. I was told at the very beginning, that this was the chain of command for this detachment."

"And you are correct, Major. However, these are currently very changed circumstances. No one foresaw the disappearance of *Standartenführer* Bock. I am certain the *Reichsmarschall* himself would understand our request."

It did not sound like a request.

Noting the look on Stroeme's face, Schelberg said, "Perhaps I may be able to persuade the major." He looked at Feldbruck. "*Herr Oberst*, may I have a private word with Major Stroeme?"

Feldbruck appeared to be avoiding Stroeme's eyes. "Of course. Use the small room on..."

"I think a short stroll would be perfect," Schelberg interrupted smoothly. Stroeme continued to look at Feldbruck. "Sir..."

"Go with him, Karl. See me when you're finished."

Stroeme got to his feet. "Yes, sir." He put on his cap, and gave Feldbruck a sharp salute, then looked at Schelberg. "Come with me, *Herr* Schelberg."

He left the room without waiting to see whether the Gestapo man was following.

When they were back at the main entrance, the two Luftwaffe guards again saluted Stroeme. Outside, the two SS men by the car snapped to attention when they saw Schelberg, and went into their stiff-armed salute routine.

"*Heil Hitler!*" they chorused.

"*Heil Hitler*," Schelberg responded, and gave them a Himmler wave.

Stroeme kept his hands firmly locked behind his back. He caught a questioning look from Dasinger in the squadron car, but greeted that with a blank, but brief stare. Dasinger would understand.

Schelberg glanced at him as they walked on. "You do not salute the Führer?" It was a mild question, but fully loaded.

"Every time I raise my hand to my cap, *Herr* Schelberg," Stroeme responded calmly, "I salute the Führer."

This was not strictly true, but the Gestapo man had no real comeback.

"Interesting," he said, "and, of course, quite correct. The Führer is the Reich, the Reich is the armed forces, and the people, who all make up the Fatherland. You salute one, you salute all." Schelberg nodded to himself. "Yes, yes. I see it. Forgive me for imagining you may have deliberately insulted the Führer."

Stroeme did not believe him for a second.

"Which, of course, you would never do," the Gestapo man continued. "I believe the Führer is himself quite pleased with you. He presented that Knight's Cross himself, did he not?"

Stroeme nodded. "It was a double honor."

Schelberg made a noise that could have been a sigh of satisfaction. "You have an enviable record, Major. A rising star of the combat arena of the skies."

"Be careful, *Herr* Schelberg. When people give me effusive praise, I tend to wonder what is really behind it."

Schelberg made his little sound again. A tiny smile appeared. "And astute with it. Impressive. May I present a little...let us call it...situation. Dashing fighter pilot, liked by the Führer, admired and respected by his men, definitely respected and certainly liked by his commanding officer and...possibly, loved by a beautiful, titled French woman. Ah, these French and their decadent titles. I have no love for the decadent German classes either; but they are useful..."

Stroeme felt a stab of apprehension. Amongst all that, the mention of Marie, certainly deliberate, was the first sign of where Schelberg was headed.

"Why have you brought Marie du Vaillon into this? Has she done something?"

The Gestapo man gave a little squeak of a laugh. "My dear Major. Of course not. The Countess is a well-known supporter of the Vichy government. Her receptions for the high-ranking members of the Reich forces are well-known and much sought after. Such Resistance groups as there may be must see her as one of their prime targets whenever they may get the chance. She knows the rules of the game. I merely brought her into the equation to illustrate how things...*may* sometimes change, without warning."

Stroeme said nothing.

"Your squadron's task," Schelberg continued, "as we all know, is to protect this area. But it must be done in such a way that the Englanders do not suspect that there is anything around here deserving of special protection. This is just another fighter airfield. If they decided to attack it, there would be help from other forces; but you do not and cannot use your squadron to...reciprocate. Your primary function cannot be jeopardized. According to the *Brigadeführer*, you have carried out this duty exceptionally well. Always on the alert, but never undue aircraft movements that might excite the interest of the watching *Tommis*.

"But suddenly, we have a crisis. A very important SS officer is missing. If a Resistance group have got him, we must assume that what is being done here may be compromised. If they have not killed him, we must also assume that they will turn him over to the English. We cannot allow that. Frankly, it would be better for him to be dead." Schelberg smiled. "See how I have taken you into my confidence."

THE RAVEN CONSPIRACY – CODE NAME: ICARUS

It was a confidence Stroeme did not want. Sharing "confidences"—willingly or not—with someone like Schelberg tended to have a price that no one in their right minds would want to pay.

"We are here, Major," Schelberg went on, "to keep the French where they belong, stop the English, cleanse the place of Jews, and to defend the Reich and its ideals. *Standartenführer* Bock is a vital part of this work. We cannot lose him to the enemy. Now imagine if it were believed—even if that were obviously not true—that there were those who would hinder, or were unwillingly prepared to help find the *Standartenführer*. No amount of Knight's Crosses—whether presented by the Führer or not—could possibly prevent both the Führer, and the *Reichsmarschall*, from independently coming to the conclusion that the Eastern Front needed the combat experience of the Cambridge Boys." Schelberg chuckled. "I like that. Cambridge Boys. It must annoy the *Tommis*. You were at Cambridge, I believe."

"Believe" nothing, Stroeme thought with an anger he did not show. It was obvious that the Gestapo man had been digging into his confidential file.

"I was. It is well known. Is that a problem?"

"No, no. No problem at all. After all. There are *Tommis* who have been to German universities. I am certain many of them are now ranged against us."

Stroeme responded with silence as they walked.

"Now if the Cambridge Boys were to suddenly move east," Schelberg said, a sly look in his cold eyes, "pity the beautiful countess without her gallant escort. She would be without anyone, and vulnerable to the vagaries of...warfare. Perhaps she would be...lucky and a new champion might appear...or many..."

The "many", with its wealth of not-so-subtle meanings, struck at Stroeme, but he did not give Schelberg the satisfaction of spotting it.

"She might even lose that magnificent 18th century mansion," Schelberg roved on. "It might be commandeered, like your headquarters building. These things happen in wartime. As for the Resistance, such as it may be..." He let the sentence die; but its meaning was quite clear.

"You are threatening me, *Herr* Schelberg?"

"I am not, Major. I assure you. Threats are an unnecessary waste of time. Helpful advice...now that, is different. So please let us not fight. Let us save it for our true enemies. Take me sightseeing."

As he Schelberg spoke, they heard the sound of a car. Both turned to look. The SS car was leaving.

"It seems the *Brigadeführer* expected you to get your flight," Stroeme said.

"Apparently." The thinnest of smiles briefly appeared on Schelberg's lips.

"Then we'd better see to it." Stroeme began walking back to the squadron car, where Dasinger was waiting. "Hans," he said when they had arrived. "We're going over to the Storch section. This is *Herr* Schelberg. He's with the Gestapo. I'm taking him up. *Herr* Schelberg, *Hauptmann* Dasinger, my second-in-command."

Dasinger looked at Stroeme with lively eyes that were full of questions that Stroeme's own eyes warned him not ask.

"My equivalent SS rank is *Standartenführer*," Schelberg dropped in conversationally as Dasinger nodded at him. "But let us not be formal. We are all officers of the Reich, after all, are we not?" He got into the back of the car before being asked.

"If you'll give me a few moments," Stroeme said to him.

"Are we not going immediately?"

"I must first report to the Commandant."

"You can do that later, surely..."

"The Commandant asked me to report to him when we were finished talking," Stroeme responded in a firm voice that brooked no argument. "You may remember that, *Herr* Schelberg. Would you have me disobey my orders?"

"Of course not, Major." Schelberg's eyes were opaque behind the glasses.

"Thank you."

"Forceful man," Schelberg said to Dasinger as Stroeme entered the building. He was not looking at the Captain, but at the entrance that Stroeme had just gone through. "Is he always like that?"

"With respect, *Herr* Schelberg," Dasinger said, "if you want to know about Major Stroeme, he's the best person to ask."

"Ah yes," the Gestapo man murmured. "Everyone is

so…'respectful'. What a polite squadron."

"He has his flight, sir," Stroeme began as he entered the commandant's office.

"I thought he might. What pressures did he use?"

"The usual about the Eastern Front then for good measure, he had the gall to threaten Marie."

The colonel nodded. "The *Totenkopf*, and the Gestapo. Malignant bedfellows. Their usual methods."

Feldbruck got to his feet, and walked over to a wide window to look out upon a garden that had taken generations to create. He placed his hands behind his back.

"Our country, Karl, is being led to disaster. Don't say anything. Let me finish. I was a 19-year-old pilot in the last war," Feldbruck continued. "That was a monumental disaster. This one will be far worse.

"Our unpleasant friends, the *Totenkopf* SS, and the Gestapo, have long pointed the way it will go. When I was that young pilot, Hitler, Himmler, and Göring, were foot soldiers. Well, Himmler scarcely was. Göring, of course, transferred to flying duties at the beginning. Now the corporal, the sergeant, and the former infantryman who became commander of *Jasta* 11, now control Germany. I will not begrudge Göring his previous flying skills, but his true nature led him to join up with Hitler, and Himmler. What is he now? A morphine addict. The failed artist, the failed chicken farmer, and a morphine addict, run our country.

"We failed to knock out the RAF. *Adler Tag* was a mistake that we will eventually pay dearly for. The *Totenkopf* murder surrendering prisoners in cold blood. The English and Canadians will not forget what was done to their soldiers when we took France. And I dare not imagine what will happen, when the world eventually sees the concentration camps. Hitler has not learned from history. He should have remembered what happened to Napoleon in the east. Barbarossa will return to haunt us." Feldbruck took a deep breath. "And Himmler, born into a conservative Catholic family, has created an unspeakably monstrous organization. For years to come, people will wonder how was it that a nation supposedly civilized, colluded so willingly to the violation of its soul. Something has to be done to save our country's honor." Feldbruck stopped, but did not turn round.

"What are you saying, sir?" Stroeme asked with caution.

"There are people, Karl...even at this early stage, who think as I do."

"These are dangerous thoughts, sir."

"I am well aware of that. Dangerous thoughts belong here. Will you report me?"

Stroeme was shocked. "Certainly not! I am advising you not repeat this, Colonel...to anyone on this squadron. As for myself, you have my word upon my honor, that I will never use this to bring you harm. Not even Dasinger will know of it."

Feldbruck at last turned to face Stroeme. He looked a sad man. "I took that chance, Karl. Thank you. Now you had better take that hound of hell on his flight. Sorry he saw fit to bring Marie into it."

"Sir."

As Stroeme left, the colonel turned back to the garden. He remained where he was as Stroeme shut the door on his way out.

He looked very lonely by that window, staring out upon a world he did not like.

He was a man twice imprisoned.

CHAPTER FOUR

Teterboro Airport, New Jersey. July 2006.
 Mary Adams had spoken to some people she knew at the airport, telling them that she was meeting a friend whom she believed was being followed by less than friendly individuals. Already geared since 9/11 to spotting anomalies, they readily agreed to keep watch. She had described Tad Duchamps as a fighter jock buddy.
 Knowing her history, they did not doubt the story.
 When she spotted him, she also spotted that he had someone in tow. She alerted her friends to the follower. They moved into an unobtrusive blocking action, while she went up to Duchamps.
 "Come with me, Captain. You've got company. *Don't* look round!"
 She took him through an aircrew exit, losing the tail.
 He stared at her. "I know you, don't I?"
 "I doubt it."
 "Yes," he insisted. "You're Air Force."
 "*Was*," she said, admitting it.
 "I knew it! You're Lieutenant Mary Adams. I saw your picture when you got your wings...in our squadron news."
 "Old picture. Old news."
 "What happened?"
 "Old story." She did not elaborate.
 "So now you fly...what?"
 "Bizjets."
 "Like it?"

"It's a good living, and I don't have to salute assholes who sleep with me, then go back to their wives. I just fly some of them. No salute, no sleeping."

"Wow, wow, *wow!* Ease up. I'm not one of them, in or out of the Service."

She paused to stare at him. "You've got *green* eyes. Never seen that before. Goes well with your complexion."

"I think that came from my grandmother's genes. She was Danish,"

"A *green*-eyed Dane?"

"Yes. My grandpa was 20, she 18, when they first saw each other. He fell like a ton of bricks. It was during the war."

"That must have been something at the time."

"It was not easy for them. She was Danish Resistance, he was a fighter pilot with the RAF."

"*The* RAF?"

"Is there another?"

"How come?"

"The USAAF wouldn't have him."

"That figures. So where are they now?"

Duchamps gave her a curious glance as they hurried. "Both dead. She did not last long after he died."

"Sorry to hear. What happened?"

Duchamps shot her another glance. "Someone killed him. All through a war with hardly a scratch, then this happens. Sniper."

"Jesus!"

"I'm trying to find out why. That's why I'm here to see you. You suggested you might have some answers."

She stopped so suddenly, he kept on walking for a brief moment.

"*Me?*" she said as he turned back to face her.

"The voice is different from the one on the phone...but you could have been faking. I'm in Teterboro, you lost my shadow, and you're in the pilot's uniform."

"Ah. Daybreak. Not me. The person I fly. She's very pretty. Dark eyes. Luminous. Don't be like your grandfather and fall for her. Too rich for your blood."

"Thanks."

"Don't mention it."

A few minutes later, they got into the company car and drove to where the Cessna was parked.

"My office," she said as they got out.

Duchamps stared at the plane for long moments. "This," he said, "is a sweet-looking ship."

"You've got taste," she said with dry approval. "The person you've come to see is inside. I'll wait out here."

"Thank you, Captain," he said, glancing at the rings on her shoulders.

"No problem, Captain."

Duchamps went up the collapsible steps and into the aircraft. He looked at Ellen with studied neutrality.

"She was right," he said.

"About what?"

"Many things." He looked about him. "This is quite a bird. I'm Tad…"

"Duchamps."

"Of course. You know that."

"Yes. Please take a seat, Mr. Duchamps. Or would you prefer Captain?"

"Whatever you feel as ease with," he said as he sat down opposite. "Tad will also be fine."

She leaned forward to offer her hand. "I'm Ellen," They shook hands.

"Just Ellen?"

"Haines."

"Haines," he said thoughtfully. "I know the name."

"Among the many Haines there must be around, one is my grandfather. Former Senator Leroy Haines..."

"That's the one. But I'm not thinking of him as a senator. I'm thinking of him as one of the men in my grandfather's old squadron; the unit no one wants to talk about; the one that's not supposed to have existed."

Occupied France. The Cambridge Boys squadron, Monday, July

1941. 0845 hours, local.

Dasinger brought the *Kübelwagen* to a halt at the Storch section flightline.

They had stopped on the way at the squadron's mission planning section, to collect an aerial map of the general search area. Stroeme had drawn a circle on the map with a fifty kilometer radius, centered on the spot where the SS colonel was supposed to have disappeared.

"This is where we get off," he now said to their unwelcome guest as he himself got out of the vehicle.

Schelberg followed.

Almost immediately and with a parting wave to Stroeme, Dasinger turned the *Kübelwagen* round, and headed back.

Watching the vehicle go, Schelberg remarked with more than a little dryness, "I think your Hauptmann Dasinger does not like my company very much, Major."

"It isn't that. He has many responsibilities to attend to."

"As do we all. I understand the situation."

Which could have meant anything.

Three of the four Storchs were in a wide, low hangar. The fourth was in front of it. All four sported Cambridge blue tails. Stroeme, followed by Schelberg, went towards the aircraft. As they approached, a ground crew senior sergeant came out of the hangar.

"*Hauptfeldwebel* Wolfgang König," Stroeme explained. "Ground crew chief. If he passes an aircraft for flight, it will complete the mission without a single failure. Only enemy action can bring it down. I trust him with my life, and have done. My 109 has never once let me down. So do not worry. This Storch will have been properly serviced."

"I am not worried."

Stroeme felt a smile he did not show.

"Is she ready, Wolle?" Stroeme said to the crew chief as all three reached the aircraft together.

"Yes, sir," König replied. "Ready to go." His eyes darted towards the Gestapo man.

"Our passenger," Stroeme informed him, "*Herr* Schelberg of the Gestapo. Find him a flight overall to fit will you, please?"

"Immediately, *Herr* Major."

Stroeme turned to Schelberg. "*Herr* Schelberg, I will pre-flight the aircraft. Go with the *Hauptfeldwebel*, will you please? Remove your jacket. Transfer anything you do not wish to leave in it to your trouser pockets. We take off in ten minutes."

The Gestapo man nodded, and followed König.

As they left, Stroeme looked up at the bright, clear sky. "At least it's a good day for it."

The Fieseler Fi 156 Storch was, like the Lysander, a peculiar aircraft. Both had vast wing areas, and both resembled, as far as Stroeme was concerned, insects. But they were also very different. Where the Lizzie looked robust, the Storch appeared spindly delicate. It also had at 270 hp, a far less powerful engine; but by virtue of its extreme low-speed capability, it came as close as a fixed wing aircraft could to emulating a helicopter. It could not hover, but it could sometimes deceive the eye into believing it. It's space frame construction, spindly, long-throw fixed undercarriage and long, broad slatted wings gave it, to Stroeme's mind, the look of a giant locust. It could fly at 32 mph, and land in as little a space as the Lysander.

Where the Lysander could climb steeply, the Storch simply floated off the ground on a wingspan of nearly 47 feet.

Stroeme had finished his checks and was already in the front cockpit with the engine running, when Schelberg—without jacket— returned, clad in Luftwaffe flight overalls. König helped the Gestapo man get into the rear cockpit.

"We should start at the point where he was last seen by his driver," Schelberg said above the noise, when he was strapped in.

"Very well," Stroeme said. "If you're ready..."

"I'm ready."

Stroeme began to taxi towards a wide expanse of grass close to the flightline, smooth enough to be a sports field. Once on it, he accelerated. The Storch floated off the ground in almost level flight, its seemingly ungainly long undercarriage making it indeed look like the bird after which it had been named.

They had been flying for about half an hour when Stroeme made a sudden, and violent bank to the left.

It was as well that he did. Streams of tracer rose from the ground and several angry things hit the aircraft, just beneath and behind

Schelberg. But for Stroeme's fast reactions, Schelberg would have been dead.

But they had not totally escaped. The Storch was handling like a bus with bald tires on an ice rink.

"I'll have to put her down!" Stroeme called to the terrified Schelberg. "There's a clearing just below. I must put her down before we get to the trees!"

"*Yes, yes!*" came the nervously relieved agreement.

Stroeme began to make a radio call, but soon discovered that the firing had smashed it. As he fought the aircraft into a turn which would take him to the clearing, he wondered why the firing had suddenly stopped.

Then he got his answer. He was scanning the area searching out the best place to land, when he saw why: *the culprit was an SS halftrack.*

"Someone ought to teach them recognition!" he said with sharp anger.

"What?"

"The people who shot at us are damned SS!"

"*What?*" Schelberg repeated, in stunned, squeaky disbelief as the aircraft gave a sudden lurch.

"See for yourself. Over your left shoulder."

Schelberg did not look. He was staring mesmerized, as the ground approached, far too rapidly, he decided.

But Stroeme made a perfect landing. At that very moment, the engine died.

"Just in time," he said. He released his harness, then removed his helmet, which he draped on the top of the long joystick. "I want words with that halftrack crew. Join me, if you want."

Without waiting for Schelberg, he got out of the aircraft and began walking with angry strides towards the halftrack and its shocked crew, barely 100 meters away.

"*What the hell do you think you're doing!*" Stroeme yelled at the SS lieutenant in command.

At first sheepish, the SS officer decided to choose belligerent contempt, instead of contrition.

"And who the hell do you think you are, yelling at me?"

"*Major Karl-Gustav Stroeme, Luftwaffe, you incompetent moron!*" Stroeme shouted. "*And I'll yell as I damned well like!*"

The SS-lieutenant fell back on outrage, seething with anger at being spoken to like that in front of his men. "I am SS! You cannot…"

"Cannot what, *Obersturmführer?*" Schelberg had come up.

The SS lieutenant glared at him. "And who the hell are *you?*"

"Who the hell am I?" the Gestapo man began mildly. "Schelberg…Gestapo…and SS *Standartenführer.*"

The lieutenant paled. His men bought themselves to attention, faces going grey.

"*And you, Obersturmführer,*" Schelberg bawled with a suddenness that took even Stroeme by surprise. "*Who the hell are you?*"

The SS lieutenant lost it completely. His lips moved, but nothing came out.

"*Well?*" Schelberg barked. The eyes behind the glasses were merciless as they stared at the SS lieutenant.

The lieutenant finally drew himself to attention, and looked into a far distance that had no pleasing visions. "Ro…Rohandt, *Standartenführer!*"

"Well, *Obersturmführer* Rohandt, the Major is absolutely correct, you are an incompetent moron, and will not long remain an *Obersturmführer!* You almost *killed* us, and had it not been for the Major's quick reactions, you would have succeeded! Have you not yet learned to distinguish our aircraft from those of the enemy? Who was the fool who fired that machine gun?"

Rohandt's lips trembled. His men seemed to be inching away.

"*Stand still!*" Schelberg roared. They froze.

"I want an answer, Rohandt!" Schelberg demanded.

"It…it was me…*Standartenführer…*" Rohandt's words died miserably.

The Gestapo man looked at the hapless SS lieutenant in wonder. "It was you," he said, almost in a whisper. "You compound your stupidity and incompetence by actually being the person *who fired that weapon?* The Eastern Front is a mild punishment! I'll see if I can do better..."

Stroeme had been scanning the sky while Schelberg had been chewing out the previously arrogant SS lieutenant when four rapidly approaching dots, coming low down from the West, caught his attention. He saw them split to go into line astern.

"*Schelberg!*" he yelled and grabbed the Gestapo man, running and dragging him to the ground, and rolling.

He was none too soon. The others, however, were far too slow.

The cannons from the first Hurricane ripped Rohandt apart, and shredded two more of his men as it swept past. It had hurtled so close to them, Stroeme and Schelberg had felt the buffeting winds of its passage. The second aircraft, hot on its heels, was not so close, but added its cannon roar to the carnage. The third completed the job, causing the halftrack to explode, and finishing off what was left of the crew.

The fourth Hurricane completed what Rohandt had started on the Storch.

The Hurricanes seemed to be curving round for a second pass, but joined up instead and keeping low, headed back towards England. It had all taken just a few terrible, ferocious seconds to eliminate the halftrack and its entire crew.

Stroeme had recognized the hostile aircraft. Raven Squadron Hurricanes. He wondered if anyone had spotted him during the fury of the attack. They had been low enough.

He stared at the smoking wreckage of the Storch, then looked at Schelberg, who was looking about him with staring eyes, mouth agape.

They had reached cover near some bushes, and were lying flat. The bushes would not have stopped the cannon shells if they had been spotted, but it had been better than nothing.

"Where...where did they come from?" Schelberg at last enquired. "One moment the sky was clear, and the next..."

"That's how it is in aerial combat, *Herr Schelberg*. Failure to appreciate that frequently results in an early death...even in this relatively quiet area."

Schelberg stared at the destroyed halftrack, and the scattered bodies of the SS men. Some had tried to flee, and had been caught in their various stages of flight.

"You should have learned to recognize the enemy!" he yelled at the dead SS crew with a vicious savagery. "Well," he continued in a sudden return to conversational tones, "that saves me having to recommend suitable punishment for that idiot." The word was yelled at the dead SS lieutenant. He turned to Stroeme. "This is the second time in a very short period that your quick reactions have saved my life, Major. I am beholden to you. Not a position I can honestly say I enjoy. But I am not ungrateful. Perhaps I can one day reciprocate."

"No need to...but you can help me out."

"Oh?"

"First, leave Marie du Vaillon alone."

"You are in love with that woman? There are many perfectly suitable Aryan women in Germany..."

"Leave her alone."

Schelberg, eyes unwavering, nodded. "Very well. You said 'first'. What's the second?"

"One of our best flak teams has been called out to join your search. I want them taken off it. We need them for the defense of the airfield. After what has just happened, you must see that this is necessary. The *Tommis* have left this area alone, mainly because we have managed to give the impression for now, that there are no valuable targets here. They are concentrating on southern Normandy and Brittany. But as you just saw, that does not mean there won't be target-of-opportunity intruder missions. If you want to recommend sending me to the Eastern Front, so be it. But leave Marie alone, and have my men sent back to their proper duties."

Schelberg shook his head slowly, a puzzled expression upon his face as both men got to their feet. "You continue to surprise me, Major. You seem prepared to sacrifice yourself for others. Even me. You could have saved yourself and left me to it. The rest of us, not possessing your quick reactions..." He paused, glancing at the bodies. "I would have been one of them. Despite everything, you risked death to drag me to safety. Now you offer yourself for the Eastern Front to protect your countess, and for your squadron. Remarkable. A man such as you can be either a very loyal friend, or a very dangerous opponent...perhaps even an enemy.

"But very well, Major. I am not unappreciative. The countess is safe. She can continue giving her parties, uninterrupted. In any case, she has German blood." Schelberg made it sound as if it was too bad she had French blood as well. "Your men will be relieved of search duties. I will speak with the *Brigadeführer*. When he hears what has happened here, I very much doubt he will refuse. As for the Eastern Front, I am certain he will agree that a commander such as yourself is of more value here on the Western Front, guarding our particular airspace. Satisfactory?"

"Very. Thank you."

Schelberg looked at the wrecked Storch. "Now how do we get out of here? Walk?"

"No need. Dasinger will be checking by radio every twenty minutes. When he does not get a reply, he will take action." Stroeme glanced at his watch. "He'll be doing a check in two minutes. As soon as he does not hear from me, he'll immediately start a search. He already knows where we're likely to be, whether we've survived or not. In a straight line, we're only 20 minutes away from the airfield by Storch. By 109, no distance at all. They'll see the smoke from the halftrack and the Storch. You'll soon be out of here."

"As I've said...a remarkable man. You think of everything."

Stroeme looked from the still-smoking Storch, to the halftrack, the bodies, and back to the aircraft. "Not everything."

"I'll see to it that your Storch is replaced," Schelberg said.

Outskirts of Macon, Georgia. July 2006.
Haines appeared to be mumbling in his afternoon sleep.

"Aaah Schelberg, Schelberg!" came whispering from between the fluttering lips. "If only you knew! If only..."

The words faded into silence.

Teterboro Airport, New Jersey. July, 2006.
Duchamps was staring at Ellen. "You knew *nothing* about the squadron?"

She shook her head. "Only what I read in the article."

"You got hold of one of the few they did not pull." There was bitterness in the remark. "Your grandfather, and my grandfather—judging by the single mention he made of the name—were not the best of friends. He said something like: Ah yes. Senator Haines. Knew him on the squadron. That was it...but the words hid plenty. A week later, he was dead. So, Miss Haines...Ellen...what do you want of me?"

"I want nothing of you. It is more about what *you* might want of me. My help."

"Why should I want, or need, your help? You are the granddaughter of the man who at best, would never have been my grandfather's friend. It was all in the voice that day. Two Southern men from the same state, on opposite sides of the racial divide. In those times...war or no war, friendship was not an option. And we all know what Senator Haines was like in his heyday. That kind never change."

"I am not my grandfather. We never agreed on anything much before I was fifteen and nothing at all, after fifteen."

"How come?"

"I think he had my mother killed."

Duchamps' eyes widened. "Run that by me again?"

"I have no proof...but it is what I think. It's in my gut."

Taken aback, Duchamps said, "And what makes you think that?"

"I never knew my father. He died when I was a baby. My mother was alone for a long time. Then one day, she met a man at a reception..."

"Works every time. Up here? Or down South?"

"Manhattan. He was a very gentle man. A lawyer."

"There are gentle lawyers?"

Both smiled at this.

"Well, *he* was. Criminal lawyer, defense. He got a lot of innocent people off. He was good at his job. She was happy for the first time I can remember. Really very happy. He seemed to be everything she ever wanted in a man."

"So what went wrong?"

"Nothing. At least, not between them. I don't believe the story they put out...after she was killed. My mother and Jack were travelling South to meet my family. It was a crazy idea of my mom's.

She should have known better. She phoned to say they were stopping off at a motel on the way. She said where it was. Next morning, we got a call. Mom had been strangled, and the police had got a black man for the crime..."

"I'm getting a bad feeling," Duchamps said.

"Your guess is right. The black man was Jack. He said at his trial that two men came into their room, and knocked him out. When he came to, my mom was dead. Strange thing was, the police were already there before he was fully conscious."

"And naturally, they did not believe him."

"No. Neither did the judge. I think the judge had an extra hatred for him because he had been so successful in getting innocent people off. Jack had a reputation that even that judge had heard about. Worse, he talked to the judge like an equal..."

"Bad move," was Duchamps' dry comment— "One thing worse than a nigger in some places, is an uppity, educated nigger."

"Jack was sent to prison...and there was a fight..."

"And poor Jack got killed."

"Yes."

"I'm so shocked." Duchamp's sarcasm was palpable.

"Only Martha and I in the family, believe he was innocent."

"Who's Martha?"

"She's been with the family before I was born. She's like a mom to me. I call her Mom. Privately."

"Is that code for she's the family maid, and black?"

"I don't see her as a maid."

"*You* may not."

"I asked Martha to try to see him. She pretended she was family, although his real family had been there at the trial. But Martha can be a good pretender. She let them see her as the kind of black person they wanted to at the prison, and they allowed her a visit. She said he looked lost, scarcely believing what had happened to him. She also said she could understand why my mom fell in love with him."

"Big crime to some people back then and in some places, even today. So you're certain old Senator Haines had it done?"

"He knew Jack was black. He could not stand to look at my mom when he found out. But she was naïve enough to think that if Grandpa got to meet him..."

"That old racist would suddenly change? Naïve is not the word."

"Instead, her crazy idea got them both killed."

"Nice man, Senator Haines. It's a very sad story, Ellen. And believe me, I am very sorry about what happened to your mom and Jack. Nothing I can say can make this better...but how does that give me information about my grandpa?"

"I wanted to give you some background so that you will understand where I am coming from, when I tell you the reason why you are here. My grandfather asked me to make the contact."

Duchamps' mouth seemed to open and close of its own volition, but no sound came out.

"Your...*grandfather?*" he said at last.

"This plane is at our disposal. We can go anywhere..."

"'Our'? '*We?*'"

"You need help. I'm it."

"Your grandfather... You've just said you suspect him of having your mother killed, the man she loved setup for the crime and miraculously, killed in prison. Now you tell me that this same Jim Crow grandfather who was on the same non-existent squadron with my grandfather—a man he hated—during the war, sends you to find me, and you *trust* him?"

"No. I don't trust him. But he had that year-old copy of the magazine; one that was not pulled. Don't ask me how he got hold of it, because I don't know. But he was interested in what you were doing. That should at least make you wonder."

"It does. It also makes me wonder if he's setting us both up to be killed, like your mom and poor Jack. There's not going to be a 'poor' Tad."

"I would think that 'poor' Tad would take information about what really happened to his grandpa from any source...even from the cranky old senator who's hiding secrets that could even get *him* killed."

"Now *that*, gets me interested."

"He gave me a valise," Ellen said, "that he got during World War Two. It used to be a secret radio. Now it's full of information about what really happened back then. I haven't looked at any of it as yet.

But the copy of the magazine was in there."

"I'll be damned," Duchamps remarked softly. "Do you really believe that what I've been looking for could be in that case?"

"I don't know for sure. But from what he said to me, some of it must be. He made a point of saying how dangerous the valise was, and that there were people who would kill to stop what's in there from getting out."

"He *is* trying to get us killed."

"He gave me a chance to refuse."

"No he didn't. A man who has sat on whatever it is for all those years, knew exactly what he was doing. He set the bait, and you took it."

"There could be another reason."

"Enlighten me."

"He's in his eighties. He probably wants to put things right before he goes."

Duchamps gave her a look that could have meant anything. "I hope you're not as naïve as you called your mom. Haines is after something...but it's not absolution."

"So what is he after?"

"Revenge. What kind...I don't know as yet. If we do this, perhaps we'll find out."

"So? Do we try to find out?" The dark, luminous eyes that Mary Adams had talked about seemed to be looking at him with an unusual power.

"Perhaps we should listen to his warning."

"Perhaps you should stop pretending and say yes. You did not come way out here, only to back off when the first real break you've had drops into your lap."

"You don't mince words."

"It wastes time."

Duchamps glanced about him. "If there are people out there who really will try to kill us, nothing wrong with going out in style, I guess. And the senator's paying. It's the least he can do."

"I hope we won't be 'going out'...in style, or not. Where do you live? You sound New York, not Georgia."

"I was born in New York. Manhattan. The Village."

"Nice place for a Duchamps."

"No relation. There's an 's' in my name."

She smiled at that. "How come your parents set up there? Were they artists?"

"My grandpa began that. When he came back to the States a few years after the war, he arrived with my grandma and my father, who was born in England. He knew he could never go back South with them. He never went back at all; not even without her to visit family. Too much had happened in his life in a short time. He could never again put up with the Southern attitudes of the time. The Village was a place they could live. It was still not easy at the very beginning, but it was the best place for them at the time. Later, of course, it did not matter anymore.

"He was already a fully qualified flying instructor, so he got a good job training civilian pilots, right here in Teterboro. Then an old squadron buddy called him from England and offered him a partnership in a flying business—charter, and training. He accepted, and spent a lot of time commuting between the States and England, and went to reunions all over the world. My grandma usually went with him when my dad was no longer a baby. She was a tough cookie. In the war, she was in the Resistance."

"Resistance? She's not American, or English?"

"Danish."

"Ah."

"Why 'ah'?"

"That's where you get your green eyes from." Before he could respond, she went on, "The business obviously did well."

"It did very well," he said, giving her a quizzical look. "It put my father through medical school. My father lived right next door when he had his own family. He never wanted a military career. That skipped a generation to me. I was away from home so long and often, I never really lived there. I only got me a place of my own when I resigned—a loft not far from the old home, which my parents inherited."

"That's not true, is it?" She was looking at him steadily.

"What's not true?"

"That your parents inherited. I think your grandfather, whom you so obviously admired, left it to you. It's something he would have done. You followed in his footsteps. You gave the place to your parents. You wanted to keep them safe. If people came after you, they would go where you lived. Your parents would be next door. Too close."

"You can tell all this from what I've just said?"

"It's in your voice. Martha taught me how to listen. She's very good at picking up what people are really saying. That's how she was certain Jack was innocent. She knew he was not lying. So? Did you give your parents the house?"

"Yes," Duchamps admitted. "I'll have to watch you," he added.

"You need the information I have, and you'll need me to tell you when people are lying to you."

He gave her another neutral stare. "Why do you want to do this? What's really in it for you?"

She answered in a roundabout way. "You want to know what really happened to your grandfather. *My* grandfather had his own daughter killed, and the man she loved wrongly sent to prison where *he* was killed. I want to know what else he is responsible for, and what's his part in what happened to your grandfather. I want to know why he decided to hand this strange inheritance to me."

Duchamps said nothing for a while, looking as if he was not sure whether to believe her. "So where do you live?"

"SoHo."

"Natch."

"What's that supposed to mean?"

"Just natch."

Over the English Channel, Monday, July 1941. 0931 hours. Local.

The four Raven Squadron Hurricanes were rushing low over the water in finger-four formation. The squadron had adapted the fluid formation, first spotted being used by Luftwaffe fighter pilots.

"Well done, guys;" Murchison said to his charges. "That was good work."

"I thought I saw..." Pew began.

"Blue Two!" Murchison interrupted sharply. "Cut it out! Radio silence, Blue Flight..." he added. "...until I say differently."

No one would speak again, until they were once more safely over Shawbridge.

Somewhere in England. At about the same time. July, 1941.

The man in shirt sleeved, *Totenkopf* SS uniform was sitting in a large, underground cell, staring at nothing. He looked the worse for wear. There were no marks upon his body but he seemed a beaten man, resigned to his fate...

There was an eerie silence about the place that went well beyond the cell, as if no one else existed within the entire building.

The cell itself appeared surprisingly comfortable, with an agreeable temperature. There was a low table and an extra chair. The camp bed against one wall was made, with better bed linen than would have been expected. Toilet facilities were clearly elsewhere. There was even a small bookcase, neatly filled with books in German.

The man stood up, and began to pace. He limped very slightly, intermittently, favoring the left foot. He took slow, aimless steps, like those of an animal that had spent too long in a zoo. Back and forth, back and forth. Sometimes, he would shift from one foot to the other, barely moving from the spot; then he would pace again.

His hard face was expressionless, the sunken cheeks making it death-like, staring eyes telling of a soul long vanished. He did not look like this from starvation. If anything, he was well fed. Despite the air of despondency, this was his natural look, born of the things he had done and for which he had sold his soul. His hair was shaven high at the back and sides, and crowned by a dark thatch at the top.

He stopped pacing, body posture assuming the stillness of a pointer that has spotted game. He thought he'd heard something. He waited, listening. Faint life crept hesitantly into the darkness of his eyes.

His body slumped. It was nothing. Perhaps the wind hissing softly through an opening somewhere along the seemingly endless corridor of polished linoleum, which was flanked by concrete walls painted a sickly hue. Unshaded bulbs hung at precise intervals from the ceiling. There were doors along the corridor, but he had never heard or seen one being opened. The sole exception was the one that opened to the shower and toilet facilities, directly opposite his cell.

The guards came every four hours daily, from 0600 to 1800, then at 2000 for the last visit of the day to the toilet. He had a bedpan for use during the night if he were caught short. It was a source of pride to him that he had never used it, in all the time he'd been there; even when there were occasions when it was a race between the 0600 arrival of the guards, and his desperate need to go. He had never given them the satisfaction of knowing it. It was, he told himself with not a little pride, a small but enduring victory.

That small victory was enhanced by the fact that neither his captors, nor their superiors had never got out of him, the secret they really wanted.

He began his pacing again. He had no idea how long they'd had him. He guessed a year, but was not certain. He had long given up counting the days.

He stopped once more, the pointer waiting. He had definitely heard something; faint, but quite unmistakable. It had not been the wind earlier.

What he now heard, was the sound of firing.

"*Gott sei dank!*" he uttered in German. The words came out of him in a wave of relief and hope. "*Endlich!*"

He rushed to the door of the cell, grabbed at the bars with both hands, and tried to peer to his right, the direction from which the guards usually came.

The firing had grown perceptibly louder, this time joined by faint shouting. He thought he heard commands in German.

"*Ich bin gerettet!*" he said in a low, happy voice. "*Ich bin...*"

He stopped. There was no more firing. No more shouts.

His entire body appeared to droop. It was obvious what had happened. The *Tommis* had killed the rescuers. He was stuck in his cell, for as long as the *Tommis* wished.

He went back to his chair, and sat down.

Bare minutes later, he leapt to his feet, excitement returning. There had been a sudden burst of firing, much closer now. There was shouting too, punctuated by screams of the dying. He again gripped the bars of the cell, and strained to look in the direction of the commotion.

More silence descended abruptly.

Bock remained where he was, at once expectant and apprehensive. Had that been the end of it? The last remnants of the rescue team wiped out?

Minutes seemed to pass. Bock did not move, eyes swiveled to his right, fixed upon the corridor. Waiting.

Then came a shout he'd been longing to hear, ever since he had been brought to this place.

"*Standartenführer Bock! Sind sie da?*" The accents were broad Bavarian.

"*Hier!*" Bock called back, excitement and relief flooding though him. "*Ich bin hier!*"

There were loud, running footsteps. Then at the edge of his vision, Bock saw four heavily-armed men hurrying towards him. They all wore flying overalls.

Their leader stopped directly in front of his staring eyes, and partially opened the overalls. Bock saw the SS uniform beneath.

The man clicked his heels, right arm shooting out. "*Heil Hitler!*"

The happy Bock grinned, stood back, and shot out his own arm, "*Heil Hitler!*"

"*Menning, Hauptsturmführer, Stardartenführer!* You have been rescued. Please stand back while we open your cell."

Bock quickly obeyed.

Another man came forward. Placed something against the cell door. All four then rapidly put a safe distance between them and the door. The explosion blew the lock without taking the door off its hinges.

"Come, *Standartenführer!* We must hurry! Here. Put this on. That white shirt is a perfect target for any sniper the *Tommis* might have out there."

Bock took the preferred overalls without question, and began to get into them.

As he did so, he paused to stare at one of the men.

"*Corporal Roberts?*" he exclaimed in startled English. His astonished, puzzled eyes turned upon Menning. "What is this?" he asked in sharp German.

Roberts had been one of the guards.

"'This', *Standartenführer*, is *Oberscharführer* Stefan Lebmann. His command of English is excellent, having worked in England before the war. He was infiltrated into this *Tommi* unit. Very successfully, as you can see." Menning gave a thin smile. "Ever since you were taken, *Brigadeführer* Forst was determined to get you back. He planned this mission. Now I must ask you to please hurry, *Standartenführer*. We...er...commandeered an aircraft to get you away. We must do so before the *Tommis* realize it is missing."

"Yes, yes! Of course!" Bock quickly continued to put on the overalls. "Excellent work!" he said to the man he had previously known as Roberts. "I will recommend you for an Iron Cross. All of you will be recommended for decorations and promotions for this."

"We'll be very happy to receive them when we're safely away from here, *Standartenführer*," Menning remarked.

"Of course," Bock repeated. "I am ready. How many men did you lose?" he went on as they hurried along the corridor.

"Two killed," Menning answered. "The *Tommis* lost everyone they had here. We achieved total surprise."

"Good!" Bock said with vicious satisfaction. "Good."

"They thought we were *Tommis* when we first arrived," Menning said. "And with Lebmann already here, it was very quick, and complete. This way, *Standartenführer*."

They hurried up a long flight of stairs, and out a door that opened onto what looked like a small parade ground. At least a dozen bodies were scattered upon it. The entire place had the air of a small, long-disused military prison. There were no structures to be seen beyond the prison's barbed wire fence. It was marooned in a landscape with few trees.

"More bodies inside," Menning said to Bock, "including our two. We have left nothing that would immediately identify them. Our blood group tattoos were removed for this mission. By the time the *Tommis* realize what the scars mean, it will hardly matter."

A single military lorry was standing near the opened main gate, engine running.

Bock took a quick glance about him as they hurried towards the waiting truck. "They kept me in this place," he snarled.

"They paid for it," Menning said.

"Their just deserts," Bock said with a snarl.

"Into the front, if you please, *Standartenführer*," Menning urged. "We'll pile into the back. There's a small airfield, normally disused and only infrequently serves as a practice diversion airfield for training. It is not manned. The aircraft is waiting there. Anyone seeing this truck will think we're a bunch of *Tommis* on military business. No one will expect the SS." He gave a brief grin.

"You have thought of everything," Bock said as he climbed into the front.

"Tell me again, *Standartenführer*, when we're safely back in the Fatherland."

Menning shut the door, then hurried to the back of the truck, where his men were already aboard.

The twin-engined, maid-of-all-work Avro Anson in RAF utility colors, waited by the single hangar on the deserted airstrip.

Its cabin seats had been removed, and it had been refitted as a training aircraft for airborne troops. Its wide door, just behind the left wing, had been removed. At the tail end of the cabin, two bodies lay untidily. One was that of a young woman, the other wore the uniform of a Pilot Officer, with undecorated RAF wings atop the left breast pocket. He had been the pilot of the Anson. Up front, someone else was at the controls.

Half an hour after leaving the prison, the lorry approached the Anson at speed.

It pulled up to one side, brakes squealing. The men in the back jumped out quickly and began making for the aircraft, leaving Menning to wait for Bock. The driver climbed out and joined his comrades.

Menning waited with controlled impatience for Bock to get out, Bock jumped down and allowed himself to be led to the Anson.

"This is rigged out as a paratroop trainer, *Standartenführer*," Menning explained as they hurried, with sling seats. "Make yourself as comfortable as you can. It will be a bit draughty without the door..."

"I am not a wilting flower, *Hauptsturmführer*."

"No, sir. But I felt it best to prepare you."

"Appreciated," Bock said as they reached the Anson. "You've already done more than enough. A well-executed mission."

"Thank you, *Standartenführer*."

Bock climbed in, and stopped, head turned towards the tail. "What are these?"

"The original pilot," Menning replied without emotion from outside. "He objected to our taking his aircraft."

"And the woman?"

"Along for the ride. He had given her a lift to a *Tommi* unit somewhere. When this plane isn't being used for paratroopers, it spends time as a flying bus."

"He was talkative."

"I told him I'd give his girlfriend to my men, then shoot her afterwards. He talked."

Bock went closer to the bodies, to peer down. The men, hands still cradling their weapons, looked at him without expression as Menning climbed in.

Without turning round, Bock said, raising his voice as the man at the controls started the first of the twin Cheetahs. "Pretty. Was she Jewish?"

"No, *Standartenführer*. I asked him. I would still have given her to my men, shot her, then thrown her body out when we were over the sea; which is where those two will be going."

"I like the way you work, *Hauptsturmführer*. When we're back, I'll arrange to have you and your men transferred to my personal staff. I can see where such excellent people as yourselves could be of valuable use. Would you like that? There will be many privileges."

Menning gave his men a quick glance. "We would be honored, *Standartenführer*."

"Good!" Bock said with satisfaction. He raised his voice further, as the second engine was started. "Pity," he went on, looking at the body of the young woman. "So pretty. I could have enjoyed her. It's been a while since I..." he paused. "Had she been a Jewess, I would still have enjoyed her, then thrown her out, alive and naked, to rid myself of the contamination." Heady with freedom, he laughed loudly for several seconds.

The men laughed with him as the Anson began to taxi. The laughter did not reach their eyes.

"Where do I sit?" Bock asked,

"Up there, sir," Menning replied, pointing towards the front of the aircraft, at one of the seats closest to the cockpit.

They made their way over, and sat down opposite each other. Bob still had a smile upon his face.

The Anson began to line-up for takeoff. A series of loud explosions suddenly cut across the noise of the aircraft. Vivid flashes briefly lit up the interior.

Bock could not control an involuntary start. "Are we being shot at?"

No one else had even flinched.

Menning shook his head. "The *Tommi* truck. We left it for them...in pieces." This time, the men grinned with a real laughter in their eyes.

The Anson rushed forwards, and lifted smoothly into the air. Then the pilot was soon throttling back to cruising speed, and kept low.

"By the time the *Tommis* realize one of their aircraft is missing, we should be well over the Channel. Too late for them to do anything."

"You hide your light under a bushel, my dear Menning." Bock was expansive. "You have thought of everything."

"We're still over enemy territory, sir."

"Cautious too. Good. A headstrong commander would be of no use to me."

There was a slight pause, then Menning said, "I have been given a message to pass on to you, sir...if we got as far as rescuing you."

Bock looked expectant.

"It is directly from *Brigadeführer* Forst himself." Menning continued.

That got Bock's undivided attention.

The men kept studiously to themselves, busy in conversation in as low voices as the ambient noise permitted. The missing door did not help.

"He said to tell you," Menning went on to Bock, "that the

documents are missing. He told me you would understand."

Bock did understand. He went suddenly pale. "*What?* What do you mean?"

"I know nothing of this, sir. I am only relaying the message as ordered."

"Yes. Yes. Of course."

"The *Brigadeführer* summoned me to his office. We were alone. He said that after you were taken, the documents went missing, and everything was halted. He said you would know what he meant by that."

"But this is impossible! In my absence, *Obersturmbannführer* Hager has responsibility for..."

"That's the problem. Hager is dead, sir."

Bock stared at him. "*What!*"

"The French pigs got him. Ambush."

"Those resistance criminals!" Bock snarled.

"With the *Obersturmbannführer* gone," Menning said, "no one was able to find the documents."

Bock thought about that, then an unnerving realization dawned. "You are not suggesting..."

"I suggest nothing, sir. I am relaying orders."

"Surely, the *Brigadeführer* does not imagine..."

"With respect, sir. I have no idea what *Brigadeführer* Forst imagines."

"But I have said nothing to the *Tommis!*"

"Sir, the *Brigadeführer* did suggest something, to be done before we arrive in the Fatherland. If we did succeed in rescuing you, I am to ask you to send a message directly to him, stating where you believe the documents to be. I am to give you a code which will confirm it is coming from you. If you agree, we must act quickly. The message should be transmitted as fast as possible, to give their *Tommis* no chance to intercept. We have a special radio which will only make contact with him. Although I am to give you the code, you must make the transmission. I am not authorized to know what you transmit. There is a sequence you must use. I will show you, then leave you with the radio. You can use open morse code. The transmission will be secure if you do it quickly."

Menning looked at his superior with unwavering eyes. "Will you do it, sir?"

"Of course! I am loyal to the Führer! I will do as the *Brigadeführer* wishes."

"Thank you, sir." Menning turned to look at the erstwhile Corporal Roberts. "The radio, Stefan."

"Yes, sir." Lebmann passed the relatively light, portable unit over, still in its canvas case.

Menning took it. "Thank you." He opened a panel in the case, to reveal several buttons, all unmarked, and topped by the SS runic symbol. He then handed the unit to Bock, who stared at it.

"What if you had failed and the *Tommis* had found this?"

"They would have found a gluey mess. There is a vial inside, containing acid. If they had tried to find out how to operate it, they would have released the acid and..."

"Which button is the release?"

"The one next to your thumb, sir." Bock moved his thumb quickly.

Menning did not smile at this. "I will give you the sequence for the code. When you have done that, send your message with this button..." He showed Bock. "That's the morse key. Acknowledgement will be three short, twice, for SS. Then we end transmission before the *Tommis* can intercept. Are you ready, sir?"

Bock nodded.

Menning gave him the code.

Bock put it in, then sent his message. The acknowledgement came almost immediately. He passed the radio back.

"Another part of the mission accomplished," Menning said as he took the radio and secured the flap.

He returned the radio to Lebmann, then glanced out the door. They were low enough for him to see water.

"Looks like it's time to dump our cargo. Will you do the honors, sir?"

"Gladly."

"If you'll go to the door, sir... We'll bring the cargo. Please be careful. Hang on to something."

Bock nodded, and got up to go near the door, ensuring he was in no danger of falling out.

Menning nodded at Lebmann, who moved with another of the men towards the tail, where the bodies lay. Menning went to the door, to stand opposite Bock.

The Anson had begun a gentle climb.

"Shouldn't he be staying low?" Bock asked.

"This is temporary. It is to confuse their radar. We'll be dropping low again soon."

Then without warning, Menning gave Bock a hard shove.

Despite the shock and being taken completely by surprise, Bock's survival instincts were in top form. He grabbed at the edge of the door, and hung on, the upper half of his body in the slipstream, his legs straining to keep him inside.

"*What are you doing?*" He screamed. "*Are you mad?*"

Menning said nothing. Instead, he had drawn his Luger, turned it butt-first, and began a merciless hammering of Bock's desperate fingers, face entirely expressionless.

Lebmann and his colleague had returned to their seats. All the men watched the scene with cold detachment.

Bock was screaming. "*No, no. Oh God no! I am loyal to the Führer! Don't do this! Please!*"

The fingers were getting bloody, turning to smears by the relentless hammering. But still they hung on, while Bock screamed in pain and terror. He desperately tried not to look down, as the Anson continued to climb.

He stared wildly at the men. "Help me! Help me for the love of God!" The men just looked at him.

The hammering seemed to echo through the aircraft. It did not stop.

At last, the pulped fingers gave way. With a piercing scream, Bock fell out of the aircraft, plummeting to the water far below.

"I thought the bastard would never leave," Lebman said in perfect English.

"You and me both," the man Bock had known as Menning said, in the same language. "God. That was hard work."

"Couldn't have happened to a better bastard," Roberts said, reverting to his true identity. He looked at the bodies. "You two can come alive again. Our pal's gone."

The pilot sat up. "I heard. A person can't get any sleep around here, damn it." He turned to his companion. "You, my lass, escaped a fate worse than death."

The young woman had also sat up. She gave an expressive shudder, and glanced at the open space where the door should be. "Better him than me." she said in accented English. She had spoken without feeling.

The Anson was descending, and heading back towards the English coast. "Shawbridge," the pilot said, "here we come." He glanced down at his wings. "This is the closest I'll ever get to being a real pilot."

"Perhaps they'll give you a commission after this, and send you to flying school," someone said. "Get you out of that office you inhabit."

"Nah," another said. "He wants to be an actor when he grows up."

A burst of genuine laughter echoed through the aircraft.

CHAPTER FIVE

RAF Shawbridge flightline, Monday, July 1941. 1115 local.

Tad Duchamps and Pew, wearing the clothes they had flown in but without the flight gear, were by their black Hurricanes. Duchamps was walking round his, carefully passing a hand over the fuselage. Every so often he would stop, peer closely, then move on. Pew tagged along.

"My dear chap," Pew began, "you have inspected that kite at least twice since we landed. It is as pristine as freshly driven snow. You have not been hit. Nary a scratch, old man."

"I'm just making sure everything's okay for tonight's training mission. Mad Murchison's idea of a training mission."

"Usually means meeting the enemy. We do know our madman. Hullo...company." Pew had stopped.

Duchamps stopped as well, to look in the direction that Pew was staring. The Anson was taxiing, seemingly towards them.

"He'd better stop in time," Duchamps warned. "If he hits my ship, I'll..."

"Still a long way away, old boy. I know you love your Hurri, but...ah! See? He's turning. Panic over."

The Anson had swung round, showing them its left flank with the gaping doorway.

"What on earth..." Pew began. "Door shot off?" He was even more startled when the passengers began to disembark. "Good Lord! Is that an SS uniform I see peeping from those overalls? We've got the SS here?"

"Look who that one is," Duchamps remarked in an even voice.

"Heavens. It's Haines!"

"Well that uniform suits him." Duchamps returned his attention to the Hurricane as the men began heading for one of the unit buses that had come to pick them up.

Pew tapped his shoulder. "I say...look who's coming to see you."

"If it's Haines..."

"Prettier than Haines. A lot prettier."

Duchamps swung round, and stared as Helle came towards them.

"Did she come out of the Anson?" Duchamps asked in an urgent whisper.

"Yep. Strange goings on...and look. Haines is staring after her." By then, she was close enough for Pew to add, "Young Helle has a lean and determined look. When women have that look, it is time for prudent men to seek shelter. My Hurri needs some tender care..."

"Coward," Tad whispered sharply.

"Well, old boy, it's you she comes to greet. Discretion beckons."

Pew went off to his aircraft, a wingspan away, to find something that needed urgent attention in the cockpit.

"Why is he running away?" was the first thing she said.

Duchamps looked into the green eyes and wondered why he had the distinct impression of being pulled into them.

"Er...er...Pew? He...er wanted to check something on his plane."

"Convenient. I think he was leaving us to ourselves." Before Duchamps could say anything she came closer, close enough for him to sense the warmth of her body. She reached out to touch to aircraft. "They look so small in the air but so close...so big. I cannot believe how you can control this." Her voice was full of admiration.

"Well...er...I'm not the only one who can."

Hand still on the Hurricane, stroking it as she would a favorite pet, she said, "I know that. But this one is yours. It looks so...powerful. Are you flying today?"

"We've already flown. We'll be doing some more tonight—Training."

"Isn't that dangerous?"

"The war is dangerous."

She nodded. "Yes." There was a wealth of meaning and

experience in that single word. "Your plane will be invisible."

"And with me in the cockpit, they won't see the pilot either," he joked.

Her reaction astonished him. "Don't you ever say that again!"

"Er...what did I say wrong? I made a joke..."

"Never joke about yourself like that. It is defensive, and beneath you. You are better than that! I never want you to say that again."

"But..."

"As long as I am spending my life with you!"

"What?" It was weakly said,

But she was already moving away, back to where the others were waiting. Suddenly, she paused, and turned round. "Did you get my note?"

"Yes." Instinctively, he touched the pocket beneath his wings.

She noted the movement. "Do you keep it there?"

"Yes."

"Next to your heart. Good."

She turned away again and continued towards the waiting bus.

"Going fly-catching, are we?"

"What?" Duchamps said again. He kept staring at Helle, as she entered the bus without looking back. Then he turned to face Pew, and so missed the malign scowl that Haines shot in his direction, before boarding the bus himself.

"Your mouth," Pew said. "Wide open, was. What brought that on?"

Duchamps turned again to look at the bus, which was now moving off. "Pew!"

Pew looked about him. "Yep. I'm the only other person here. Must be me he's calling for."

"Pew," Duchamps said in a hushed voice. "I never thought I'd see her again. She just said she'll be spending her life with me. With *me!* Oh God. I...I cannot believe it!"

"Barring the efforts of a little war getting in the way...sounds like a cozy future to me. When a woman sets her hat, she sets her hat."

"Pew..."

"That's three times in less than three minutes. I am popular. Thank you Lord."

"She's white..."

"Great recognition skills. The CO will be proud."

"You know what I mean."

"Alright, she's white. So?"

"Where I come from you get invited to a lynching party for less, with you as the guest of honor."

"But you're not where you come from, old son, and even if we do have our own dozy versions, nothing like that over here. Besides, no one has the right to dictate whom the old heart ticks for."

Duchamps looked at him with renewed interest. "That sounds like experience talking."

"I'll tell you about it one day. Word of advice...don't let anyone, or anything stop you. You'll never forgive yourself."

Pew looked so serious, Duchamps did not probe further.

Outskirts of Macon, Georgia. July 2006.

"Goddam nigger! Stole my girl, you black bastard! You stole Helle!"

Eyes closed, Haines was deep in his reverie and had no idea that Emma-Mae, who had come out to check on him, had heard every word.

She put her hand to her mouth to stifle any sound she might make. Her face crumpled, a redness coming to her eyes. Although she had long known that her husband had loved someone else all his life, it still hurt to hear it so bluntly.

She turned, and ran back into the house.

Haines was locked in his memories and was quite unaware of either her shocked presence, or her humiliated departure.

Galen Private Archives, New York, July 2006

Duchamps closed the diary with a slow reverence tinged with revulsion. "Jesus! I know the guy was SS, and it was wartime...but the way your grandfather describes how he killed him. So cold-blooded..."

Ellen was herself shaken by the revelations.

They had driven back to the city in Duchamps' car, a reincarnation of the Ford GT40, his pride and joy. She had directed him to the building where she worked, and they were now in her office, reading through one of the diaries she had taken out at random. Duchamps had leafed though it, emulating her and stopping at random to read aloud.

He looked at her, seeing the shock in her eyes. "He is some piece of stuff, your grandpa. I can only imagine what else could be in the rest of this, and the others. One thing's for sure...you're sitting on a whole pile of dynamite. He sure as hell did not give this to you, or made you contact me, for altruistic reasons."

"Meaning?"

"We watch our backs. There'll be people out there who won't want this known. They buried the story after the war; but had no idea that old Senator Haines—war hero—had set it all down..."

"And if we start asking the wrong questions..."

"The wrong questions that are also the right questions."

"They'll come looking." Ellen paused. "Do you want to lock it all away and forget about it?"

"Commonsense, and self-preservation, say yes."

"What does Tad Duchamps II say?"

"Your grandpa was jealous of my grandpa...and how!" Duchamps opened the scrupulously hand-written diary once more. "Just listen to this..."

"*I looked at that nigger standing by his damned plane talking to the woman I wanted, But her eyes were all for him...*"

Duchamps slowly closed the diary a second time. "That's it. That's the connection...or one of them. Your grandpa was crazy about my grandma. I won't call it love. In his own words, he wanted her. In those days, seeing her with my grandpa would have made him go apeshit. Worse for him, it was *her* choice. She chose this black guy over a good old home boy aristo. No wonder he hated poor old Jack so much. He envied my grandpa's ability as a fighter pilot, and hated him even more because of my grandma. That must have twisted something inside of him. God knows what it made him do. Ellen, if that bastard's responsible for getting my grandpa shot..."

"Knowing what I do about him, I would not put it past him. But we don't know the whole story yet. We know just this tiny part of it. It's all in those diaries, and what we've got to find out there. Let's see how far we get first."

"And stay alive while we're at it."

The dark eyes surveyed him. "Scared?"

"It's smart to be."

"Then we'll be okay."

"You know that, do you?"

"If you'd said to me—hey, I can leap buildings in a single bound, I'd be worried."

"Well, I can't. I left the springs back in my apartment."

She smiled at that. "I think I'm going to like you, Tad Duchamps II."

"Wha, missy? This lil' ol' black boy?" he joked in a step'n'fetchit voice, thinking of what Haines had done to Jack, and his antipathy for the original Tad Duchamps.

"Don't do that," she said, eyes very serious. "Ever."

He was surprised. "I just made a joke..."

"Don't make jokes like that about yourself."

He stared at her, bemused. "Okay. Okay. You got it."

"What do you think those documents he killed that Nazi Stand...Standa..."

"*Standartenführer*. That's the SS equivalent of a colonel."

"So what do you think the senator killed him for?"

"Who knows? Could be anything. After the war, the Allies parceled off a few Nazis between them—mainly the States and the Russians—but they all had a hand in it."

She nodded. "We've got some private documents here, in safe deposit boxes."

"Bet they've got a few stories to tell."

"No one has access to those, except the people to whom they belong."

"What if those documents the senator killed that guy for, are here?"

She shrugged. "Perhaps. I've always had the feeling he arranged this job for me. I know the inventory. His name's not on it."

"It wouldn't be, would it?" Duchamps suggested. "Those

documents—whatever they are—could be about the kinds of weapons the Nazis were working on, or maybe even a list of the names of people involved with them—collaborators, traitors, shady business people, or deals—that no one wants made public. There must have been a few of those. As I said—could be anything. But whatever it was, it was important enough for them to run that scam to fool the Nazi colonel..."

"And then kill him."

"Dead men don't talk."

"But documents do."

"Maybe the senator's scribblings will tell us," Duchamps said. He paused. "What the hell was grandpa's unit involved in?"

Office, Intelligence unit, Whitehall, London. Monday. July 1941. 1143 local.

"Haines appears to have done an excellent job. Go far, that man."

The man who had spoken was a former First World War colonel—one of the youngest—who had been dragged back into uniform, with the rank of Brigadier. He sported a moustache that gave him the look of a benign walrus. During combat in the previous war, he had been anything but. His ferocity had gained him one of the fastest sprints up the promotion ladder; that, and his ability to survive.

The man in civilian attire he had spoken to, looked uncannily like the late *Standartenführer* Bock. They could have been identical twins.

"We've got what we wanted," the Brigadier continued with satisfaction, "and you, my dear Alistair, must return to the hornet's nest to fetch it. Time for your miraculous 'escape' from the French Resistance. Are you game?"

Alistair James grinned. "Would I miss out on the best part I've played in my career so far? Of course I'm game, sir."

"Well, take no chances. You're only returning long enough to filch what we're after, and get back here as fast—*and* as safely—as you can. You cannot afford to remain any longer than is absolutely necessary. Your explanations might hold Jerry off for a short while; but he's a suspicious bod. He'll check and check again, until he finds an anomaly. Get back here to while away the rest of the war behind a desk in that proper colonel's uniform we've given you, and not that Nazi muck. You've earned it. Like the invaluable intelligence you've already given us, your experiences will be as invaluable to the newer people we'll be sending out all over the shop. And when this madness is all over, you can return to the stage a hero, but unsung. Way it is with what we do."

"I've long understood that."

"We'll be sending the excellent Haines along. Keep you company, and to watch your back. See that you both return safely. No good to us dead. Either of you."

James gave a quick smile. "I won't forget. And I'm looking forward to that desk." He went out with a slight wave.

The brigadier touched his moustache briefly as watched Alistair James leave. His expression was studiously neutral; but his eyes betrayed a concern he could not quite hide.

When the door had shut, he muttered under his breath, "And God help you if they catch you. We won't be able to."

Occupied France, Midnight, July 1941.

"Looks as if we were lucky," Alistair James, back in his guise as Bock, said.

They were standing in the yard of a disused farm, next to an SS *Kübelwagen* that the Resistance had supplied. "Whatever the Raven boys did upstairs tonight, it kept the jerries busy...and uninterested in us."

Haines felt a sudden rush of anger at the mention of the Raven pilots. He knew Duchamps was flying, and the praise uttered by James annoyed him. He did not let the anger show.

The vehicle's markings were fully authentic. The Resistance members had themselves long disappeared into the darkness, and there were no enemy patrols around.

James now said, "You'll have to hit me to make it look believable."

Haines stared at him in the gloom. "Sir, you're a real colonel, and I am a lieutenant..."

"I promise not to put you on a charge. Now hit me."

Perhaps it was the flash of anger over the mention of the Raven pilots.

Perhaps. Whatever it was caused Haines to strike James far harder than expected.

The blow felled James, who protested in real pain, "My God, man! Did you have to hit so hard? I'll have a swelling on there!" He got to his feet groggily, and climbed into the passenger seat.

Haines, now a *Sturmbannführer*, settled behind the wheel. "Sorry, sir. You've got just two days. Can you do it?"

"Yes. My plucky escape should keep them occupied for at least that long. I get the documents, then out again before they start looking too nosey. We'll meet at the rendezvous, and I can say a final goodbye to *Standartenführer* Bock. I'll be glad to get out of there for good," he added with some feeling. "Damn! That hurts. You almost broke my jaw."

"Sorry, sir," Haines repeated. "How long have you been playing the Nazi?"

"A whole damned year. I'll be glad when it is all over. I'll be glad when my jaw stops aching."

Haines said nothing as he started the vehicle. It sounded loud in the darkness. "Don't know how you managed it."

"It wasn't easy," James said. "Strange irony our Resistance friends getting Hager before I could discover the whereabouts of those documents. Had that not happened, I would not be going back into the lion's den tonight."

"Let's hope your luck holds and you get out again."

Fifty minutes later, the *Kübelwagen* was halted by two SS guards, just before the barrier that blocked the entry road to the big chateau that housed Bock's special unit. Unsmiling, they positioned themselves on either side of the vehicle.

Then one stared in shock at the disheveled passenger. "*Standartenführer* Bock!" He clicked to attention, and shot out his right arm. "*Heil Hitler!*"

The false Bock, bare-headed and looking tired, uniform dirty with buttons missing, barely nodded. The other guard, staring in equal shock, had also snapped to attention.

Haines, eyes cold beneath his peaked cap in the glare of the sentry searchlights, shouted, "*Well? Are you going to stand here all night like a pair of idiots? The Standartenführer has escaped from the French pigs. I found him on the road several kilometers from here. He's hurt. Are you going to keep him waiting? I've got to return to my unit. Now move!*"

"At once, *Sturmbannführer!*"

They roused themselves, and hurried to lift the barrier.

"*And take those damned lights out of our faces!*" he yelled at them.

"At once, *Sturmbannführer!*"

The lights went out as the barrier was raised.

Haines drove through, and up the long road.

"That was well done," James remarked with approval when they were well away from the sentries. He spoke in German. "Quite the SS officer. I could almost smile if it weren't for my damned jaw. Hope you *haven't* broken it. I would not be amused."

"Sorry, sir," Haines apologized for the third time. "Forget it. I'm just having a good moan."

"As for the SS officer...a good shout seems to work."

"It does indeed. But be careful. They're not as stupid as some would believe. Will you be alright making your way back out?"

"Yes. Just make sure you're at the rendezvous in time. I'll have to leave without you if..."

"No you won't. Those documents are far more important than either of us."

When they eventually pulled up before the high, gated entrance to the chateau, more lights came on.

Both knew there were machine gun posts beyond the lights, the weapons undoubtedly trained upon them, just in case.

They remained unmoving, the vehicle's engine idling loudly.

Then the gate opened, and an SS captain came through. Like the guards, he stared at Alistair James, stunned expression upon his face.

"*Standartenführer!*" He clicked to attention. The right arm stabbed out. "*Heil Hitler!* I could not believe it when the sentries said you were on your way, sir! You're hurt!"

James nodded tiredly. "Relax, Henk." He began to get out.

"*Are you going to help him?*" Haines snapped.

The captain appeared to see Haines for the first time. "Of course, *Sturmbannführer!*" He hurried to help James climb out. "Where...?"

"Did I find him? Some kilometers from here, looking much the worse for wear, as you can see. It seems he had been taken by those French pigs, but managed to escape. As you can also see, they were not gentle with him."

"They'll pay for this!" the captain snarled.

"They should. I'll leave *Standartenführer* Bock in your capable hands. I must return to my unit."

The captain glanced at the vehicle's markings, noting the unit, and the Iron Cross Haines wore. "Your unit has a fierce reputation, *Sturmbannführer*," he said with respect.

The unit Haines was supposed to belong to had a dedicated mission: to hunt out the Resistance, a duty it carried out with implacable ferocity the captain had mentioned.

"We aim to keep it so," Haines said with the ease of someone who had no qualms about what he did.

"May I know..."

"We also do not give out our names."

"Of course, *Sturmbannführer*. That is known."

"Then why ask?"

"I...I apologize, *Sturmbannführer*."

"Now see that the *Standartenführer* is attended to. *Quickly.*"

"Yes, *Sturmbannführer!*"

Haines nodded imperiously at him, and without a backwards glance, turned the vehicle round to head back down the road. Neither Haines, nor James, had exchanged the slightest of glances. James as Bock, was apparently so done, he could barely lift his head.

The sentries snapped to attention to let Haines through when he got to the barrier. He did not look at them as he drove away.

Standartenführer **Bock's office, Château Eloise, Normandy, Occupied France, 0120 local.**

Apart from the swelling, courtesy of Haines' too-enthusiastic punch. James had been given a clean bill of health. He was at his desk, still in the rumpled uniform with the missing buttons. On the wall behind him was a portrait of Hitler, hanging between two red banners with the black swastika on its white, background disc at the center of each.

A sharp knock sounded.

"In!"

A meticulously uniformed Forst, accompanied by Schelberg, entered the large office.

James got to his feet, and began to raise his right arm in preparation for the customary salute.

Forst waved him back down. "So good to see you back, Heinrich. I came as soon as I heard. We've been turning this part of France upside down looking for you" He came closer to peer at James' cheek. "Nasty swelling. You should make the French pay."

"I shall."

"Oh ho! That sounds like a promise. Excellent." Forst looked very pleased. "But you should be in bed, Heinrich."

"I'm fine, sir. I was just making certain everything was in order."

"No one's been allowed to touch anything."

Schelberg had stood to one side, looking at James with interest, but saying nothing.

Forst glanced at him. "Ah, Heinrich," he began to James, "You haven't met Schelberg. Gestapo, *Standartenführer* equivalent rank. We called him in to investigate your kidnap."

James looked at Schelberg "*Herr* Schelberg."

"You've made me redundant, *Standartenführer*. Spoiled my party." Schelberg gave a thin smile. "I was so looking forward to being rough with the French; but seeing that bruise and having heard your intentions, I might get the chance, after all."

"You will, *Herr* Schelberg, if I have anything to do with it." There was no mistaking the grimness of James' tone.

"Then I accept the invitation."

James seemed to sway briefly in his chair.

"Look," Forst said. "You should get some sleep. I insist. You need it. We can catch up in the morning."

James nodded weakly. "I think you may be right, sir," He glanced about him, an absent-minded look in his eyes. "Yes. I could do with it."

"We'll make them pay, Heinrich. Count on it. Oh one more thing...your return has saved your driver a posting to the Eastern front."

"I want him reinstated. None of this is his fault."

Forst nodded. "Very well. See you in the morning."

Again, James gave a weak nod.

As they walked away from the office, Forst said to Schelberg. "Well?"

Schelberg had the tiny smile pasted upon his face. "The French seem to have roughed him up. The doctors have given him a clean bill of health, so this is temporary."

"But?"

"There is no 'but'...for the moment." Schelberg kept on his little smile.

James waited until he could no longer hear footsteps, then stood up, and went to the unsmiling portrait of Hitler. He lifted it. The thin outline of a movable panel showed. He pressed at it. It sprang open to display a wall-mounted safe.

Supporting the portrait with one hand, he dialed the combination with the other, and opened the safe. The documents were there.

"So bloody close", he whispered to himself, careful to do so in German.

He left the documents where they were for the moment, shut the safe and the panel, and allowed Hitler to hang again in his customary position.

James knew how he was going to make good his escape, with the documents.

On the second day of his return, looking as smart as he had the day he'd gone painting, he stepped out of the chateau and towards his waiting car, carrying his usual portfolio. His driver, SS *Scharführer* Marius Löringer, was standing smartly with the passenger door of what everyone knew was *Standartenführer* Bock's personal *Kübelwagen*, held open.

"Glad to see they let you out, Marius," James greeted.

"Thank you for getting me out, sir."

"No need to thank me. You were entirely innocent. They over-reacted."

"All I can tell you is that I'm grateful, sir," the Sergeant said with feeling. "I was looking at a long, hard winter with the Russkis." Löringer shut the door when James had got in, then took his place behind the wheel. "Same place?"

"I think not. Let's see what we can find."

"Yes, sir."

As Löringer was about to start the vehicle, a soft voice asked, "Tempting fate are we, *Standartenführer?*"

James looked round at Schelberg, "Not really, *Herr* Schelberg," he replied easily. "If one survives an aeroplane crash, it is wise to get back into the air as quickly as possible, or one may never do so again. If one falls off a horse and can still walk, one gets back into the saddle for the same reason."

"I think I understand. I have recently been in an air crash."

"Oh?"

"You will not have known of it. It happened while you were...away. I was in fact, searching for you."

"I see. How did it happen?"

"One of the Luftwaffe pilots, a Major Stroeme, was piloting me in a Storch. Unfortunately, a unit of SS troops had poor recognition skills. They fired at us. We crashed, but thanks to Major Stroeme's remarkable skills, we survived."

"I hope you had those troopers punished."

"I would have, but the *Tommis* intervened."

James looked surprised. "The *Tommis*?"

"Four aircraft. Out of nowhere. They raked the area and vanished as quickly as they had come. Again, Major Stroeme saved my life by reacting quickly. The troopers were not so lucky. Fate is a strange thing."

"Indeed. So will you get back into the saddle, so to speak?"

"Oh yes. I agree with you."

"Then we are in accord."

"We are indeed. Enjoy the painting."

"I shall, *Herr* Schelberg. I shall."

"Should you not have an escort?"

"I do not want a company of troopers hanging around while I paint. Disturbing. The *Scharführer* and I will be quite alright." James patted the machine gun that had recently been mounted on the vehicle. "We are well armed this time."

"Then I leave you to your painting, *Standartenführer*." Schelberg touched his hat in a brief salute.

James gave him a parting wave as Löringer sent the *Kübelwagen* charging down the road.

Schelberg watched it go. This time, there was no smile upon his face. His eyes were lifeless.

Löringer glanced at his superior. "Expecting the French to try something, sir?"

James had been glancing behind from time to time. "Not really, Marius. Isn't this area supposed to be now clear of the swine?"

"Remember that last time, sir."

"How can I forget! Still..." James glanced back again. He was not expecting the Resistance. At least, not here. He was expecting Schelberg to come sneaking up, with a company of SS. "...you never know."

"Are we going to the same place?"

"That," James said, "would be taking the hair of the dog a little too far. Some bocage country, perhaps. Plenty of inspiration to be found there...excellent ambient light values. Somewhere near a small stream. I'll know it when I see it."

"Yes, sir. I suppose I had better stick with you this time. I don't think I would escape the Eastern Front if I leave and you are taken again."

"That won't happen."

"I'll stand guard by the machine gun. I won't disturb you, sir."

"I know you won't, Marius. I know you won't."

The bocage country James had spoken of was the patchwork of fields bordered by irregular hedgerows, created over time to protect the orchards and fields, and the cattle within those fields. Some of these hedgerows were only about 6 feet or so, and could easily be penetrated. Innumerable others were, however, more than 10 feet tall, thick at the base with solid earth and vegetation, from which trees of varying heights grew, forming mounds that were virtually impassable. Many unpaved, narrow roads passed between them. Streams meandered their way through. The bocage country offered great defensive positions.

"There!" James said after a while. "Turn into that small road over there. To the right. See if it leads to a stream. If not, we'll try another."

Löringer had no way of knowing as he followed James' instructions, that this was just a few fields away from the farmhouse—well hidden by a screen of trees—where the Resistance had left the SS vehicle that James and Haines had used.

After about ten minutes of working his way along the twisting road, Löringer spotted a stream flowing through a small clearing.

"Stream, sir," he said.

"Yes. I see it. Perfect. Plenty of light. Rich vegetation. Quiet, and secluded. Exactly what I need. Pull up by the stream, but not too close. The bank might not be secure. We would not want to bog down our only transportation out of here, would we?"

"We definitely wouldn't, sir."

James nodded. "Alright, Marius. Stop somewhere safe, and position the vehicle so that you have a good field of fire across this clearing, for the gun. And stand by that radio in case we have any trouble."

"Yes, sir."

They were protected on three sides by tall, impenetrable hedgerows with a single entry for small vehicles in one corner only. The stream formed the fourth border.

Löringer drove slowly round the clearing, looking for the best position to site the gun, while James set up his painting gear, facing the stream.

James heard the vehicle stop, and turned to look. Löringer had parked in a far corner, facing the entry point, but also enabling him to swing the gun to his right, to cover the stream, if need be.

"How's that, sir?" he called softly. James nodded. "Good. Good."

***

Trailing some kilometers behind, Schelberg was at the head of a small column of SS troops. While not company-sized as James had imagined with some concern, there was nonetheless a sufficient number to make life very awkward for Haines, and the people James expected to make the rendezvous later in the day.

Schelberg had no inkling of what was really going on; but his inherently suspicious nature had driven him to obtaining Forst's permission to take out a "covering escort" for the man he knew as Bock.

"Lightning is not supposed to strike twice," he'd said to the *Brigadeführer*, making no mention of his own true reasons. "And even if this area is supposed to be free of the French terrorists, lightning has been known to strike twice."

Forst had bought it, and had authorized the "escort".

As he rode in the lead vehicle, Bock's intentions occupying his mind, Schelberg said, quietly, "You're up to something."

"Sir?" the SS captain sitting next to him in the back, queried.

"Just talking to myself."

"Er...yes, sir," the puzzled captain said.

He was the same captain who had helped the supposedly battered James out of the SS *Kübelwagen* that Haines had driven.

It would take Schelberg more than two hours to head in the direction of the route into the bocage that James and Löringer had taken.

It was Löringer who spotted them first.

Some instinct made James look up from his easel, a fraction of a second later.

"Marius! No!" he shouted.

Löringer, ready to fire, turned to look sharply at James in astonishment, "Sir?"

"These are..."

"You'll be dead in a second if you try to fire. Or reach for that radio. A sniper has you in his sights." James was on his feet, waving urgently to someone Löringer could not see. "*Stop!*" he heard the man he knew as Bock shout in *English. Then in French.* "*Do not fire!!*"

James moved rapidly to Löringer's position, clearly blocking someone's line of fire.

Löringer was staring at him. "*Sir!* You'll get shot if you stand there! I have a clear line of..."

"Please do as I say, Marius!" James interrupted, switching back to German, "if you want to live. Let go of the gun, slowly, and clearly, so that's there's no misunderstanding. And do not touch that radio. Those woods are full of Resistance. Now leave the vehicle. Climb out. Slowly."

"Sir, but..."

"*Marius!* No time for pointless heroism."

"Are we surrendering?"

"Not quite. Now just wait. They're checking the immediate area to make sure it's clean..."

"Of our men?"

"Yes. Now just wait," James repeated.

They stood there, waiting, knowing that guns were trained upon them.

It was a good fifteen minutes before anyone approached them. It was Haines, still in his Waffen-SS uniform. His pistol was drawn, and pointed it at Löringer who watched him, seemingly mesmerized and uncomprehending, in stunned surprise.

Haines raised the pistol and was about to shoot, when James chopped at the gun arm with the edge of a palm. Haines gasped with the pain of the blow as the weapon fired into the ground.

Löringer paled, shocked by the close shave.

"*Are you mad?*" James snapped in a sharp, low voice at Haines..

"He's the *enemy!*" Haines said furiously, rubbing at the arm, but holding the gun down.

"He's the enemy, *sir!*" James corrected harshly. "In future, you will await my orders before taking action. Is that clear?"

Haines continued to hold the weapon pointed at the ground. His mouth worked, but no sound came out.

"*Is that clear?*" James repeated, emphasizing each word.

"*Yes...sir,*" Haines finally acknowledged.

"Now take his machine pistol, and his sidearm. And that is all you do."

James reached into the vehicle as Haines began to comply with the order, and picked up a thin portfolio by the handle.

Having listened to the sharp, low-voiced exchange spoken in English, Löringer was staring wide-eyed from one to the other, than stared at Haines who took the MP40 out of the vehicle, then snapped fingers indicating he should remove the ammo pouches about his waist, and his pistol.

"You…you are *English, Standartenführer?*" Löringer said as he handed Haines the belt with the pouches, and the weapon.

James looked at him. "Do you *understand* English?"

"Yes…yes, sir," Löringer replied in that language. "I worked in a cabaret bar in Berlin, before…before the war. Many Americans and English came…" He paused uncertainly, still looking from one to the other. "…newspaper people, writers…I learned from them…" He stopped again, looking beyond them.

Two armed men in civilian clothes were approaching in a hurry.

"The *Boche!*" one began with some urgency. "I don't think they were close enough to hear that shot, but we should leave now." He glanced at his companion. "Jacques…fix that *Boche* car," he said quickly in French. "Leave a nice surprise for our occupiers."

"I'll leave something nicely ugly." The man began to booby-trap the vehicle.

"*Germans?*" James said to the leader of the group. "Where?"

"A small convoy, still on the main road. But according to one of our lookouts, they're heading here. They seem to be looking for something, she thinks."

James' mouth tightened. "Schelberg. I *knew* it. I agree with you. We must hurry…"

The man looked at his comrade, switched back to French. "*Jacques!* How long?"

"Don't be so impatient! Nearly there!"

The leader turned a hard stare on Löringer. "And this *Boche?*" he asked James. "Should we leave him for his friends to find? Dead, of course."

"He comes with us…"

"*What?*"

"He comes with us," James repeated firmly. "Or they will kill him themselves."

"So?"

"So he comes with us." James turned to Löringer, still in English, "Marius, you must come with us. You will be safe with Antoine—not his real name, of course. He's an honorable man, and even if you are his enemy, he will treat you honorably. Won't you, Antoine?"

"So this *Boche* understands English?"

"Yes."

"I see. Come, *Boche*..."

"His name is Marius Löringer."

Antoine gave James an exasperated look, before turning back to Löringer. "Come, Mr. Marius Löringer, I have been placed upon my honor. I will not kill you. For now." He looked at James. "Okay?"

"You will not kill him. Period."

Antoine sighed. "Let's get out of here before his friends arrive. Are you *finished*, Jacques?" he added sharply to his comrade.

"One last thing to...do. There! Done."

"Thank God. Now let's move!"

"I get no appreciation," Jacques grumbled.

As they hurried away, with Haines walking ahead behind Löringer, Antoine said, "Why are you so soft with this *Boche?*"

"He's a good man..."

"He is *SS!* We hate the Germans, but most of them are ordinary soldiers. The SS...*they* are animals. It will be difficult..."

"He is a good man, Antoine. He has been my driver for all the time I have been playing this role. He was punished with military detention because of my last 'disappearance' and was due to be sent to the Eastern Front..."

"Good. Let the Russkies have him..."

"This time, his punishment will be more severe, perhaps execution..."

"Even better."

"And his family might well pay too..."

"They chose Hitler

"Antoine…"

"I shoot Frenchmen who collaborate—Vichyists, Milice... Why should I hesitate to kill a *Boche?*"

"Because I have asked you not to. Because of humanity. Because he could be useful..."

"What is he...a sergeant? How useful is that?"

"It isn't only officers who can supply valuable Intelligence. You know that. Use him here to give you information that can help you..."

"Look after a *Boche* for the rest of this war? This is crazy..."

"Or get him out to England."

"You can take him with you tonight."

"No room."

"*Merde!*" Antoine said in his native French.

A little later, James began to slow down perceptibly. Antoine instinctively kept pace, while the others drew ahead.

"What is wrong?" Antoine asked.

"It's Haines. Something about him worries me. Keep an eye on him whenever he comes over."

"Why?"

"He enjoys killing."

"War does that to some people. I have seen..." James shook his head. "Haines does not need a war."

"You are saying he is sick in the head?"

"Worse. He isn't sick. At least, not in the way you mean."

A silence fell as they made their way through the bocage. Then Antoine glanced at the portfolio.

"Some of my favorite daubs," James explained.

"Of course," Antoine said, not believing it. "So who is this Schelberg?" he added.

"Gestapo. First name Heinrich. High rank. He recently arrived. Don't let that lull you into believing because he's new, he could be easy to fool. He's a veteran, and very cunning. He did not get that rank for being stupid. You should hope your paths never cross. He smiles too much. It's the smile on the face of the tiger...and its owner is as dangerous. For someone of the rank, he is not an office man. He likes being out in the field. He likes to hunt. Remember that."

"Then we shall be careful. Perhaps leave the area for a while. How do I recognize this...Schelberg?"

"You can't miss him." James gave Antoine a detailed description. "He's following me. He's suspicious about me, but my supposed rank makes him cautious. He has the same equivalent rank, so he has enormous authority. But, as I've said, he needs to be careful. If he makes a mistake, he will pay for it; but if he is proven right..."

"But he will not get the chance. Your part here is finished."

"Yes. Thank God."

They did not stop at the farmhouse, moving on to the pick-up area, which was still some distance away. They moved through the bocage quickly, but without haste, leaving nothing to chance. Counting Haines, James, and Löringer, there were twelve people in all, including two women. The two women were ahead of the spread-out group, acting as scouts. The one who had warned of Schelberg's approach, would rejoin the group, some kilometers from where she had made the sighting.

"This is good defensive country," James said to Antoine. "An invasion will come one day. If it's in this area and the Germans set up defenses among these hedgerows, there'll be the devil to pay when the force comes ashore."

Antoine glanced at him. "We already know about how good it is for defensive purposes. We use it...and the Germans are already aware of its potential. There are three snipers with us today in this group. They play hell with the Germans. The rifles we use were taken from their own dead snipers, and we have plenty of ammunition for them. The Germans are already conducting trials. They will definitely use the bocage. We watch them. They position their snipers in burrows in the bocage. They have little tunnels, so that they can escape after shooting. We watched the ones we killed, for days. Then we took them, and their weapons, one after the other. The *Boche* went crazy, but they never got us. But," Antoine continued, "it would be madness to invade this part of France. Better to start at Calais, then spread north, east, and south, isolating their armies."

James was looking about him, seeing how the hedgerows would allow the enemy to take a murderous toll of the invading Allied troops.

"Perhaps," he said. "Some of these things have been here for what...a thousand years? If I were a German commander, I'd use them." He would mention this serious, potential danger to the general when he got back, he decided. Perhaps it was indeed madness to invade via Normandy.

Which was exactly what the enemy would think. Calais made tactical and strategic sense.

But, James thought, never do what the enemy expects of you. He said nothing further on the subject.

CHAPTER SIX

Schelberg's column was forced to stop. The three halftracks, full of heavily-armed troops, could not go further into the bocage at that point. Only the lead vehicle—the *Kübelwagen* in which Schelberg rode—could make it along the unpaved narrow, twisting roads, some of which were bordered by deep ditches between the hedgerows.

The troops disembarked and fanned out to cautiously make their way into the bocage, weapons ready for immediate use. A trooper had remained at the mounted machine gun in each halftrack.

"Stop!" Schelberg ordered his driver. "We should continue on foot," he added to the SS captain next to him. "If anyone's out there, we'll be heard long before they see us, or we see them. They've probably heard us already."

He climbed out. The captain followed.

"Go back to the halftracks," Schelberg ordered the driver, who seemed relieved to get out of the bocage trap.

"Yes, sir!"

"Don't look so happy," Schelberg said. He took a lightweight radio, in its slinged canvas case, out of the vehicle and handed it to the captain to carry. "I might call you back," he went on to the driver.

"Yes, sir."

If the captain entertained any thoughts that he did not consider himself a radio carrier like an ordinary trooper, he wisely kept them to himself.

Schelberg watched in silence as the driver took several tries to turn the *Kübelwagen* round on the narrow track, going back and forth on short jerks before finally heading back the way they had come.

"Lucky for him there were no ditches in this section," Schelberg muttered balefully to the captain as the vehicle rounded a bend and went out of sight. "Alright. Let's see what's in there."

It took them a good half hour to find the vehicle that Löringer and James had used.

Schelberg and the SS captain went carefully towards it, while the troopers took up defensive positions within the immediate area. Schelberg stopped about three meters from the abandoned *Kübelwagen*. He stared at it for long moments; then looked towards the stream where the easel belonging to the person he knew as Bock stood, a lonely sentry at the water's edge.

"What the hell happened here?" the captain asked. He stood a little distance from Schelberg, looking about him with a frown that was both puzzled and angry.

"Lightning, it would seem..." Schelberg replied, more to himself, "striking twice."

Instead of his usual pale suit, Schelberg had for the occasion splendidly attired himself in the black SS uniform that the Gestapo also wore. He was the only one wearing a peaked cap. All the others, including the captain, wore helmets. He carried an MP40 submachine gun slung from a shoulder, and a pistol at his belt. Like his subordinate, he looked about him, but more slowly, as if searching for something. Whether he saw it or not, he gave no indication.

"Stay here," he ordered, and moved closer to the vehicle.

He walked around it slowly, peering at it but not touching it. At times, he crouched to peer beneath. Finally, he saw something, grunted to himself, then straightened from the crouch that had enabled him to spot it. He went back to the captain.

"Booby-trapped," he said. "With our own grenades too."

"Swine!" the captain snarled.

"Oh I don't know," Schelberg said, remarkably unruffled. "I would have done the same. Know your enemy, Henk. That is the key to defeating him."

Without waiting for comment, Schelberg walked towards the water. Giving the vehicle a wide berth.

Henk followed, knowing his superior expected him to. "Are we going after them?"

"Certainly. But this hedgerow country is a maze. It will serve us well if the *Tommis* invade. But for now, we are the attackers, and the French terrorists the defenders. They know this country. Let us not give them any sacrifices. Get the men moving."

"And the *Kübelwagen?*"

"Leave it. It's lost to us. Perhaps an unsuspecting terrorist will try to steal it and save us the trouble of having to kill him one day."

It was a bizarre sight: a small, lonely chapel at the edge of a field, backed up against a solid hedgerow that seemed more than capable of withstanding a massed charge by a tank squadron. It was over four meters thick at the base and reared a good six meters behind the little chapel. From its high summit, solid trees shot skywards, their branches merging to form a perfect screen. Tightly laced vegetation covered its steep flanks; as would have been expected of such a massive hedgerow.

It was a very long example, and curved in a wide horseshoe, descending slightly towards each end. Another, shorter hedgerow, scarcely less high and massive, partially blocked the mouth, leaving just two narrow points of entry which would have defeated even a *Kübelwagen*.

James stared at it. "This is huge!"

Antoine grinned. "And perfect for cover and defense. The chapel is invisible from the air. We call this place *Croissant*. The shape, you see."

"Why not *the* croissant?"

"If those who should not know ever hear it mentioned, they will think we are talking about a member of the Resistance; a code name for someone, and not a place. We have been using it from the time the *Boche* arrived in France. It has been safe since."

"Perfect trap too."

"Without an exit, it would be."

"So there's a way out?"

"The very best, as you'll see."

"A Lysander could probably land here," James mused.

"Perhaps, but that would not be a good idea. We should never use this field. The *Boche* might spot, or hear an aeroplane. Then this place would be compromised for good. We need to keep using it."

James nodded in agreement.

They moved on to the chapel, which the others had already entered. On either side of the near-ruin short poles, surviving parts of what might have once been a fence, were stuck crazily into the ground. They looked as if they hadn't been touched for years.

When Antoine and James arrived inside, they found the others waiting for them expectantly. James could see no exit. Save for the entrance and the few, tiny arched windows that had long lost their original glazing, there was not a single opening to be seen. The state of the little church betrayed the fact that it had not served its original purpose for a great number of years. Although there were some dilapidated pews, none were the right way up, and they lay at haphazard angles upon the earth-covered flagstones. The place also stank of years of animal droppings and urine. Upon the thick layer of earth, the recent footprints made by the men were clearly to be seen.

In the dim of the chapel, Antoine noted the expressions on the faces of James, Haines, and Löringer.

"Yes," he said with a tiny smile. "It stinks."

"You said there was a way out," James began. "I can't see..."

"Jacques, Maurice." Antoine interrupted him to call. "Show our English friends our exit."

Jacques and Maurice hurried outside, then quickly returned with two of the nondescript poles that had seemed like the remnants of an ancient fence. Each pole had a chiseled tip, protected by a metal sheet bolted to it. They moved one of the pews, and began using the poles to shovel at the covering of foul earth. Soon, a flagstone with a clearly defined border came into view.

To the astonishment of the three, Jacques and Maurice jabbed the poles at one end of the flagstone and began to lift, pushing the poles further as they gained purchase. With a metallic groaning, the flagstone began to lift. Antoine went forward to grab it. Haines helped him and together they raised the flagstone until it balanced itself in an upright position.

James stared at the dark hole the slab of stone had covered. "The exit."

Antoine nodded with satisfaction, took a small torch out of a pocket, and shone it down. A short ladder was displayed.

Maurice put down his pole to join Haines and Antoine. "I can hold it this way."

"We'll go down here," Antoine said. "Maurice and Jacques will stay behind to make things look as they were, including removing our footprints; then they'll go their own way. The rest of us will meet them later after you two have gone to your pick-up point. Come. Let us go down. Mr. Löringer, you first. And do not try to run away. You won't make it."

They filed down the ladder and into a small space from which a narrow tunnel led off. The tunnel itself was high enough to allow ease of movement at the barest of crouches. The only light was by Antoine's torch.

"This seems like a very old tunnel," James observed.

Antoine had taken the lead, closely followed by James. "It is," he replied. "From the time of the Huguenots. According to legend, this was an escape route during the religious wars. I can't tell you whether this is fact or not. There are many stories about Huguenots and Catholics. Some are true, some are myths. But whoever built this tunnel, we are glad of it today."

"How far does it go?"

"Three kilometers, but not all like this. Further on, you'll be able to walk upright. It also widens. We have made use of that, as you'll see. It is also deep enough to be safe from bombs if the *Boche* decide to bomb the area above, for whatever reason."

"What about our people? This will happen one day when we retake Europe."

Antoine shrugged. "It will still be safe...unless the *Boche* finds it. Then it won't be safe at all for them. We will leave it as a booby-trapped present. The people who built it could not know about bombers; but for now, we thank them for being smart enough to go deep. The end of this tunnel is in a farmhouse."

The tunnel was not straight, but meandered as it continued. About half a kilometer before the end, they turned a corner and a faint glow warned James that they were approaching the "widened" part that

Antoine had spoken about. The glow led them into a big, cave-like excavation, lit by several naked bulbs. A low hum spoke of a generator running somewhere.

"This is some 'widening'," James commented, studying the place in astonishment.

Antoine grinned. "We did not make this. The same people who built the tunnel did. The stories say they used this place to rest, before moving on. We are using it for this."

"This" turned out to be an all-in-one weapons cache, dormitory, and supply unit. There were a few more Resistance people about, some lying on camp beds, fast asleep. Others were reclining, and looking at the newcomers with sharp interest, particularly at the German uniforms of James, Haines, and Löringer. Despite seeing Antoine and his small group, they kept their weapons close to hand.

"We'll rest here for a while," Antoine said.

At that moment, one of the sleepers came awake and opened baleful eyes. A smallish man, he got to his feet and picking up his weapon, a British Sten submachine gun with silencer, approached slowly.

"*Juif!*" Antoine greeted in genuine surprise. "Didn't expect to see you here today."

"I arrived an hour ago. Catching up on some sleep. They sent me to warn you to watch out. The SS are more active than usual, for some reason. News is the Gestapo are behind it." He looked at Haines, James, and Löringer. "Are these the reason? You have captured them?" The man called Juif looked hungrily at the supposed prisoners.

"Sorry to spoil your appetite, but these are not real Germans. They are English agents. And you've never seen them."

None of the group who had accompanied Antoine said anything about the lie that had included Löringer.

Juif looked at each of the three supposed agents. "Pity," he said, turning away. He seemed very disappointed that these were not more Germans to be killed, especially SS.

Antoine took them to one side as Juif went back to his camp bed. He looked at Löringer. "You must go with these two..." he began in an urgent whisper.

James stared at him. "*What?*" he exclaimed. Like Antoine, he kept his voice to a low whisper.

"It's to do with Juif," Antoine began to explain. "You are supposed to be three English agents. If your...driver stays, Juif will be suspicious. I doubt the charade will last for long after that. Juif will kill him, no matter what I say, or do."

Löringer's eyes widened, and avoided looking towards Juif, who was still staring in their direction.

"What's going on, Antoine?" James asked.

"His name is not Juif, of course," Antoine said, speaking rapidly. "And he is not a Jew. He used to be a schoolmaster...until the SS came." Antoine did not look at Löringer. "The schoolmaster was, however, married to a Jew. They had two small boys. The wife had herself been born in the village and had grown up there. They were childhood sweethearts. In that village, being a Jew was no more to be remarked upon than having black hair, brown hair, or blonde hair. Or so everyone thought. He was at school doing his job, when the SS turned up at his home. It seems someone in the village had told them a Jew was living there. That day, his parents were also in the house.

"Those particular SS..." Antoine glanced at Haines. "...were from the unit you are pretending to belong to. They literally burst in, breaking the door down. They grabbed her. The parents tried to stop them, and got shot for their pains. In the melee, she managed to pull free, and did the unthinkable; a brave, desperate thing. She was somehow able, screaming, to pull a weapon from one of the soldiers and shot him. Dead. God only knows where she found the strength to disarm an SS soldier. But she had not finished. She killed two more, before they got her. They were completely astonished to see three of their number shot dead by a Jew—with one of their own weapons—and a woman at that. As you can imagine that also made them crazy. They went into a killing rage. People said they turned into savage animals. They mutilated her body. Then they kicked the boys to death. When they were finished, they went looking for the husband.

"But one of his friends had already gone to warn him. He escaped. When the SS were finally gone, he returned to his house. He found a nightmare waiting. They had left the bodies as they lay. The place seemed painted in blood. His beautiful wife was unrecognizable. They had smashed her face until it had become pulp. People say he never uttered a sound. His friend watched him look at each body as if at a piece of furniture; even the boys. Then he left the village that night. No one knew what became of him, until news of a Resistance group with an astonishing reputation for SS kills, began to spread through the whole movement. The thing that gave a strange edge to the stories was the fact that on many of the bodies, a small yellow star of David had been left. Before long, people started talking about the Juif, the killer of SS. To those in the movement who know him, he is therefore 'Juif'. His real name no longer matters to him. He has no other identity. The SS would love to get their hands on him. No one is certain whether they have yet worked out who their nemesis happens to be. So many enemies to choose from."

Löringer had listened to this in appalled silence. "I am not like that!" he whispered in protest.

"You are SS," Antoine said without mercy. "I do not think Juif would accept your defense. I do not think many people would. You are still alive by the grace of a British agent. Never forget that."

While Antoine had been talking, James had glanced in Juif's direction. Juif had left his bed, and was foraging through some clothing material. Every so often, he would pick up a piece to spread it out, and study it with a critical eye.

"What is he doing?" James whispered.

Antoine looked. "He must have run out of stars."

"What do you mean?"

"When he finds a suitable piece, he will cut it into small stars and keep them to mark his next kills. As I said earlier, the war can change us all...and in ways we would never have imagined. Now let's get you something to eat, and to drink."

Schelberg had radioed the halftracks and the *Kübelwagen* to a rendezvous some kilometers west of where they had parked. This was in a field close to a road that was just wide enough to allow the halftracks access between the hedgerows.

He had little idea of where the group that had taken the man he knew as Bock, and Löringer, had got to; but he gave no indication of this. He and his men arrived to find the halftracks and the car parked in defensive positions in the encroaching dark of the July evening. He noted with satisfaction that no lights were showing, and that the machine gun on each vehicle was manned.

Henk posted guards, and the rest settled down to a meal of field rations. Henk and Schelberg sat in the *Kübelwagen* to eat. Schelberg had sent the driver to eat with the other men.

"Tell me, Henk," Schelberg began. "That *Sturmbannführer* who brought in the *Standartenführer*...you had a good look at his unit's insignia, did you not?"

"Yes, sir. Very clearly. One of the perimeter searchlights was fully on the vehicle when it arrived. The unit insignia is well-known: red full shield, upon it SS runes outlined in black, with a single, diagonal key in white going from right to left upon that. The key has a looped head, the tip at a right angle, pointing upwards. The whole is supported by two silver oak leaves. The *Sturmbannführer* did not give his name. That unit is very secretive."

Schelberg nodded. "Yes. It is."

"Permission to speak freely, sir."

"You have permission."

"Although they are ostensibly part of *Oberkommando West*, they take their orders directly from Berlin..."

"As do we."

"Yes, sir."

"What are you driving at, Henk?"

"Not even generals—SS or Wehrmacht—can give them orders. If you wish to find out who he is, I would advise caution."

"Worried about me, Henk?"

"I am certain you are quite able to look after yourself, sir. But that unit has a ferocious reputation that even other SS units treat with respect."

"I can be very fierce when I want to be," Schelberg said, in a voice whose very mildness made it sound strangely ferocious.

"Yes, sir."

"Have a safe flight back," Antoine said.

James glanced up at the clear night sky. "With a bit of luck, we should have a trouble-free run."

The battered 1930 vintage Citroen C4 Fourgon van that would take James and Haines part of the way to the pickup point, was outside the farmhouse in which the tunnel ended, engine idling and lights out. The three of them, plus Löringer, were standing a short distance from it. The driver was already behind the wheel, but out of earshot.

After a meal and a rest, Antoine had arranged for the van to take them.

He now turned to Löringer. "Marcel will drop you off first. This will be near two trees growing in V-shape. It is in fact one tree that split for some reason underground, and ended up looking like two. We call it the twins. The position is on high ground, with a clear view across a wide field. Wait there. There's plenty of cover. When Juif has gone back to his group, I'll come for you. *Don't* move from there. There's plenty of Resistance activity tonight. An unarmed SS soldier on his own won't survive long enough to tell them otherwise. An armed one would not either, so you have no chance at all if you try to get away. You're welcome to try if you feel up to it, because I know I'm not risking anything. You won't get far enough to tell anyone about us."

"I will not run away."

"I have your word?"

"Yes!"

Antoine made a sound full of skepticism. "The word of an SS man?"

"The word of Marius Löringer."

"We'll see."

Antoine was about to turn to the others when James said, "Just what we need."

The way he spoke made Antoine turn to look. The night was clear enough for them to see Juif approaching, carrying his Sten.

"*Merde!*" Antoine whispered.

"I was busy with my stars when you left," Juif began in English as he drew up. "Come to say goodbyes to our English friends." He was looking at Löringer. "You are doing a very dangerous job helping us kill the *Boche*. You must be glad to go back for a while, eh?"

"Yes," Löringer replied in the same language, hoping that single word would not betray his accent.

"I used to be a teacher," Juif said. "I have good English." Löringer nodded, while the others watched Juif carefully.

"Tell your friends in England," Juif continued to Löringer, "that we appreciate what you are doing."

Löringer dug into his memories to think of a phrase that he'd heard from his British customers during his days as a Berlin barman, that he could use in order to escape Juif's curiosity.

Then one came to his rescue. "I will," he said. "Cheers, mate." He started to turn away, to head for the van.

But Juif had not finished. He held out a hand. "*Vive l'Angleterre! Vive King George! Vive Churchill Vive de Gaulle!*" He gave Löringer's hand a firm shake with each salutation.

Löringer gave what he hoped was an easy smile in the gloom, as he allowed his hand to be shaken.

Juif gave a little nod, went to Haines and James, and repeated the performance with each. Then he went back to the farmhouse.

Antoine stared at Löringer. "Where did you learn that?" he whispered, astonished by Löringer's escape.

"A bar in Berlin."

"It just saved your life. Juif would not have expected an SS man to say that. Had it gone bad, Juif would have shot first, and I would have explained later...too late for you. Get into the van before he thinks of something else and comes back. *Hurry!*"

Löringer needed no second bidding.

The Fourgon's fully enclosed rear body was secured by a double-paneled door at the back. They were currently swung open, their slatted inner sides clearly visible, even in the gloom.

Antoine shook his head in wonder as he looked at James. "Such a small thing, and a man keeps his life..."

"Or loses it."

"Yes. Sorry we don't have better transport tonight. This is a working farm vehicle. It carries small farm animals, among other things. The smell in there may not be too good...but it's clean."

"We'll manage."

Antoine held out a hand. "Take care of yourself."

James shook it. "You too. Thank you for everything. And remember what I said about Schelberg."

"Thank me over a cognac at a nice place I know in Paris, after the war." Antoine grinned in the dark. "We can bore each other to death with our war stories."

"I look forward to that."

"And I'll remember."

"Good."

They both knew he also meant Haines.

Antoine extended the hand to Haines. "I expect we'll be seeing a lot of you. Have a good trip."

"Thank you, Antoine. See you around." As they walked to the van, Haines added to James, "Who's Schelberg?"

"Someone you never want to meet," James replied. "Gestapo. I'll tell you about him on the way. You sit with the driver. I want a word with Marius."

"Okay," Haines said, and got in next to the driver.

James climbed into the back. Antoine shut the doors behind him.

The van began to move off. Sitting on the floor, James and Löringer, could at first not see each other's outlines; but there was the faintest of backglows from the slits of the masked headlights that came through the small, glazed window at the front. Then as their eyes grew sufficiently accustomed, they were able to see each other's shape reasonably well in the vague twilight of the vehicle.

"Take Antoine's advice very seriously, Marius," James cautioned in a voice that was just loud enough for Löringer to hear above the noise of the van. "Stay out of this war as best you can. If you survive it, marry that girlfriend of yours."

"If *she* survives..."

"Indeed. If you both do, have many children, have grandchildren..."

"If we do have any and one's a boy, I'll name him after you, sir."

"You don't know my real name."

"The one I've known you by."

"Just look after yourself," James said, more gruffly than he'd intended.

"Yes, *Standartenführer*."

The van came to a halt some time later. They heard the driver get out of the front and after a short pause, the back door opened. Despite the dark of the night, light seemed to flood in.

The van had stopped in a narrow track between two hedgerows that were so close, it seemed as if the Citroen had squeezed itself through and would not be able to get out again.

"Go round to your right," the driver said to Löringer. "You'll see the twins. Wait there. Wait until I come back with Antoine. We have just this car tonight. Okay?"

Löringer nodded, paused, and held a hand out to James. They shook hands firmly. Neither spoke as Löringer climbed out.

The driver was equally silent as he closed the split door on James.

Löringer stood there as the driver got back in, and the van lurched off along the narrow path. He looked up and realized he could only see a small patch of starlit sky. Then he realized why. The trees lining the top of the hedgerows were close enough for their branches to form an almost seamless canopy above his head.

He suddenly felt very lonely, exposed, and vulnerable. He decided to look for the twin tree and get into cover as quickly as possible. With a sense of relief, he found the twins exactly where the driver had said. He also discovered that Antoine had been correct. There was plenty of cover, with an almost unrestricted view of the field. It was a perfect ambush position.

He wondered how many of his comrades had already died in that field, and how many more would. Or would it be the British, when they invaded?

Löringer was certain there would be an invasion. It was inevitable. He was not one of those who believed that the Reich would last forever, although he would never have been mad enough to say this aloud. The man he knew as *Standartenführer* Bock was right. He must try to survive this.

"If I can," he muttered.

As he thought of the colonel, his mind wandered to the one in Waffen-SS uniform who had been so eager to kill him. There was something about that one which made him uneasy.

Löringer paused. He'd heard a sound. He froze, waiting. How

much time had passed since he'd been dropped off? Fifteen minutes? Half an hour? He had no way of knowing. They'd taken his watch, even if he could have seen it in the darkness.

Soon, there was no doubt about the sound. The van was returning. Allowing for time to the drop-off point and back to his position, it could not have been so far away.

The van went past without even a slackening in speed. It was as if the driver had no idea he was hiding by the twin tree.

Löringer waited until he could no longer hear the vehicle. Something continued to nag at him, giving him an uncomfortable feeling he could not shake off. He could not explain it, but it forced him to do the very thing both Antoine and James had advised him not to.

He left his hiding place.

"How much further to the pickup point, sir?" Haines asked.

"According to the instructions," James said, "should be no more than half a mile from here. We've been walking for twenty minutes since we were dropped off. We'll be in time. We are to be met, and we'll know the field by the lights for tonight: two yellow, one blue. I'll certainly be glad when we're safely back."

"Amen to that, sir."

"You'll be doing this a few times. Remember to watch out for Schelberg."

After being dropped off, they had continued cautiously towards the rendezvous with the aircraft. James had decided to give Haines as detailed a brief on Schelberg, as he had to Antoine.

"That is one individual I'm going to watch out for," Haines vowed.

"If it ever gets to the point where your paths cross and you can do it without getting caught...shoot him. Make that shot count."

"I hear you, sir. Was it worth it?" Haines continued. "Coming back?"

"It was."

James said nothing more, and they continued in silence.

THE RAVEN CONSPIRACY – CODE NAME: ICARUS

* * *

Löringer had followed the track in the direction the van had taken to drive James and Haines to the drop-off point. He was running, not certain why, and not sure of what he intended to do when he caught up with them, if at all. He told himself he was behaving irrationally; that when Antoine came, he might well not have returned in time; that any marauding members of the Resistance might catch him, or shoot him as he ran past.

But a strange feeling of loyalty to a man he did not really know, and a sense of foreboding, drove him on. He kept running.

Just after the twin tree, he had found what he had thought was a branching off from the track, and for some uncertain moments, had hesitated before checking the "turnoff"; only to discover it to be little more than a small clearing that went nowhere. He had returned to the track.

I'll never catch up, he now thought. *This is hopeless. I'll get lost. I should go back.*

He ignored his own advice, and kept going. He discovered that he could see quite well by the starlight; and when he could spot the bends ahead, he would cut straight through fields to rejoin the track further along, hoping to make up the time this way.

Throughout, he expected what he feared most: being spotted by the Resistance. Yet he continued, a man driven beyond concern for his own safety.

He almost did not realize he had found them. He stumbled on something yielding. He stopped, turned to look down.

There was no mistaking what he was looking at. The light of the night was strong enough.

He dropped to his knees in shock—"*Standartenführer!*"

"And so, the faithful little man comes to save his master," he heard a sneering voice say from somewhere. "Too late, Löringer. And so noisy. I heard you coming. You should have listened to good advice, and remembered what curiosity did to the cat."

With a growl of rage, Löringer began rising to his feet. He was already far too late.

He felt a terrible, painful blow, and he dropped almost perpendicularly, onto James' body.

The night had turned impenetrably black.

Haines arrived at the rendezvous. The colors for the night were correct. He could hear the aircraft approaching.

"Where's the other one?" a voice asked. "He did not make it."

The voice did not ask further, and Haines did not explain. The Lysander approached steeply.

"Wave off the second plane when I've been picked up," Haines said.

"Yes. Now hurry. When you get back, tell them not to use this field again. It might be compromised."

"I will."

The Lysander landed and took off again, almost with barely a stop for Haines to climb aboard.

Outskirts of Macon, Georgia. July 2006.

"Löringer. Never expected Löringer to come by. Never expected him to be there to see that. Man risks his life for someone he never really knew...an enemy soldier at that. Who would have expected it? Goes to show. Never can be too careful."

Senator Haines was in his study, sitting in front of the old desk, and staring at it. He was totally oblivious of the fact that his wife had peeped in, and had gone away again.

In the kitchen, she said to Martha, "He's just sitting there, looking at that old desk, and talking to it."

Martha, who had long decided she knew far more about what made Haines tick than his own wife, said, "He's talking to something...but it ain't that desk."

"What do you mean?"

"His conscience, perhaps. If he had one."

Galen Private Archives, New York, July 2006.

Tad Duchamps II, closed the diary he had again chosen at random. He did so with a caution that almost spoke of a fear that it would suddenly attack him.

"Jesus!" he muttered, as he had done before. "Your grandfather is something else. He killed that British officer in...in *cold blood*. An *ally*, God's sake! Then the Waffen SS guy turns up, and bang. Down *he* goes too. Who'd have expected a German running to try and save a Brit in those days, from one of his own side?"

"I think that at that moment," Ellen said, "in some weird way, Löringer only had in his mind the thought of saving a commanding officer he respected, I think that for him, there was no German, and no Brit. There was just the man he knew as his CO, in danger..."

"And he gave his life for that." Duchamps shook his head slowly. He stared at Haines' ancient valise. "Your grandpa's sure given us a poisoned chalice."

"You can always put it down...and forget all about trying to find out what really happened to *your* grandfather." Her eyes were challenging him again.

"Are you saying I'm chickening out?"

"I'm not saying anything. The choice is yours. The chalice, or nothing."

Duchamps rubbed at his face briefly. "Who the hell was that old man really working for? And what happened to those documents? Why were they so important?"

She tapped at the valise. "The answers could all be in there."

"Maybe only some of them. He did not give you that plane to park it at Teterboro."

"So maybe we should go to the places he mentions in there. There may be more answers."

"As long as there are no snipers waiting."

"Look..." she said, "are you hungry? I'm hungry."

"After what we've just learned, I could use a shot of something strong. But I could eat," he admitted.

"We've got four choices..."

"Four? I just want to eat."

"I know some places, I'm sure you know some places. Or my place, or your place. Four."

"Neutral ground."

"Okay. Let's find one together. That do you?"

"That do me."

The two men in suits in a parked, dark green SUV had been watching the Teterboro carpark for some time.

The radio held by the one in the passenger seat squawked. "Anything?"

"Nada," he said into it. "I think he towed us here. No one's been near the damned car since."

"Stay put."

"That's a rog." He made a face as the transmission ended, but said nothing to his companion.

Another SUV, similar in color, was parked within eyeshot of Duchamps' apartment building. There were two suited men in that one as well.

The occupant of the passenger seat glanced at the driver. "What the hell's he playing at now? We've been watching that guy since he went public with that article. We watched him bang his head against walls, getting nowhere fast. Suddenly, he rushes off to Teterboro, where some people run interference, and he disappears. Our people don't see who he meets, so that avenue's closed...for now. Is he still at the airport? Or was he picked up by someone and could be anywhere..."

"Well, he hasn't left the country," the driver said. "We'd know by now."

"In case you'd forgotten—new security measures or not—it's a goddamned big country."

"You know what I mean."

But the other was not listening. "Who the hell did he meet? After months of nothing, where did the sudden excitement come from? One thing's for sure...he's found an informant; or thinks he's found one..."

"Who could have that kind of information? And who would be prepared to give it to him?"

"No one I can think of who would be crazy enough. It would be a death warrant."

"There you go."

"But someone's out there. Perhaps someone we know nothing

about."

"Not good."

As they left the building, Duchamps took a quick glance around.

"Expecting company?" Ellen asked.

"Dark green SUVs. They've been my constant companions since that article. But we should be okay. The people in them are probably still watching my car at the airport. They couldn't know I'd get a chopper ride back to town. And as Mary got her buddies to do some nice blocking when I arrived, they don't know we've met. Don't know how long that's going to last. Another reason why we can't go to my place. They've got sentries there too."

She was staring at him.

"You talked to the magazine," he said. "You put it together."

"Poisoned chalice," she said.

"Oh yeah. Still want to eat?"

"More than ever."

"How about over there?" He indicated with a brief, sideways nod.

"*Hot dogs?*" She looked scandalized.

"It's food."

"*No*...way! Next choice is mine. You've had yours!" She waved at a taxi.

"What I like," Duchamps said. "Solidarity."

The taxi took them to a bistro not far from Broadway.

"Early 20th century French chic," Duchamps remarked, looking at the warehouse-like exterior. "I've heard of this place. Don't you have to book?"

"Let's see."

They were greeted inside. "Miss Haines!" the greeter said with enthusiasm. "So nice to see you!" He gave Duchamps a welcoming smile.

"Is a table free?"

"For you...always. And it's your favorite."

She responded with one of her own best smiles. "Thank you."

"If you'll please follow me."

"She doesn't have to book," Duchamps said to himself as they were led to the table near one of the wide, partially frosted windows.

They sat down, and the menu and wine list were brought. "Hope you like French," Ellen said.

"I've got French genes in the mix. Why would I hate myself?"

She looked at his tiny smile. "Are you making fun of me?"

He took a quick glance around. "Make fun of someone who can get a table without booking, among the Broadway celeb crowd? Never."

She gave him a faked, cross stare. "You've got to admit," she said, "it's a good place to hide while we eat. If your green SUVs would never come looking, and even if they did pass by accidentally, they can't see us through this window."

"And we can't spot them."

"If you stand..."

"Stand to eat?"

"Duchamps..."

"What?"

"Can we order?"

"That's him!" the driver said.

"*What?* Where?"

"Getting into that taxi. There's some woman with him."

"What are you waiting for? Follow the damned cab!"

A third SUV had been prowling and as Ellen had said, it had indeed come down the street by chance. A little earlier, and it would have gone right past. A little later, and it would have missed the taxi.

In the taxi, the cab driver said, "You guys celebs going incognito? If so, I've got a great idea for a TV series..."

"What makes you say that?" Duchamps asked.

"Say what? About the series?"

"About being celebs."

There was a smile in the driver's voice as he answered, "I know the score. You get into a cab—limo too obvious—but the bodyguards follow..."

"What bodyguards?"

"Guys in that green SUV..."

"Ah those," Duchamps said with a calm he did not feel. "We'd like to lose them."

The driver gave a huge grin. "Just like in my idea. Secret celebs get into a cab...only, they're really government agents and they need to lose the bad guys..."

"You got it," Duchamps said, straight-faced. "Can you do it?"

"Is the Pope Catholic? Am I Catholic?"

"So am I," Duchamps said.

"Triple turbo power," the driver said, and proceeded to demonstrate how he could lose the SUV.

In the pursuing vehicle, the driver swore. "He's made us."

"Don't lose him!" the other snapped. He continued into his radio, "He's in town! Don't ask. All I can tell you is that he's in a cab with a woman, and they're trying to lose us."

"And succeeding," the driver interrupted.

The cab had vanished.

"*Shit!*" the driver snarled. He smacked the steering wheel in frustration.

They stopped the cab a sidestreet away from the Galen building, and got out quickly. "My card," the driver said, handing it to Duchamps as he paid. "Call anytime."

Duchamps gave a tiny wave of the card before putting it in a pocket. He'd given a handsome tip.

The driver grinned. "Have fun!" He sent the cab surging in a squeal of wheels.

"Someone's going to put him in the movies," Duchamps said, watching it go.

"So are you a Catholic?" she said as they hurried back.

"Someone way back must have been. I took the liberty."

"Huguenot, more than likely."

"Could be."

"What are you going to do now?" she asked after a while.

"Well...my apartment is out, and they know I'm in town. And my car's still out at the airport. Plenty of time for them to put some kind of tracer on it. It's no longer passive surveillance. They'll be wondering if I've got some new information, and where from. They won't stop now, until they know. Damn it. Who could have expected them to be passing just as we got into that cab?"

"Do you think they saw enough of me to make a connection?"

"Unless they had a camera on you, I don't see how. They're trailing me, not you. Different ballgame if they realize you're the senator's granddaughter."

"Conference time in my office, I think." They made it without further incident.

CHAPTER SEVEN

Bocage country, Normandy, France. July 1941. 0155 local.

Someone was urinating like a mini waterfall.

"Can you make that a little louder?" came a sarcastic voice. "I can't hear you."

Subdued guffaws followed.

"*Quiet!*" Henk ordered in a sharp hiss. The men immediately fell silent.

Sitting on the ground and propped against the *Kübelwagen*, he had been snatching some sleep.

Schelberg was in the vehicle. He had not been asleep. He was listening to a far-off sound.

"*Aeroplane!*" he whispered to himself. "*Henk!*" he called in an urgent, low voice. "Do you hear that?"

Henk sat upright, listening. "No, sir, I don't..." He paused abruptly. "*Aircraft!*"

"Exactly. And it's slow. The *Tommies* are either picking someone up, or dropping off an agent...or dropping supplies for the French. Mark that position. Get the men ready."

The sound of the aircraft was already fading.

"It's far away, sir, and seems to be on its way back. It will be long gone before we get there, even if we find where it landed..."

"Henk..." Schelberg was patience itself. A bad sign.

"Sir?"

"I realize that. Now get the men *moving*."

"Yes, sir. At once."

***

0210 local.

"He's not here!" Antoine exclaimed softly.

He had thoroughly checked out where Löringer was supposed to be hiding; but there was no sign of his erstwhile prisoner.

"Did you give him correct directions?" he asked the driver.

"I was very clear. There could have been no mistake. It wasn't far for him to go. Face it, Antoine. The *Boche* ran away. You should have killed him long ago." The driver barely kept the reproach out of his voice.

"*Merde!*" Antoine said to himself. "We'll have to evacuate the tunnel until we're certain it hasn't been compromised."

"That could be for a long time..."

"Don't you think I know that? But I can't risk it."

"Perhaps someone will get the *Boche* before he makes it back to his comrades."

"Let us hope so." Antoine gave a weary sigh. "These English and their sense of fair play. I should not have listened. There is no 'fair play' in this kind of war." He looked about him, then gave another sigh. "Let's go back. We have a lot to do...just in case he was lucky enough to make it."

The four black, Raven Squadron Hurricanes had prowled in a wide double pair formation, looking for trouble; but none had come as they shepherded their charges safely across the Channel. Earlier, they had kept enemy interest away from the two Lysanders by deliberately attacking ground targets a long way from the flight path of the slower aircraft. They had been supported in this diversion by aircraft from other squadrons operating along the coast, whose pilots had no idea of the true reasons for their mission.

Now they swept in to land at Shawbridge, doing so with panache in a darkness that had begun to show the first indications of the approach of the new day. Murchison had again led the mission, with Duchamps leading Blue section, composed of himself, and Pew. Fernando was Murchison's number two.

THE RAVEN CONSPIRACY – CODE NAME: ICARUS

The aircraft had barely taxied to a halt on the flightline, when Murchison jumped out, and approached Duchamps' aircraft. Duchamps had just freed himself of his harness.

"Mr. Duchamps!"

He paused in the act of getting out, and looked down at the shape in the gloom, wondering what he had done wrong. "Sir?"

"You were good tonight. In fact, you were excellent. And those flak emplacements you shot up was very neatly done, if a little close for my nerves. But well done!"

Duchamps grinned with relief. "Thank you, sir!"

"Next time, try not to get so intimate with the gun crews. Wouldn't want to drop in permanently for some Schnaps, would we?"

"Er...no, sir."

"Must have terrified the bastards, though, before you got them! Get to debriefing." Murchison walked away, and seemed to be chuckling.

"Yes, sir!"

Duchamps climbed down to find Pew hurrying up.

"Was Murch-the-Yank tearing you off a strip?" Pew asked.

"In a nice way," Duchamps said, removing his helmet. He related what Murchison had said.

"Well, you were close, old son," Pew said. "It cost me a few beats of the ticker, watching that. Were you trying to recognize their faces?"

"Just making certain."

"Any closer, and they'd have been inviting you in for Schnaps. Oh. Murchison's already said that." Pew grinned.

On the way, Fernando joined them. "What were you trying to do, man?" he began. "Stamp on their bloody heads?"

"The wing commander's already been there, and Pew. You're last in the line, Jamie."

"But they were nice bonfires," Jamie admitted. "I'll say that for you." After debriefing, Hamilton was less sanguine than Murchison. He called Duchamps into his office.

"Mr. Duchamps," he began, "I've had Wing Commander Murchison's report on the mission. He sings your praises. He also told me of that pass you made along those flak guns. I agree with him it was excellent work, well executed. Where we part company very slightly, is in reaction to your...let us call it...keenness. I am all for pressing the attack to the enemy. Frighten him. Make him fear you as if he were facing the devil himself. But I would also like that devil to come home safely. In the very short time you have been here, you have impressed both of us with your skills. You have taken to the Hurri and to nightflying, as if you've been doing it all your life. I want that life to last a little longer. This is not a reprimand, Tad. Just some friendly advice."

"Yes, sir. Thank you, sir."

"Now go get some rest. You've earned it."

"Yes, sir."

After Duchamps had gone, Murchison entered with a sideways smile. "Good cop, bad cop routine. Shame on you. I'm supposed to be the bad cop around here."

Hamilton glanced at the door. "A change of role now and then is no bad thing. Keeps them guessing. I was just making certain that young life lasts a little longer."

"Going to stick my neck out," Murchison said. "If the folks back home thought differently, they'd be looking at one of their youngest generals-to-be."

"If he lived long enough..."

"And *we*...are looking at perhaps our youngest squadron leader-to-be..."

"If he lives long enough," Hamilton repeated.

"I'll stick my neck out again," Murchison said. "Barring accidents, I don't see him going down in this war."

"That's as bold a prediction as I've ever heard. This is *war* we're talking about. People are dying in their droves as we speak, many of them pilots."

"Yes, we're talking about war; but that kid's good, Richard. He's better than good. Watching him operate tonight was a revelation. Though it seems to look like it, he does not take chances. He just seems able to squeeze into margins that would kill a lesser pilot in a heartbeat. Including me."

Hamilton stared at him. "You are waxing lyrical."

"If you'd been there, you'd be singing too. He went along a line of light flak...six of them! Pew was off to starboard, watching out for surprises. Those cannons can swing 360, as you know, with a hit-range of 4800 meters. Jeez. That's nearly five klicks. What does he do? He goes way down, almost hugging the ground, so he's not pasted nicely against the nice bright starlight like a sitting duck. He's moving fast, and they can't see him in time. The sound of the Hurri must have seemed to come from everywhere.

"One crew panics, and starts to fire. The others follow, giving away their positions. They're firing in the *wrong* goddamned direction! Duchamps opens up. The first gun blows. He must have hit some ammo. By the time the others realize where the attack is coming from, he's on them, he's going so fast. He got five that way. Pew came in to take out the sixth, that had finally begun to get things right. But Pew got them before they could get near Duchamps. Those two work like a dream. It's all in my report."

"Yes. I've read it. But reading it, and hearing you tell it, are two very different things."

"If we were in the medical business, I'd call him a surgeon."

"We're in the killing business,"

"He's a surgeon," Murchison repeated. "Go fly a mission with him. If you're lucky, you might get to see him in action. We both know that 'Cagey' Stroeme's one of the best fighter pilots around. Before much longer, that kid will be good enough to take on someone like him…and win."

Hamilton was still looking at Murchison with amazement. "When we welcomed our new intake, I told them you were a man of few words. That's the most I've ever heard you say in almost one breath. You've whetted my curiosity."

"Go satisfy it one day. Take him on a rover across the Channel. Look for some game. As I said…you might get lucky."

"Put that way," Hamilton remarked with a fleeting smile, "how can I pass it up?"

Outskirts of Macon, Georgia. July 2006.

"Duchamps…Duchamps…*Duchamps!* That's all I heard when I got back. Duchamps and those goddamned flak guns. I spent my time behind enemy lines; but you'd think he had suddenly begun to walk on water. That nigger was already haunting me, and would haunt me for the rest of my life."

Haines was still staring at his desk. His lips tightened as he remembered that July night in 1941.

Galen Private Archives, New York. July 2006.

"'Duchamps...Duchamps...Duchamps!'" Ellen read softly, continuing from the diary they had been reading before their eventful meal. "'*That's all I've been hearing about since I got back. Duchamps and those goddamned flak guns. I spend my time behind enemy lines; but you'd think he has suddenly begun to walk on water. That nigger is haunting me...*'"

She stopped, and looked at the younger Duchamps. "I'm...I'm sorry..."

"What for? That's not your diary. Those are not your words. My grandpa and his buddies protected that murdering, racist bastard's ass that night..." He glanced at the valise. "...just so he could continue doing whatever it is he's been doing all those years. But my grandpa survives the war, only to get killed later by some sniper that your grandpa either knows about...or is responsible for..."

"Or he did it himself." Ellen was quite serious. "We already know he could kill easily. What we don't know is how many more he is personally responsible for. The senator stayed fit most of his life. He was certainly fit enough back when your grandpa got killed. After Jack and my mom, and what we've seen so far, nothing about the senator going to surprise me."

Duchamps glanced at the valise again. "I think you've got more surprises coming. A lot more." He gave a sudden smile, "Sounds like my old gramps was quite a flyer."

She cocked her head to one side, and gave him a look that was perilously close to being fond, and intimate. "Have you any idea how proud you sound?"

"Shouldn't I be?"

"Yes. You should. He was quite a warrior. Even the senator was forced to write down what he'd been told about that attack on the guns."

"Yeah. But it chewed at him..."

There was a knock on the outer door; muffled, but insistent. "Ellen?" a male voice called faintly. "You still here?"

"Shit. That's Dean Howe." She glanced at her watch. "Time does fly when you're having fun. I think most people must have gone. Perhaps only the security staff are here."

"And Dean. Boyfriend?"

"He wishes." She stood up. "He's not a colleague...but the security staff know him, so they let him in when he comes over. I'll...go get rid of him. Don't come out."

"Going nowhere."

She gave a tiny nod, and went into the outer office, closing the door quietly behind her. She went to the outer door, and opened it.

A tallish, patrician man in his thirties in a neat, summer-weight suit and wearing a ready smile, was standing there. Dean Howe possessed a fine head of blond hair that was parted in the middle and surgically styled, so that two precisely cut wings fell carefully on either side of his face. The wings allowed him to absently brush them back at selected intervals.

"Hi, Dean," Ellen greeted.

"Hi. Are you free for dinner? It's an impromptu thing. The parents are having dinner in the town house. Just family. Mother and Father always look forward to seeing you, and even Daphne will be there. She's up from LA. Something to do with the fashion mag she writes for..."

"Your sister does not like me very much. She considers me a spoilt Southern bitch..."

"Come on, Ellen. Daphne's a bit strange. You know that. She does not even like her own family. I'm amazed she's even decided to honor us with her presence tonight. Normally, she either checks into a hotel on her expense account, or stays with friends, whenever she comes to New York. So...are you on?"

Ellen shook her head. "I'm so sorry, Dean. Please give your parents my regrets. I'm stuck on a very important matter that will take a lot of time..."

"I am disappointed, of course...but I understand. How about the coming weekend? The parents are having a small entertainment at the country house. I know they'll look forward to seeing you there..."

Again, she shook her head. "Oh, Dean...this is so...awkward. I'd love to, but this thing I'm working on really is going to take some time. On top of that, my grandfather is not too well these days. He is getting on, and..."

Howe's eyes had widened. "The senator's unwell?"

"He's not exactly young, anymore..."

"So you could be going to Macon at the weekend?"

"I might. It all depends."

"Look, if you need company, I can..."

"If I do go, it has to be..."

"Yes. Yes, of course."

"And besides, there's that weekend at the country house. How would it look if the only son were not there?"

Howe smiled to hide his disappointment. "As usual, you're quite right. Let me know when you've got some time."

"I will."

He leaned forward, intending to give her a quick kiss on the lips; but she turned her head slightly, and the kiss landed on her cheek, close to the corner of her mouth. A tiny frown briefly appeared, but he covered that with another smile.

"Till then."

She nodded. "Okay."

She remained where she was until he had entered the lift that would take him down to the lobby. He gave a little wave just before the doors closed.

She waved back and when the lift had gone down, she shut and locked the outer door, before rejoining Duchamps.

"Wouldn't take no for an answer?" he began.

"He tried, and failed."

"What's the story there? You don't have to answer if you feel I'm poking my nose where it doesn't belong."

"I don't mind answering. Dean comes from an old banking family."

"Ah..."

She stared at him. "What do you mean 'ah'?"

He waved a hand briefly. "Look at this place. Not exactly a

supermarket checkout. Good-ol'-boy senator's granddaughter, old banking family son...match made in Heaven. It's a natural."

"You're a matchmaker now?"

"Hey. Peace. Just kidding. None of my business."

The dark eyes were fathomless. "That's right."

"Uh-oh. Guess I pushed a wrong button there."

She was still staring at him. "Can we continue now?"

"Hey. It was only a joke. I'm sorry."

"So don't jump to conclusions."

They stared at each other, Duchamps wondering what had got into her, she seemingly annoyed with him.

The tension, for some moments, was electric. Then it dissipated. Slowly.

"I'm sorry," he repeated. "Okay?"

She drew in a deep breath, then let it out. "Okay."

About an hour later, she said, "I think we should stop for today."

He rubbed at his face. "I agree. Let's lock the poisoned chalice away for now. You should go on home, and I should..."

"You can't go home. Remember?"

"I can get home without being seen by those..."

"Do you really want to risk it, after what happened when we left the restaurant?"

"You have a suggestion?"

She nodded. "I have a suggestion. We go down to my car in the basement garage. You stay low. I drive to my apartment block. We get out in the garage there, go up to my apartment. They're not watching me..."

"Not yet."

"So? And in case you're wondering, I've got two bedrooms. You're safe."

"I never imagined otherwise."

The dark eyes held his. "Okay. We'll do that."

The dark green SUVs were not yet watching Ellen, but someone else was.

When her Mercedes SLK left the Galen garage, a big Mercedes

coupe followed at a discreet distance. It trailed all the way to her apartment block. She was quite unaware of it; and Duchamps, keeping low, was unable to spot their shadower.

The Mercedes coupe stopped near the entrance of redbrick-and-glass building that was the converted loft apartments, as the smaller car entered the underground garage. The driver hurried out, to enter the lobby. The person who was the discreet security man, doorman, and concierge rolled into one knew him, and looked up in a friendly manner.

"Mr. Howe! Nice to see you, sir..."

"Hi, Danny. Can I just rush up to see if Miss Haines is in?"

"Of course, sir. You know the way."

"Thank you."

"You're welcome."

Howe rushed to the lift, and took it to one floor beneath Ellen's apartment; then he hurried up the flight of stairs to her floor. He did not leave the stairs but peered through the glass panel of the access door. He was just in time to see her arrive with Tad Duchamps.

"So that's how it is," he muttered to himself. His mouth turned down. "'stuck on a very important matter that will take a lot of time'. I see."

He went back down the stairs, and took the lift to the lobby.

"She's not in," he said to the man he'd addressed as Danny.

"Thanks again."

"You're welcome, Mr. Howe. Have a nice evening."

"You too," Howe said, seething inside.

The "town house" was a classic urban mansion on five floors. Howe drove to it in a cold rage. The entire basement had been converted into a big garage and he drove in almost too fast for the remotely controlled, up-and-over door. He screeched to a stop in his parking space, inches from the wall. There were other cars already there: his father's chauffeur driven Rolls Royce, and his mother's blue Mercedes saloon, also chauffeur-driven. He sat in his car for several long minutes, controlling the anger he felt. At last, he got out.

The rest of the full complement of the immediate Howe family were waiting when Howe finally made it to the vast lounge that took up an entire floor.

"Darling, you're late," his mother began. "Where's Ellen?"

"She can't make it."

"Oh, what a pity."

Daphne had been looking closely at him when he'd entered. It was not the look of a sister who loved her brother.

"So the Southern belle has dumped you?" she said, the needle sharply toxic.

"She did not 'dump' me, sister mine, as you so charmingly put it."

Daphne glanced at her parents. "Something's wrong. His eyes are so tight. They look ready to burst."

A business-suited Augustus Howe, standing a little way from the women, hands in pockets, looked at his son with unblinking eyes. "What's the problem, Dean?"

"She's...busy."

"And the rest?"

After some moments of hesitation, he told them about what had happened.

"You actually *followed* her?" Daphne asked with open contempt.

"Why not?" he retorted. "She was lying."

"Far be it for me to defend her, but what right have you to follow her? She's doing her job."

"Taking this...man to her apartment?"

"So what? She's not your wife. She's not even your girlfriend."

"Something's not quite right. That man was in her office when..."

"Dean, it may be news to you, but people do have clients in their offices."

"Yes. They do. But they don't sneak them out in their cars and take them to their apartments...unless there's some funny business going on. She did not know I was following her. He was hiding from *someone else!* Why would Ellen Haines take a black man to her apartment..."

"A black man?" all three exclaimed, for three different reasons.

"I take it all back about her," Daphne continued. "I'm beginning to like her already."

"You would," Dean Howe remarked, with more than a hint of poison.

Her eyes blazed at him. "What's that supposed to mean? *Dean?*

What's that supposed to *fucking mean?*" she shouted.

Her mother was scandalized. "Daphne!" Charlotte Howe scolded, horrified.

"What's wrong, mother? That little word bother you? Don't you know what Dean's getting at?" She looked at her father. "Don't *you?*"

Augustus Howe was remarkably calm. "Can you describe this man?" he asked his son. "Are you positive he was black?"

"No. Well, I did not exactly get a clear view..."

"Peeping toms never do," Daphne cut in.

"Daphne," her father said. "Please. Go on, Dean."

"At first, I thought he could be Italian, or perhaps Puerto Rican. On reflection...I think he's a light-skinned nigger..."

Daphne leapt to her feet—"*Jesus Christ, Dean!*" she yelled. "Don't you get enough of that shit with your dinosaur pals at the tennis club, the golf club, or any other fucking club these types of people infest? Do you have to bring it here?" She glared at her father. "And you! Keep on pretending you don't know what he's getting at. I came here tonight against my better judgement. I knew it was a mistake to come. I should have listened to myself. I need some air!"

She turned to go.

Charlotte Howe tried to save what was left of the evening. She got to her feet, and went over to Daphne. "Darling, listen..."

But Daphne's eyes were strangely unforgiving. "Mother, I've never said this to you, but here you are, so liberal, so supportive of affirmative action...unless one of them falls for your daughter. And you, father. Thanks for the support you never gave me when I needed it. What are you, really?" She glared at Dean. "God. I'm so embarrassed to have you as a brother!" She looked at each in turn. "As I said...I need some air."

She walked out on them.

Dean was unrepentant. "Guess we won't be seeing her for some time."

His mother rounded on him. "Dean...just...*shut up!* You've ruined the evening with your stupid jealousy!" She too, left the room.

A long silence descended between the two men. Augustus Howe seemed to be deep in thought.

At last, he said, "This man you saw...would you say there was something...military about him?"

Dean looked surprised. "Why that question? Why would Ellen...I don't understand..."

"Just think. *Was* there?"

"Well...to be...to tell you the truth, it was hard to tell. His hair was not military in cut. He did not look like your average nigger...Military?" Dean shrugged. "He had an air of assurance. That's the best I can do."

"Thank you. And don't ever use that word in this house again!" Augustus Howe's voice was soft; but there was no mistaking the force of the censure. "This may be common coinage among the people with whom you associate..."

"I've heard you..."

"And don't interrupt when I'm speaking to you! You do *not* use that word in this house, or any other house or building I own. And never again in my presence. Am I getting through, mister?" Howe's eyes were cold.

"Er...yes. Yes."

"Good. Well. I think the evening's pretty well dead now, don't you? Nice work. I'll be in my den. Stay, or see yourself out."

He strode out of the room, leaving his son with the ruins of the evening.

Daphne Howe was an impressive woman to look at. Younger than her brother by four years, and nearly as tall, hers was a vibrant beauty. A statuesque body and rich shoulder-length blonde hair completed the picture. Many friends and colleagues had told her she belonged on the cover of the magazine she worked for, and could not understand why she would never countenance doing so.

The cab dropped her off at the entrance to Ellen Haines' apartment block.

Ellen had just finished giving Duchamps a tour. They were in the vast kitchen and she was raiding the fridge to see what there was to eat.

"Great space," he said to her with undisguised enthusiasm, glancing up at the sunken lights in the 12-foot high white ceiling. "All this, and a roof terrace all to yourself. Nice, nice."

The apartment had mainly white walls where there were not high and wide areas of glass, and a polished, dark wooden floor. On one side in the huge living room, white columns rose to the ceiling

"Thank you. I expect you to reciprocate one day. I've shown you my loft, you show me yours."

"You've got a deal." He peered into the fridge. "Looks like mine."

"What do you mean?"

"You eat out a lot, or order."

"You too?"

"Me too."

"I can cook, you know."

"I believe you. Shame to waste such a kitchen."

"Martha taught me."

"I believe you."

The security phone rang. They looked at each other. "Expecting company?" Duchamps asked.

"That's my line."

"Not this time."

She picked up the phone. "Yes, Danny?"

"Miss Haines," the man in the lobby began, "I've got someone here who wants to speak with you. A Miss Daphne Howe. She says she's Mr. Howe's sister..."

Ellen's eyebrows rose in astonishment. "Put her on."

"Here she is, Miss Haines."

"Ellen?"

"Daphne! This is a surprise..."

"I'll bet it is. Can I come up?"

"Er...sure. Danny will tell you where."

"Okay. Be right with you."

As she put the phone back on its hook, Ellen said to Duchamps. "I can't believe it. Dean Howe's sister! What's she doing here? She's never been here before. Once, she was in the car when Dean dropped me home...but she never came up. She practically hates me."

"Come to plead for bro?"

"No chance. She likes him like you like a verruca."

"Happy families."

"Tad, you've got to..."

"Yep. I know. Lock myself in my room."

"Sorry. At least until we know why she's here."

"You got it. I'm a dot."

Daphne arrived at the door just as Duchamps made it to the bedroom Ellen had given him for the night.

"That's an uncertain smile," she greeted when Ellen had opened the solid door. "So many questions must be going through your mind."

"Hi, Daphne. Come on in."

Daphne entered, and looked about her. "Nice place. So? Where is he?"

"Where is... What do you mean?"

Daphne gave her a sideways look. "Ellen, this is Daphne. I come in peace, believe it or not, and I bring news that will be of interest to you. I've just come from the Howe family home...or what passes for a family home. It's a house, not a home."

"You're not making sense."

"My brother came to your office."

"Yes."

"He invited you to dinner at the family home...house."

"Yes."

"But you could not make it."

"Yes."

"A good thing. Did you know he followed you?"

Ellen was shocked. "He *what?*"

"He did. And he ran all the way home to cry about it. He was spitting mad...and jealous...*and* nasty." Daphne was still looking about her, as if expecting to see someone leap out from behind a sofa. "He came into your building, and sneaked up the stairs."

Ellen was staring at her, wide-eyed. "Is this some kind of joke?"

"No joke. He saw you arrive with your...friend. He peeked through the access door. I don't know what's going on, and I am not sure I want to know. But I thought I should tell you what happened...if it helps."

Ellen had sat down in her shock at this piece of news. Then her face hardened, eyes going cold "Why did he do this?"

"Because he's a little shit?" Daphne suggested, sibling love conspicuously absent. She peered at Ellen. "You've got an expression on that tells me this is more than being pissed because of what my jerk of a brother did."

Ellen stood up. "Wait." She left a puzzled Daphne to go to Duchamps' room, and knocked softly. "Tad," she said in a sharp whisper. "Open up. We've got to talk."

Duchamps opened, eyes telegraphing questions.

Ellen entered quickly, and shut the door. She moved away from it, a curious Duchamps following.

"Dean followed us here!" she began, keeping her voice a low whisper.

"*What?*" Duchamps glanced at the door, and kept his own voice low.

"My reaction too."

"He's that crazy about you?"

"He's crazy. Period. The question is what do we do? He came up the stairs to sneak a peek, and..."

"Saw me."

"Yes."

"Shit."

"And some. He went to his parent's home and—according to Daphne—raged about it."

"'Raged'?"

"He was...angry, and nasty. What she said."

"Jealous. He thinks we were..."

"It does not matter what he thinks! What matters is that in his mood, he's going to talk more than he has already. He mixes with a club crowd who would be at home in the old days of the South. Sooner or later, someone we would not like to will get to hear..."

"And we'll have more problems..."

"And Daphne's here. *She's* not going to leave."

"Until she's satisfied her curiosity."

Ellen looked at him closely. "We could make this work for us."

"How? I thought she didn't like you."

"Dean's little trick seems to have changed her...perhaps. She did come here to warn me."

"Or to nose around."

"She writes for a magazine."

"Ah!"

"Not 'ah'. It's a fashion magazine."

"A magazine is a magazine. Remember my last experience."

"Somehow," Ellen said, "I don't think she'll write anything unless we allow her."

"How can you be so sure?"

"Intuition. Let me tell you something about Daphne. When I first came to New York, the Howes took me under their wing. I'm certain the senator had something to do with that too. And before you say it, I'm paying for this place with my own money."

"I said nothing about that."

"Just so you know. Dean," she continued over whatever Duchamps had been about to say, "got...'attached', but it was all strictly one-way. Daphne never warmed to me. I was Southern, and spoilt. That's what she thought. There was a reason behind it that I did not understand until much later.

"She'd met someone in Washington where she'd gone for the magazine. It was at some reception, and he was there. It was love at first sight. Really. She saw him, he saw her, and bang. She thought he was a reporter. It was only later she found out he was military. Worse, from her point of view and what happened later, Special Forces. He was a captain. She introduced him to the family. That didn't go down well."

"Meaning?"

"He was black."

"Ah. I begin to see something in the murk. You keep saying 'was'."

"He's dead."

"Ah." Duchamps repeated.

"Some friends of his came round to see her. He was missing, but not to worry, they said. He was good in the field. He'd make it back. He didn't. She moved to LA and never forgave her family."

"And now you think she feels some kind of solidarity...because of me?"

"Who knows? She obviously thinks we...er..."

"'We...er' what?"

"You're not stupid. Don't act it. Well? Do we tell her? She can be our eyes and ears, and the people in the green SUVs would be no wiser."

"Until they find out, and she becomes a target."

"We've got to tell her something. She's no fool."

"But nothing about the diaries."

"Of course not. Now I'd better get back before she comes looking. Come out a while later."

He nodded.

She began moving back towards the door, then paused. "Oh. she's...a looker."

"Meaning?"

"She looks good. She's tall, got real blonde hair to her knees, and blue-on-blue eyes..."

"Hair to her knees. Blue-on-blue...that's a phrase sometimes used to describe friendly fire..."

"It could come to that," Ellen said in an ominous tone. "She's got very blue eyes. Okay? And I'm only warning you so you don't make a fool of yourself."

"Does that worry you?"

"Why should it?" she remarked airily, and went out. Duchamps smiled at the closing door.

"Oh...my..." Daphne began when Duchamps entered. "And *green* eyes too," she continued as he drew closer. "No wonder Dean's so jealous." She held out a hand, and as he took it, said with a slight frown, "Green...eyes...er...I'm..."

"Daphne," he said. Her eyes, he noted, were indeed an astonishing blue. "I see Ellen has warned you."

"Yes. I'm..."

"Tad Duchamps," she said, stunning him and Ellen, by adding, "And no, Ellen did not warn me."

Ellen stared at her. "*Daphne?* How do you..."

"Know?" She was still holding on to Duchamps' hand. "Those green eyes. I knew I'd seen them before, and that face." To Duchamps, she went on, "every female member of our editorial staff wanted us to find you, to put you on our cover. You and that jet of yours."

"You saw that article?"

"Surely did. And we did try to find you. But, as Wiley used to say, you went off the radar."

"Who's Wiley?"

A sudden, faint moistness appeared in the blue eyes. "Someone I used to know."

And Duchamps understood she meant the captain who had died.

But Ellen was looking at their hands. "You *can* let go of him, Daphne."

Daphne gave a quick smile that was not at all apologetic as she turned to Ellen. "Sorry. Carried away by the surprise. And what a surprise. The guy who's off the radar is here, in *your* apartment." She looked at each in turn. "So who's going to tell me? And don't say tell me what. I wasn't born yesterday. Are you guys hungry? I am. The dinner I thought I was going to have didn't happen. So how about we order something? Then you can tell me while we eat." She looked at them with a mild air of triumph. "So what do we order? Chinese, Thai, Malaysian, wings and ribs...?"

"Wings and ribs," Duchamps said. "With flaming aviation fuel sauce."

"The hot stuff," she said. "Hmm. Ellen?"

"Me too."

"Hmm," Daphne said again, sounding relieved. "Thank God. I feel like gnawing something."

In his study, Augustus Howe was making a call.

"A problem may have reappeared," he said to the person he had called. "I am not as yet certain, but it could be that our turbulent pilot has found an unlikely, and unexpected, ally."

"And who would that be?"

"Hold on to your hat. Ellen Haines."

"*What!*" It was an involuntary shout. "Who gave you that information?"

"My son," Howe said with distaste.

"Is he certain?"

"That's just it. He did not make a positive identification. He did not even say it was our inquisitive pilot; but he did say enough to make me believe it could be. The circumstances of the sighting make the possibility very likely."

"If he *is* in touch with the senator's grandchild, what's the worst-case scenario?"

"He knows more than he should, and is attempting to use her."

"And the best case?"

"He's still banging his head against walls, and hopes to use her."

"I have a different worst-case scenario."

"Which is?"

"That Haines, in his winter years, is having an attack of conscience."

"I thought he lost that as a baby."

"Who knows with people? Outlandish as my suggestion might sound, it should not be ruled out."

"Perhaps we should find out if she visited the senator recently," Howe said. "That, would be a good place to start."

They were seated at a table that seemed overloaded.

"Did we order *all* that?" Daphne asked no one in particular, eyes an avid blue.

Duchamps looked at the accompanying sauces. "I can smell the flames from here. Let's get to it." He paused, observing that Daphne was looking at him. "What?"

"You remind me of Wiley...just a little. You don't look at all like him. It's just...a manner."

"The Special Forces guy..."

She glanced at Ellen. "So Ellen's told you."

"Yes. And I'm sorry...both for what happened to him...and how your family behaved."

She picked up a rack of ribs and tore one off. It was almost as if she were dismembering someone. "My oh-so-liberal family. 'We're only thinking about your best interests'," she mimicked. "'We're not responsible for the way the world is, darling.' This, from my *mother!* Too dumb to see she was perpetuating it!"

"I don't think she's that dumb," Duchamps said.

"Guess not." Daphne dipped the rib into one of the hot sauces, and tore into it with a vengeance.

"That's not your family you're eating," Duchamps joked.

"They would not taste this good. And that's not a joke." Daphne cleaned off the rib and tore off another, pausing to say. "Don't tell me anything. Hear me out first, then you two decide."

Duchamps glanced at Ellen's watchful expression, before saying to Daphne. "Okay..."

Daphne rolled the new rib in the sauce. "When the issue with that article disappeared, it left more questions than answers."

"Tell me about it," Duchamps said, not hiding the bitterness,

"We got to see it because a member of the staff had gotten hold of an early copy. She'd known the guy at her local news stand since she was a kid, so when she was late getting home on the nights we put the magazine to bed, he would give her the next day's paper or magazine, depending on what she wanted. That night, she chose the issue with your article, as it was already in. He told her later that less than an hour after that, he got the call not to sell it. He said nothing about the one he'd already given away."

"And that's how you got to see it."

"Yes. She brought it in, saying we had to find this guy for our cover. The editorial staff agreed—the women more than the guys." Daphne bit into the sauced rib with a tiny smile.

Ellen's expression was stony.

Daphne demolished the second rib, and tore off a third. "We rang the magazine to ask about contacting you. That's when we found out all issues with that article were being pulled. Then they hung up. Redials got us nowhere. The staff member with the only issue still around, it seemed, decided to take it home. That was a mistake. She was in the company garage, car door open and was about to get in, when the passenger door opened, and some guy just reached in and took the magazine off the seat where she had put it. She yells at him, and goes after him. Another guy blocks her. Forget the magazine he tells her. He says this in a way that leaves no doubt what will happen to her if she does not take his good advice. She drove home, shaking all the way. And you, had dropped right off the radar. Now here you are, in Ellen's apartment." She grabbed a fourth rib, held it poised just beneath her eyes, and looked at Duchamps and Ellen over it. "So what brought you two together?"

She began to roll the rib in the hot sauce.

Duchamps glanced at Ellen, then said, "I got tired of getting nowhere. Every route I'd tried had been blocked. I did not stop. I just preferred to stay low, after what had happened. I took no calls about the subject, and generally made myself unavailable. That did not stop the people in the dark green SUVs from following me about..."

Daphne held the half-finished rib in the sauce, and paused. "Green SUVs? You're being *followed?*"

"The reason Ellen brought me here. To avoid being seen by them. I lay out of sight. That's what your brother misinterpreted."

"Jumping to wrong conclusions never stopped Dean before. He was just following a well-established practice." Daphne toyed with the rib in the sauce. "These people who are following you around...would they be the same ones who frightened our colleague, Janine?"

"Could be some of their buddies. I can't know for sure...but since they were after the article, it's got to be. But how did they know she had one?"

"That was easy...for them. All they had to do was demand a full outlet list from the magazine, then pay some visits. The local guy at that news stand said he had some visitors. He was so sorry when he told Janine, she had to tell him it was okay. They scared him too. What stones are you digging under?"

"I don't know," Duchamps replied, not looking at Ellen. "As the article said, all I'm looking for is some answers about what happened to my grandpa, and why."

"Looks like you've been poking at some kind of hornet's nest."

"Not what I expected."

"I'll bet." Daphne bit into the rib. "And your grandpa belonged to a unit that never officially existed."

"Yes."

"Like those missions Wiley officially never went on, but bigger."

"A lot bigger. At least, Wiley was officially listed. To make sure that his unit was never confirmed as having existed, they listed my grandpa in a known outfit he was never part of. They didn't like my saying that in public."

"So they follow you around, and try to make out you're some crazy pilot with a head problem, and who's no longer fit to fly."

"My resigning made it easy for them."

"You must have loved that old man."

"I do. His death does not change that. He did a hell of a job back then. For what? To get shot down like some goddamned dog?"

Daphne paused in her eating, noting the gruffness that had come into Duchamps' voice.

They all ate in silence for a while after that.

Then Daphne said, "So what made you go to Ellen?"

"I did not go to her as such," Duchamps said. Again, he did not look at Ellen as he spun his story. "I'd gotten so desperate with getting blocked all the time. I thought I should try a different route. Public institutions were no help. There always seemed to be some hotline that alerted the pals of the guys in those SUVs. I had the bright—aka desperate—idea that just maybe, I might make some headway if I tried a private archive that gave public access. I thought I might find something—letters, photos, even train schedules of the period—anything, that might give me any clue. Sometimes, even a newspaper clipping that looks like it has nothing of interest, can point a way. I was hoping I'd find perhaps a picture in an old British newspaper that would show my grandpa out there. They didn't have those annual reunions for something that never existed. And my grandpa was not the only former member of that unit to have died suspiciously. Someone, somewhere, wants them all terminated. There has to be a big reason, or there'd be no SUVs."

"If this unit was so secret, wouldn't they have made damned sure that no compromising photo of that time got into the papers?"

"I thought of that. But we all know people on all sides took private photos during the war. Lots and lots of them. I was hoping to find some that might help. I went to Ellen's archives. Some person in there pointed me to Ellen, saying she was one of their archivists. We broke off for a bite to eat, went to a restaurant...and were spotted by the guys who love dark green SUVs..."

"And here you are."

"Here I am."

"Well, you're right. You don't kill off members of a unit that never existed."

"The line is that no one is being killed. They're all dying naturally, or by accident."

"There are accidents, and then there are 'accidents'."

There was another silence, which was again broken by Daphne. "I think I can help you kids."

Duchamps shot Ellen a surreptitious glance while Daphne was occupied with making a choice between a wing and a rib.

"How?" Ellen asked.

"I can ask around discreetly. I write for a magazine."

"A fashion magazine."

"So? We don't have only articles about fashion. We have special features that do not cover fashion. I could be researching for one of those. No one would expect me to be connected."

"If they even suspected you were working with me."

"I know the rest. I am a big kid now, Tad. And I still have contact with Wiley's buddies. If I get into trouble, they'll come running."

"They may not arrive in time. Always consider that. I have already dragged Ellen into this. I don't want to."

"You let me be the judge. Okay? So...do I help? Or not?" Ellen and Duchamps looked at each other.

"She's got a point," Ellen said, as if she had never considered the idea.

CHAPTER EIGHT

Bocage country, Normandy. July 1941.
The first glimmers of the July dawn were beginning to appear when Schelberg and his men found what they at first believed were two dead bodies. There was a small yellow star on each.

Schelberg was still some distance away when someone yelled, "*It's the Standartenführer! And Scharführer Löringer! They're dead!*"

"That's right," Schelberg muttered to himself as he hurried. "Let every Frenchman in this part of France know we're here."

Henk, who was close by, only caught something indistinct. "What's that, sir?"

"Have words with your men, Henk. They shout too much."

"Yes, sir." Henk hurried ahead.

By the time Schelberg had arrived at the scene, there was enough light to betray the sheepish expressions on the faces of two men who had made the find. Henk had obviously relayed his version of the order.

Schelberg looked down at the bodies. Both were face up, Löringer lying across James. He saw the yellow stars, and frowned.

"Anyone touched them?" he asked.

"No, sir," one of the men answered. "Good."

"The *Scharführer* was hit right in the heart, sir," the other said. "Look. But we can't tell about the *Standartenführer* until..."

"Yes. I can see. Until we move them."

Schelberg lowered himself to peer closely at the wound in Löringer's chest. The bullet had entered via the left breast pocket. A wide patch of blood had spread from the entry wound, darkening a large patch of the uniform. He picked up each star, stared at them briefly, then put them in a pocket.

"What do these mean, sir?" Henk asked.

"Yellow stars of David on two dead SS men. What do you think it means?"

"Jews daring to attack us? They will pay for this!" Henk said tightly. "Our comrades had no weapons! This was an execution!"

Though without doubt well aware that the SS routinely executed the defenseless, Schelberg said in a mild voice, "They are already paying. Serve your rage cold, Henk. It may not necessarily be Jews. Those still around may be too busy getting away from France." Then he gave another slight frown, and straightened. "Get our medical man here," he said to one of the men. "Quickly!"

"*Sanitäter!*" the man yelled.

Schelberg glared both at Henk, and at the shouter. "If you want to alert every French terrorist in the area, you're doing a very good job. The next time you shout while under my command, your next unit will be on the Eastern Front. *Do you hear me?*" Schelberg hissed.

"Yes...yes, *Standartenführer!*"

"Now go and find that medic and bring him here!"

"At once..." He stopped.

The medic was already hurrying up to them.

Henk reserved a particularly poisonous look for the shouter.

The medic, an SS sergeant named Neuermann, had a strangely calm face. He looked down at the bodies with no visible sign of emotion.

"Marius," he said to the top body. "What did you get into?"

"You knew him?" Schelberg asked.

"Yes, sir." Neuermann, still looking down at the body, paused. "What the...!"

"So you see it too."

"Yes, sir. But I can't see how." Neuermann knelt quickly and began to inspect Löringer's body, putting an ear close to its chest. "It's impossible, but he's still alive!" He felt gingerly near the wound. "Something solid in the pocket."

"A cigarette case?"

"He never smoked. I need light on this pocket. Quickly!"

Schelberg ignored the tone of what seemed like an apparent order from a lowly subordinate, and said to Henk. "A torch or two on there."

Henk and one of the other men obeyed.

Neuermann studied the wound again, and began speaking without looking up. "He was hit at close range, by someone above him. Whatever's in that pocket, and the angle, saved him. He was very lucky. The bullet went through far enough to penetrate the body, but not far enough. It's in the flesh, but I can see it. The blow was enough to put him out and that again, saved him. If he'd moved at the time, whoever did this would have fired again, to finish the job. As it is, he obviously thought Marius was dead."

"Can he be moved?"

Neuermann finally looked up. "No, sir. Not with that bullet where it is. I've got to remove it first."

"Would that not risk finishing him off?"

"Yes. But we don't have a choice...except to just leave him here for nature to take its course."

"He fought this long to stay alive. Let's give him the chance. Besides, I want to talk to him."

"Yes, sir. I'll need more light."

"You shall have it. Henk...more torches, and set up guards to make sure the French don't surprise us."

"Yes, sir."

Neuermann was eventually surrounded by six soldiers, all shining their torches on Löringer. Carefully, he began to cut off the upper half of the pocket, and peeled it back to reveal what did look like a cigarette case.

"I thought you said he did not smoke," Schelberg remarked from above.

"He doesn't. This is the case in which he keeps a photo of his girlfriend, and the last letter she sent him. I've seen this before. His girlfriend seems to have saved his life...if I don't end it, that is. I'm going to try to remove the case, and hope it will come easily. The bullet might have pinned it..."

Neuermann stopped talking, and began to inch the case upwards so slowly, it appeared he was not moving at all. At one point, the weakest of groans came from Löringer. Neuermann did not pause.

It seemed to take forever, but the case came away cleanly. There was a bloom of metal where the bullet had exited from the tough case, lacerating the flesh around the bullet itself. The blood had coagulated, sealing the area.

He held the case upwards. Schelberg took it.

"Coagulation's good," Neuermann said. "Now to see what the bullet does. I'll need to work fast to prevent heavy bleeding. If I can get the bullet out, I'll sterilize the area as best as I can, and stop any bleeding. If his luck still holds and I'm lucky, he won't wake up, even if he makes a sound. If we're not lucky, he'll wake up screaming to wake the dead, before he finally joins them by bleeding himself to death. If we make it, he'll need at least a field hospital. Fast. A lot of ifs..."

"Leave the hospital to me," Schelberg said. "You get to work."

Löringer did give a whimper as Neuermann gingerly worked at the bullet. It took even longer than the case, but in the end the round came out, with very little additional bleeding.

"I'll take that," Schelberg said.

Neuermann passed him the bullet, then quickly dressed the wound, and finally rested on his heels with a sigh of relief. "Whoever's watching over him, just did extra duty."

Löringer was still out.

They took James' body and Löringer, to the nearest military medical unit. This happened to belong to no other than the same SS unit, one of whose members Haines had pretended to be. They arrived at 0600.

They had made Löringer as comfortable as possible on a journey that took two hours at the necessarily slow pace through the bocage before reaching normal roads. Löringer was still in relatively good shape, all things considered, when the medical team took charge.

Schelberg met with the unit commander, Ulrich Brödl, someone he knew. Brödl, an *Obersturmbannführer*, was subordinate by one rank to Schelberg; but under no circumstances could Schelberg ever give him, or members of his special unit, orders. Schelberg was well aware of this.

Brödl had come to the medical unit to see what the commotion was all about.

"My dear Schelberg!" Brödl greeted expansively "I never expected we would see you in Normandy. We need more people like you down here to teach the French to behave themselves."

"I hear your unit is doing that quite effectively." They shook hands.

"We have our successes," Brödl said with some pride. "But the more pressure the better, eh? As you're out and about so early, why don't you have breakfast with me in my quarters? Whatever the failings of the French, their cooking is superb. I have a sympathetic chef. Good type. Hates Jews with a vengeance." Brödl barked a laugh. "Come. My medical team will look after your sergeant. And your men can go get something decent to eat in the Mess. All ranks eat together here. The food is excellent."

"More sympathetic chefs?"

"Let's put it this way...none have tried to slit our throats." Brödl gave another laugh as they walked to the big, commandeered house he had made his quarters.

"Charming place," Schelberg observed as they entered.

"Once belonged to a schoolmaster. Big for a teacher. Her family obviously had money. The fool was married to a Jewess, and they even had children—two boys. The obscenity of it! They have no further use for this house now."

"What happened to them?"

"She *resisted*." Brödl's face grew dark with anger. "Damned Jewess. She fought back! Actually disarmed one of my men and shot him dead, and two others, before she was stopped. Permanently."

"She *killed* your men?"

"Yes, damn her Jewess soul! But she paid for it. My men can be...enthusiastic when driven to it. She drove them that day. Mother and children paid."

"And the husband?"

Brödl removed his cap. "Robert!" he called. "A breakfast guest! The husband...weak coward, *ran*. He was clearly warned. We cleared the entire village after that, and the citizens relocated under the tender care of their fellow French, the Milice. The place became our operating base. No French person is here without permission. The house had to be cleaned of her remains and the children's, and his parents who stupidly tried to intervene. They too, paid for that stupidity; but as you can see, no trace remains. She grew up here, you know. Born here too, I believe. But she was betrayed by one of her own villagers. And the world tries to make out we are the only ones who hate Jews." Brödl sighed at the injustice of it as he saw it, and at the hypocrisy of the world. "Let's go in to breakfast. Robert will already have things prepared."

Schelberg removed his own cap. "Mmm! I can smell coffee."

Breakfast was over.

"Excellent cooking," Schelberg commented with appreciation.

Brödl grinned. "I told you."

Brödl pushed his chair back, took out a gleaming cigarette case with embossed SS runes, snapped it open, and offered the opened case to Schelberg, who shook his head.

"Still don't, eh?"

"Still don't."

Brödl withdrew the case, took out a cigarette, shut the case, tapped the cigarette briefly upon it, before returning the case to a breast pocket. He lit up, drew long upon the weed, and blew out a long plume of smoke.

"American," he said. "I have a friend out there who finds ways to send me these. He supports our ideas." Then abruptly, he got to his feet. "Something to show you."

Schelberg followed Brödl out of the room and into another that was only a little smaller.

"This serves as my personal office. The mayoral building is the unit HQ. All the village buildings have been commandeered to suit our needs. Officers have the bigger houses; the local tourist hotels—three, small—and the pensions, are the men's billets. We all eat in the same building." Brödl gave a fierce grin. "...the church. As I've said, except for occasions like this when I have senior guests." Brödl smiled at this. "St. Jean-Bocage—this village—is locked down. Every access point is guarded, round the clock. Roads big enough for vehicles, like the main road that goes through, have barriers."

"I'm assuming you've got an in-depth defensive screen..."

"You assume correctly. We've got hidden positions as far as several kilometers out. We saw you coming."

Brödl had gone to a desk that must have once belonged to the schoolmaster, to unlock a drawer. He pulled it slightly open, and reached in to take out a handful of something. He held the hand for a brief moment over the desk, then opened it. A shower of yellow seemed to fall slowly, to spread across the surface.

Schelberg found himself staring at several yellow stars of David. "Dead Jews?"

"Dead SS," Brödl corrected.

Schelberg stared at him. "*What?*"

Brödl drew on his cigarette, exhaled, mouth tightening, eyes cold. "We seem to have an avenger."

"The husband."

"My first reaction when these started to come in. But we are not the only SS unit to take these casualties. Had it only been this unit, I would have said so..."

"He could be moving around. Avoiding being pinpointed."

Brödl nodded. "I thought of it too...but our schoolmaster is nothing like that. The informer was questioned when we picked up the first of these. By all accounts, the schoolmaster was mild-mannered; retiring, even...almost shy once out of the protective cloak of his school."

"He lost everything of value to him. That could have created a great change. In fact, it almost certainly did. I'm a policeman, as well as SS. There's nothing about my fellowman that surprises me."

But Brödl would not accept it. "That schoolmaster has not got the guts...or the capabilities, to take on my men. You know what we are, Schelberg. We are fierce wolves."

"Yes...but a badly wounded wolf can hunt even other wolves—even the fierce ones—because he no longer cares for his own safety. The schoolmaster was not physically wounded, but his soul was."

Brödl gave Schelberg a long scrutiny. "You almost sound as if you're justifying him."

"Not at all. I repeat, I am a policeman. I leave nothing out. Understanding your enemy gives you a far better chance of defeating him. If I may say something to you that I said to Henk when we found Bock's body, and Löringer...serve your anger cold. Your schoolmaster, if it is he, is doing just that." Schelberg glanced at the yellow stars. "And succeeding."

"'*I swear to thee Adolf Hitler*'," Brödl began to quote,
"'*As Führer and Chancellor of the German Reich,
Loyalty and Bravery.
I vow to thee and the superiors whom thou shall appoint,
Obedience unto death,
So help me God.*'"

Brödl stopped, and continued looking at Schelberg.

"I know our Oath as well as you do," Schelberg said. "It is not disloyal to face the reality of a situation. It may *not* be your schoolmaster. It may be several French terrorists copying what someone has started; but if that Oath is to mean anything..." Schelberg pointed at the scattered stars. "...something has to be done about this. Otherwise, as far as your unit—and other SS units—are concerned, only the dying part of that Oath will matter."

"We take reprisals..."

Schelberg picked up some of the stars, and let them trickle through his fingers. "And sow a fresh crop of these. Have you reported this?"

Brödl shook his head. "But I can't speak for the other units."

"Until today, I knew nothing of these stars."

"Then everyone else is sitting on it too."

"What's morale like?"

"Strong...but there is plenty of anger, and rage."

"Anger is good. Even rage. But this must be cold, and calculating. Rush-of-blood reprisals are not the way."

"What do you suggest?"

"Play cat-and-mouse. Starve him of his prey. If it is your schoolmaster, he'll come to you...and he'll have to work his way through your defensive screen..."

"Keep my men here like frightened women and children? We'd

soon be a laughing stock. We did not gain our reputation by hiding."

"Make him *believe* you're hiding. Keep the bulk of your men 'visible', so that the news spreads you're pulling in your horns. But send out small hunter-killer teams. Let them stay out as long as it takes, so that it almost looks as if they were never part of your unit. Use their well-known sniper abilities to good effect. Get them to know his stamping grounds as well as he does. I am certain you have excellent, accent-less French speakers among your personnel. Use them. Try some infiltration. I know your unit thrives on combat, and this will take time; but that's far better than seeing more of these stars...or getting a summons from Berlin."

Brödl still looked reluctant. "I'll consider it."

"I can't give you orders, Brödl; but I can offer advice. It is your choice to take it, or leave it. By the way," Schelberg continued before Brödl could say anything. "How many majors do you have?"

"Four, plus a doctor of major rank. Why?"

"One of them found the *Standartenführer*, just a few hours over two days ago, escaping from a kidnap attempt. He gave him a lift to our unit. The *Standartenführer* was kidnapped again. But this time, he's dead. When you told me about the schoolmaster, I first thought it might be him—if he *is* your avenger." Schelberg dug into a pocket. "My turn to show you something." He pulled out the two yellow stars. "One each on Löringer, and the *Standartenführer*."

"He certainly gets around," Brödl said, expression grim as he stared at the stars.

"Let us work together on this," Schelberg suggested, "if you've a mind to. I will not interfere with the anonymity of your personnel, nor their autonomy. I'll command my men, you command yours as normal. You and I liaise, co-operate, but do not encroach upon the other's territory. If you ask my advice, I'll give it. If you do not, I won't. You continue to be answerable only to Berlin. Most of the time, I will be back at my unit, but we will keep in touch. Do you have a mind to?"

Brödl hesitated briefly, then nodded.

Schelberg gave one of the smiles James would have called the smile of the tiger. "Now about that major..."

"Two are out in the field, one of them our youngest major..."

"How young?"

"Young," Brödl said, making it clear he would say no more about the major. "Two are here;" he continued. "The doctor is where he should be. I'll talk to them. Not you. You wait somewhere."

"Of course."

"You should realize that whoever rescued your *Standartenführer*, may not have thought it worth mentioning officially. We have...other priorities."

"I understand."

"But he might have said something in passing to one of the others."

"Let's find out."

In the event, it was neither of the two combat majors at the unit, and they had not heard of any rescue.

"When the others come in," Brödl said, "I'll ask them. Our practice as you know, is autonomy in the field, wherever that may be. This goes for every rank. Our unit is more...flexible than most. They contact us only when they need to. Rather like your idea for hunting our man with the yellow stars."

Schelberg nodded, saying nothing.

"Now let's see how your Löringer is doing."

They began walking towards the former schoolhouse, which was now the unit hospital.

A doctor—a captain—came out of the building as they approached. "Remarkable," he began, looking at Schelberg. "Your man will recover, sir."

"*Good.* That's very good!"

The doctor smiled. "Not much for me to do. Astonishing work by your medic. He did everything correctly. As good as any doctor, myself included. If he hadn't done what he did on the spot, that man would now be dead. Wherever he got his training he was well-taught and he, a good student."

"I'll tell him," Schelberg said. "Can I see your patient? I'd like to talk..."

But the doctor was shaking his head. "I'm afraid not. First, he's still out. Secondly, if he were conscious, I would not advise stressing him."

"I am certain he has something to say. He forced himself to stay alive. I'll wait..."

"With respect, *Standartenführer*, I am talking of *days* before your man will be ready, either to be moved, or to be questioned. More than a week, at the very least."

This did not please Schelberg, but he had little choice. He knew Brödl would support the doctor's stance.

"Very well. We'll return to our unit, but I want to be informed the moment he is ready." Schelberg looked at Brödl when he said that.

Brödl nodded.

Schelberg turned back to the doctor "May I at least see the *Standartenführer's* body? We'll be taking him back with us."

"Of course, sir. The *Sturmbannführer's* in the process of examining..."

"Take me there. I want to be present." Schelberg again looked at Brödl, who nodded to the doctor.

"I'll come with you," Brödl said to Schelberg.

"I expect you to."

The first thing the senior doctor said when they entered the room where the naked body of Alistair James was being examined was, "Shot from behind. Close range. Bullet from a Browning Hi-power. No exit wound. The bullet lodged in the ribcage. I've extracted it. Died instantly. I'm finished. Just cleaning up."

"Many of us use this Belgian weapon," Brödl said to Schelberg. "We prefer its 13-round magazine. It also has excellent stopping power."

"The French take weapons from those they have killed," the doctor said. He did not introduce himself to Schelberg.

Schelberg took the spent bullet that had been extracted from Löringer's chest, out of his pocket. "And this?"

The doctor studied it for brief moments. "Similar weapon."

Schelberg nodded to himself. "Thank you." Glancing at Brödl, he put the round back into his pocket.

"One other thing," the doctor said, looking steadily at Schelberg. "I don't know who this man is, but he isn't Heinrich Bock."

"*What!*" Brödl and Schelberg exclaimed together. They looked at each other, then at the doctor, as if he were mad.

"What are you talking about?" Schelberg demanded.

The doctor stood his ground. He pointed to the body's feet. "What do you see?"

Schelberg still looked at him as if he had really gone mad, then looked at the dead feet. "Two feet, ten toes. Should I be seeing twelve?"

"Thank you for the sarcasm, *Standartenführer*, but I am not mad, I assure you. I knew Heinrich Bock since childhood. We once went to the same school, but lost touch during our late teens. Unless he's seen a surgeon since then, those are not his feet."

"What are you telling us, *Sturmbannführer?*" Brödl almost barked.

"Sir, when Bock was a boy, he broke a toe in his left foot, playing football. He always kicked with his left. It never healed properly, but curved to the right. This sometimes gave him trouble, catching the big toe now and then. He always said he would have it re-broken and reset properly. But the same toe on this body, has *never* been broken. At *any* time. Take my word for it."

Both Schelberg and Brödl now stared at the perfectly straight toe.

"This man," the doctor went on, "is an uncanny double. He could be Heinrich Bock's twin. I know for a fact, that Bock never had a brother. At least, for all the years I knew him. So unless he had a secret brother somewhere this man, as I've said, is an impostor." His eyes held Schelberg's. "Check his personal records. Something about that toe should be in there, somewhere."

Schelberg considered the implications, expression giving nothing away. "Thank you, Doctor," he finally said. "Get him dressed. We're taking him back." He left the room.

The doctor glanced at Brödl, who nodded, and followed Schelberg. They walked in silence until they were once more outside the building.

"An infiltrator," Brödl at last said. "How much damage?"

Catastrophic potential, Schelberg thought. *I knew there was something about him.*

Aloud, he said, "Hard to tell at this stage. I'll have to investigate when I get back. It makes talking to Löringer vital. Contact me the moment he wakes. I may not have the luxury of the time the doctor suggests."

"I'll see to it."

Another silence fell as they continued walking towards Brödl's commandeered house.

It was an irony of life that Martin Brödl's physical stature closely resembled that of the man his soldiers had turned into an implacable enemy; but their faces were very different. Brödl had a cliff face of a forehead and a brow which jutted above his sunken eyes like an overhang. A sharp nose, a thin gash of a mouth, and a weakish chin completed the picture. He topped that with a Himmler-like haircut. But Brödl led, as he had said to Schelberg, a pack of fierce wolves; and he was the fiercest of them all. And merciless.

Then Brödl began, with some uncertainty, "It would seem our interests are...more connected than first appeared. My yellow star casualties, your...impostor, a *Sturmbannführer* from my unit..."

"I must talk with him..."

"As soon as is possible. We must consider," Brödl continued, "Berlin's probable reaction."

"Are you making a suggestion?"

"Perhaps we should indeed work closely together to resolve this problem...before Berlin becomes curious..."

Schelberg glanced at him. "You are suggesting we keep Berlin in the dark?"

"I am saying Berlin will want solutions...not problems."

"I agree, Martin."

Office, Intelligence unit, Whitehall, London. July 1941. 1540 local.

The brigadier looked as if he'd just lost a cherished member of his own family.

He stood at a window, hands locked behind his back, looking down upon a small courtyard. A young Wren officer was talking animatedly with an RAF pilot.

"Young love?" the brigadier wondered softly. "Madness in this. But if so, enjoy it while you can." He sighed. "Damn it, Alistair," he went on. "I told you to be careful. What possessed you to play the hero?"

A diffident knock sounded.

The brigadier cleared his throat, and turned to look at the door. "Come in!"

Haines, in civilian attire, entered. He too looked as if he had lost a valued brother.

"Ah, Haines," the brigadier greeted. "Bad show, eh?"

"The worst, sir."

"Don't look so glum. Not your fault. You did everything correctly. I've read your report. Typical of Alistair to go dashing off playing the noble hero."

"He ordered me to split direction, while he led the Jerries off, and on no account was I to go back to help in case he got into trouble."

The brigadier nodded. "Classic Alistair. Selfless disregard for his own safety. Remarkable man. Quite, quite remarkable, and incredibly valuable. Brave. Terrible loss. But nothing you could have done, Haines. He gave the order. You had to follow. Nothing gained getting both of you killed."

Haines, looking dejected, remained silent.

"Cheer up, old boy. Best medicine is to stick it to the damned Hun where it hurts. Pity we did not get what he went for."

"Maybe it's not lost, sir. He said he'd got what he went back for. Maybe he's hidden it out there somewhere, when he realized he wasn't going to make it."

The brigadier did not look so sure. "A possibility, of course. Anything's possible in this damned war. Needle in a haystack, though. Could be anywhere in that damned bocage country."

"I'm beginning to know the area. I know roughly where we were. Perhaps one day I could go back..."

The brigadier was looking at him steadily. "You *want* to go back?"

"I feel I owe it to the colonel, sir."

The brigadier seemed thoughtful. "I was going to offer you a desk job for a while. Alistair was due to spend the rest of this jape behind a desk, impart his considerable knowledge to those we'll be sending out. After what happened, I considered that even with your limited experience so far, what you've learned in the interim could be of use." He paused. "Are you certain you want to keep on being that SS major? Could be even more dangerous, given the current circumstances."

"I don't always have to play him. Only when it is tactically useful. That uniform is very powerful out there, even among the enemy."

"And what about that Gestapo man Alistair warned about...Schelberg? The one who pursued you and sprang the ambush?"

"I'll watch out for him, sir."

"Well, it might give you some comfort to know that Alistair's instincts were spot on. We've done a little checking on your man. He *is* known. Bit of a villain, but very clever with it. Implacable. Fearsome. Cunning. You might want to read up on what we have on him. Carefully garnered information, even before the balloon went up. If you're serious about going back, that is."

"I am, sir."

The brigadier looked at Haines for a long time. "Good show," he said at last. He went over to a tall cupboard that seemed more appropriate in some baronial mansion, than in his office. He pulled the double doors open. "Take a look at this."

Haines went to look. "A valise?"

"Not for clothes, old boy. But for something you'll be taking with you at some point. When that time comes, it will be your almost constant companion. There will sometimes be safe places where you can leave it. At other times, you must use your own ingenuity. Never let the Hun catch you with it. You'll be for the chop in double-quick time if that happens, assuming you escape the very painful interlude which might precede it. The Hun's a dab hand at inflicting pain. Open it very carefully. It is booby-trapped. Nasty surprise for Hitler's chummies when you no longer have any use for it."

"Which means I'll either have dumped it..."

"Or you're dead."

Taking his own advice, the brigadier showed Haines how to open the valise. And Haines looked down at the secret radio it held.

"Marvelous piece of kit, if I say so meself," the brigadier said, shutting the case again. "This remains here until it's time to hand it over to you. When will you be heading back to your unit?"

"Today, sir...when we're done here."

The brigadier nodded to himself as he began shutting the cupboard. "Hope the Hun give Alistair a decent burial...but all things considered, that is probably too much to hope for. Your pursuers never did get a glimpse of you, did they?"

"No, sir. One of the reasons the colonel gave. He wanted to protect my...disguise. He said as this was his last trip, anyway, he was the more expendable. Brave man, sir."

The brigadier nodded again. "Indeed he was. Just the sort of thing he would do. We shall miss him around here." He held out a hand. "Get a few days rest when you get back. You deserve it." They shook hands. "Good luck, Lieutenant Haines."

"Thank you, sir."

Haines emerged from a sandbagged entrance that was a long way from the brigadier's office. The two armed guards saluted him. He nodded in acknowledgement, and walked on, heading towards Trafalgar Square. When he was some distance away from the sentries, a man in civilian clothes caught up, and briefly matched pace.

They did not look at each other.

"Did you get it?" the man asked, lips barely moving, and looking straight ahead.

"Yes."

"And?"

"It's in a safe place."

"Good work."

The man moved on, looking about him, as if searching for a street, then crossed over, veering right to head up St. Martin's Lane.

Haines walked on without looking to see where the man had gone, eventually turning right towards the Strand.

St. Sauveur was a pocket-sized town a mere five kilometers in a straight line, from Brödl's locked-down village. By road, it was almost ten kilometers away. Barely larger than a big village, it was at a lower elevation than St. Jean-Bocage.

About the time that Haines was heading for the Strand, Juif made his way through the backstreets of the town, making for a house he knew well. He was unarmed, a risk he considered worth taking. He slouched along, giving the impression of being much older than he actually was, and in poor health. He was less likely to attract unwelcome attention, than someone who looked fit and young.

He arrived at his destination without once running into a patrol, either of Germans, or Milice. In fact, despite the relative proximity of Brödl's SS unit, there were hardly any enemy troops in the town, none of these few being SS.

Juif found a back door open, and entered. There was no one home. In the living room, he took a chair into a dark corner, and sat down to wait.

Odile Laurent, in her forties and widowed by the war, returned home from a trip to a local market. Juif heard her moving about the kitchen, but remained where he was.

"Ah," he heard her say in annoyance, "I left that door open again."

She shut the door, and continued moving around. At last, she entered the living room. She gave a tiny squeal of alarm when she saw Juif, put a hand to her chest, and the other to her mouth.

She took that hand away, and was about to say his name. He put a finger to his lips. "No names."

"You nearly gave me a heart attack! What are you doing here? If they find you."

"I won't be staying long."

"But why take such a risk?"

"I came to see someone. I've heard that since St. Jean was emptied, some were brought here to St. Sauveur."

She looked at him steadily. "You're looking for her, aren't you? You are Juif, aren't you? Everybody whispers that name..."

"Who's this Juif?"

Odile got the message. "Are you hungry? I can make..."

"Perhaps later, if there is time. I *must* see her."

"*Why?* It is too dangerous..."

"I want to know why she did this terrible thing to me. What have I done to her to deserve it?"

"Don't you know?"

"Know what?"

Odile gave him a look of heartfelt sympathy. "Oh you poor man.

She was jealous."

"*Jealous?* How could she be jealous? She's a married woman!"

"To the wrong man who never stopped telling her he was her second best choice, and that she was a reject. She never forgave you for marrying Sarah."

"*What? She destroyed my life because of that?* There was never any chance that I was going to marry her. We were just friends. *All* of us—Guillaume, Annette, Sarah, and me. I was always with Sarah."

"Yes, but she was only with Guillaume because he was *your* friend. She hoped you would choose her. When you went away to university in Grenoble, and Sarah's family moved to Paris to join the family business there, Annette was glad, and hoped you would come back, now that Sarah was gone. When you did come back to be the schoolmaster, it was the shock of her life to see you arrive with Sarah as your wife. She hated both of you ever since."

Juif was stunned. "She never showed it."

"But she was waiting for her revenge. When the war came, the *Boche* gave her the chance."

"My God. How could anyone do something so terrible?" Then in a voice that was at first almost a monotone, he went on, "When I went back to my house, I saw them there, on the floor where those animals had left them. My Sarah was something I could not recognize. She...was not a person anymore. They had done horrible things to her. Her skirt was raised almost to her head, and she had no...underclothes. There was blood from below...they had...they had...blood from both... areas...down there..."

Odile had put a hand to her mouth again, as if to stifle a cry of horror, her eyes seeing the hell of Juif's torture mirrored in his own, began to moisten.

"And her face," he went on, "was just not there anymore. My beautiful, beautiful Sarah... And my little sons...my babies...were just lumps of meat...as if wild dogs had got at them, then decided not to finish the meal."

Odile held her hand tightly against her mouth, but a tiny squeal of horror escaped. She felt trickles drip from the corners of her eyes, but did not wipe them away.

Then a tremor he could not prevent, came into Juif's voice. "I wonder when they did those things to her...down there? Before, or after they killed her? Were they happy to 'contaminate' themselves on a Jew?" He looked at Odile's weeping eyes, her hand still at her mouth. Abruptly, the voice returned to the almost lifeless monotone, as if he were discussing a lesson. "I have never cried, you know. I don't know if I ever shall." The voice became colder. "So I ask again...how could Annette do something so terrible?"

"You ask this question?" Odile Laurent was finally able to say, in a voice that was itself shaky. She wiped at her eyes. "People are doing terrible things every day in this war. Look about you. There is a man called Juif who is doing terrible things too. Of course to the enemy; but before that, he was an educated man...a loving father and husband. Now..."

"I must see her! I want to look at her face."

"To kill her?"

"I have thought about it...*yes!* But now, I want her to look at *my* face, and I want her to live with her guilt."

"Well, you will find it difficult to get to her. She has the Milice guarding her."

"The *Milice?* Why?"

"Do you think you are the only person who may want to kill her?"

"What do you mean?"

"She is not so much guarded, as a prisoner...not of the Milice, but of this town. In the whole of St. Sauveur, she is alone. She already has her punishment."

"And Guillaume?"

"He has killed himself. He too, is her victim." Juif put his head in his hands.

"Go back," Odile told him gently. "Do not risk your life for someone so worthless. Fate will attend to her. Whether you are Juif or not, go back to what you have been doing. You serve France that way."

Juif gave a laugh that did not sound quite human, and glanced up at her. "Serve France? I think I am serving myself."

She was relieved he when looked down again, unable to cope with his ravaged eyes. "You will get yourself killed for nothing if you try anything now. I will make you something to eat, and then you must go back,"

Head still in his hands, Juif nodded.

RAF Shawbridge flightline. July 1941. 1910 local.

The black, Raven Squadron Anson from Northolt which had gone there to pick up Haines, taxied to a stop. Moments later Haines, carrying a kit bag and still civilian clothes, climbed out from the passenger cabin.

Both Hamilton and Murchison were there to meet him.

"Mr. Haines," Hamilton began. "Glad to have you back safe and sound."

"Thank you, sir."

Murchison nodded at him. "Lieutenant."

"All go well?" Hamilton asked.

"As well as could be expected, sir."

Both senior officers knew Haines could not give details of his mission.

"Good show." Hamilton pointed to a waiting squadron car. "Get along to your tailor in Supply. Dump your kit, then get some sleep. You look as if you can use it."

"Yes, sir."

They watched as Haines went over to the car, and got in.

"Is it me?" Hamilton said as the car moved off. "Or is there some tightness about Haines's eyes?"

"Stress of the mission?"

"Not so sure. Haines was picked for this kind of work because he is supposedly stress-immune. It's something else."

"Do you want me to find out?"

"Only if you can do so without alerting anyone." Hamilton was still following the car with his eyes.

"Do my best."

"You could do with a trip to London, could you not?"

"Now that you mention it..."

Haines got out at the special supply section, and went in to see the man who made the clothes he would need to wear in enemy territory. Even the manufacturer's labels were good enough to pass as authentic.

"Mr. Haines!" Axel Phillips, part-German and Jewish, greeted effusively. "No holes in the nice uniform I gave you?"

"None at all, Axel."

"And it passed muster?" Axel's accents belonged to north London's Finchley, with the barest tinge of German.

"In the best possible way. Right in the lions' den."

"Bravo! So...let us see what you have in there." Axel opened the kitbag that Haines had put on the counter and slowly pulled out the SS uniform. "My best work, so far. And it gives me a shiver to see it. I have family who..." He paused. "I think you know what I mean."

"I do."

"You are a very brave young man, Mr. Haines."

"Thank you, Axel."

"I will keep this here until you need it again. If you will please sign it back in, and I will countersign..."

Haines did so on the form Axel had pushed over. "Any excitement while I've been gone?"

"Everybody is talking about young Mr. Duchamps and how he destroyed many of the enemy flak guns last night. Such a *Mensch!* That pleases me."

"I'm sure it does," Haines said, hiding the annoyance he felt at the mention of Duchamps. He passed the form back.

"Thank you," Axel said. "A war does not stop the paperwork, eh? And now me." He countersigned. "And we are finished." He peered at Haines. "You need some sleep. Go get it."

Haines gave a tired smile. "On my way." He waved a finger at his forehead in a casual salute. "Later, Axel."

"Ja," Axel said quietly, watching Haines leave. "So brave," he added to himself.

He began to put the uniform away.

Ellen's loft, SoHo, New York. Tuesday, July 2006. 0010 local.

They looked at the wreckage on the table.

"I cannot believe we just did that," Daphne said with a lopsided smile. "We've eaten all that stuff!"

Ellen pointed at the empty wine bottles. "And drunk that too."

"Yep," Duchamps joined in. "Couldn't fly tonight...if I still had my jet."

Daphne looked at him. "You miss it."

"Sure I do. But it's important to me to find out what's behind all this. I owe it to my grandpa. Losing the jet—though it hurts—is small beer against that."

She nodded, more soberly than she actually was. She looked down at the table, eyes focusing inwards as she retreated into a memory.

Ellen and Duchamps glanced at each other.

Daphne roused herself. "'kay, kids. Gotta go. Got to interview a guy in the morning. We're doing a series on best-dressed young business tigers. If the conversations I've had with him is anything to go by, he's going to try to peek at my tits and my legs, and see if he can get me into bed. I think I'll go dressed as a nun."

She stared at the table again. "Only once in my life did I go to bed with a guy the first time I saw him." She played idly with a rib that had been picked clean, for another moment returning somewhere into the past.

Ellen and Duchamps knew she was thinking of Wiley. "Why don't you stay the night, Daphne?"

Daphne looked up. "Are you saying I'm drunk?"

"Well..."

"Yes," Duchamps said with a tiny smile.

"A man who tells it like it is. But I'm not really drunk."

"You are, and you should not refuse the offer."

"Okay," she said after a moment's hesitation. "I'll take that couch over there."

"You take the second bedroom," Duchamps said. "I'll take the couch."

"And if you want to go to..."

"I've had the grand tour. There's a bathroom in each bedroom, and a cubicle for couch guys like me." He grinned, then got to his feet. "You two argue about it. I'm going up to the terrace to enjoy the night view."

Both women watched him leave.

"And?" Daphne said to Ellen when he'd gone.

"'And' what?"

"Well? You know! I'm not that drunk."

"I just met him."

"So? I saw Wiley, and *wham*."

"Not the same situation, Daphne."

Duchamps was enjoying the nightscape on one of the four recliners on the terrace, when Ellen appeared with a half-full bottle of wine, and two glasses. Half an hour had passed since he'd left.

"Some company?" she said.

"I see three more empty places."

There was a recliner next to his, with a small table between them. She put the bottle and the glasses on it.

"Some wine?" she suggested as she sat down.

"I'm not driving, I'm not flying...and this is a great view."

"I love coming up here at night," she said as she poured.

Somewhere, sirens wailed like lost souls.

"Has she gone to bed?"

"Yes."

"Was it a smart thing to do? Telling her?"

"You did a good job of telling her, but not telling her. I think we're okay." Ellen raised her glass. "She asked if there was something between us. I think her eye's on you."

"That's crazy. She still dreams of Wiley. You saw her."

"And if she didn't?"

He peered at her. "Now that, *is* crazy."

"To your grandpa," she said, switching tack and keeping her glass raised.

He raised his. "To grandpa." After they had drunk the toast, he added, "I'll have to watch you. You don't play fair."

"Of course not. I'm a woman."

They spent the next hour in almost complete silence. They did not touch each other, simply happy to enjoy their proximity in the night.

They went back down, and cleared the table quietly so as not to disturb Daphne, again barely speaking to each other.

When it was all done, she said, "Thanks."

"Come on," he said.

"You'd be surprised how many people would not. I'll go get you some bedclothes."

"You can just hand them to me."

They had to pass Daphne's bedroom. A sound made them pause. A soft weeping was coming from inside.

Ellen stared at the door. "Perhaps I should..." she mimed.

Duchamps placed a hand on her arm and shook his head.

She glanced at the hand, then the dark eyes seemed to engulf him.

He took his hand away, breaking the moment.

They went on, and she got him the bedclothes.

As he made his way back, he murmured to himself, "I am not going to fall for this woman. Mary is right. Waaay too rich for my blood." He began preparing the couch. "Hope you guys outside my place have a nice night, and enjoy my timed lights.

Ever since he became aware that he was being followed, he had got himself a selection of timed light switches. In his absence, they would switch the lights on and off at random intervals in different parts of the apartment, then switch all lights off as if he had gone to bed.

"Have fun," he said, as he lay down.

Outside Duchamps' apartment building, the men in the SUV watched the lights go out.

"How the hell did he get back without our seeing him?" one asked.

"Friends, neighbors. They let him into their place, and he takes it from there. Easy. That's why we never spot him coming or going...unless he wants us to see."

"Not sure I buy that."

"Well his car's still at the airport, he's been seen near Broadway, and now he's back home."

"He may have been a goddamned jet jock, but he's not superman.

He can't fly to the top of the goddamned building, or through a fucking window."

"Why don't we just take him out?"

"Oh sure. Very smart. We're trying to make sure this guy is frozen out, kept in the cold so no one takes him seriously, and you suggest we kill him. The media would suddenly rediscover their memories and balls, and have a field day. The supposed emotionally disturbed jet jock with his mad conspiracy theories would become someone whose story should be investigated, after all. The Pulitzer Prize hunters would be out in their droves, making up as they went along, what they could not substantiate. Don't you think he would have been taken down a long time ago, if our people thought it was worth it? Killing off at random, old soldiers that everyone's forgotten and don't care about is one thing. Killing off an Air Force pilot who's been doing some digging will do what...?"

"Okay, okay. You don't have to paint me a picture."

It was six a.m. when Tad Duchamps opened his eyes, sensing a presence near him. The bluest of eyes were inches away. Daphne, fully dressed and looking as if she had never been near a glass of wine, hand poised, it seemed, to stroke his cheek.

"Daphne!" he said, sleep in his voice, not daring to move. "What...what are you doing up? It's..."

"Only six. I know. But I've got to get myself ready for the interview with this..."

"Don't say it. Too early in the morning."

"And the city's wide awake."

"Did it go to sleep?"

"I was just about to say goodbye."

Duchamps began to get up. She did not move away.

"Don't," she said. "I can see myself out. Then I'll grab me a cab..."

"At least some coffee..."

"I'll have something at the hotel."

"Still time to change your mind about what we said last night..."

"Not on your life."

"These people are playing for keeps."

"I'll be okay. Say goodbye to Ellen for me."

"Ellen's here," came her voice. Ellen, barefoot, in a kimono-like dressing gown.

Daphne straightened, and turned. "Oh. I did not want to wake you."

"You didn't. I'm usually awake at this time." She shot Duchamps a wide-eyed glance, before adding to Daphne, "Sure you won't have that coffee?"

"I'm sure." An enigmatic smile appeared on Daphne's lips. "Great evening. Beats some awful family dinner any day. Well, gotta go, kids. I get to hear anything, I'll be in touch. Let's do this more often, Ellen."

"Sure."

"Tad...you watch yourself."

"All the time."

She gave him a little smile, then allowed Ellen to see her out.

Ellen waited until she had entered the lift and it had started down, before shutting the door slowly, and turning to face Duchamps.

"She was nearly licking your face. I thought she was going to fall all over you."

"She wasn't."

"Then the floor was leaning, and she was standing straight." She headed for the kitchen before Duchamps could say anything. "Coffee?" she called from there, just short of a yell.

"Er...sure."

"Breakfast?"

"If you're making it..."

"I wouldn't ask if I were not making it."

"I'll help..."

"No! And you can have your shower...although her smell's probably still in there. You'll like that, I guess..."

"This," he said to himself as he got up and picked up his clothes, "could be a bad day."

Carrying the clothes over one arm and the sheet wrapped about him, he made for the bedroom he would have slept in, but for Daphne's unexpected visit.

He did not see Ellen poke her head out of the kitchen to watch him, nor her tiny, calculating smile.

CHAPTER NINE

Château Eloise, Normandy, Occupied France, July 1941. 1911 local.

On the way back, Schelberg had decided that he would say nothing to anyone about the impostor. At least, not yet; not until he had done some quiet investigation. He had spoken to Brödl, and each had tacitly agreed to keep the entire thing under wraps. Each had his own reasons for doing so. Brödl, in complete control of his subordinates, would ensure that the doctor spoke of it to no one.

And so, another of the many little conspiracies that belonged to the sum of the parts of the main conspiracy, came into being; but it was an open question which of the two would be the first to renege on their mutual protection pact.

Schelberg now looked on with studied calm, at the coldly brutal expression on Forst's face.

"So the bastards decided to kill him," the commander of the chateau Eloise-based SS unit said in a quiet snarl.

They were in the mortuary section of the huge medical research center, housed in a building that was scarcely smaller than the chateau itself, and of similar architectural style. James's body, once more fully clothed in SS uniform, lay on its back upon the examination table, effectively hiding the entry wound. In addition to Schelberg and Forst, only a single doctor was present.

"He will be buried in these grounds, with full honors," Forst continued. "It is only fitting that it should be here, where we carry out our important work." The muscles around his jaw seemed to dance, betraying his controlled rage. "They kidnap him twice, then kill him for managing to escape that first time. I'll make them pay heavily for this!"

"If I may suggest..." Schelberg began in a mild voice.

"Of course you may." Forst kept looking at the body.

"Before taking any action, we should wait to hear what Löringer has to say when he wakes up. We should find out whether they interrogated Bock, and whether he said anything to them. They would not have expected Löringer to be still alive."

Forst thought about it, then nodded. "Some luck for us. You're right."

"And, I'd also like to do some investigating. Something about all this worries me."

Again, Forst nodded. "That's what you're here for, Heinrich. Do as you see fit."

"Thank you."

Forst looked at the doctor. "Prepare him for burial."

"Nothing for me to do, *Brigadeführer*. They already did a perfect job in St. Jean-Bocage."

"I see. Well, make arrangements for the coffin. He'll be buried tomorrow at 0800, with a full guard of honor. He was an atheist, but I'll read something over him."

"Yes, sir."

More like Church of England, Schelberg thought, *if Brödl's doctor is right.*

Forst was looking at him. "I'm finished here. Are you coming?"

"If I may, I'd like a word with the doctor."

"Then I'll see you later. Bock's office?"

"Yes, sir," Schelberg said.

Forst nodded, and went out.

Schelberg turned to the doctor. "I would like to look at the *Standartenführer's* medical records."

The doctor nodded, "At once, sir. Please come with me."

As they went out, the doctor saw one of his senior orderlies approaching. "Prepare the *Standartenführer* for burial at 0800 tomorrow," he ordered, pausing briefly.

"I'll attend to it immediately, *Sturmbannführer!*"

The doctor gave a curt nod, and moved on with Schelberg in tow. They came to a locked, unmarked door.

"Only the senior doctors of this department have access to this room," the doctor said, unlocking the door. "The medical records of all the senior officers of this center are kept here. Yours will soon be included."

"How comprehensive are they?"

The doctor glanced at Schelberg with a brief frown, wondering at the question. "As comprehensive as necessary."

Schelberg nodded, not elaborating. "Where can I view Bock's file undisturbed?"

The doctor opened the door. "In here. The room's quite big, and there are chairs and a large table. High, secure windows give plenty of light, and there are reading lamps on the table. This used to be the château owner's personal library away from the main house."

"Where are its previous contents?"

"Berlin."

"Of course."

Schelberg followed the doctor into the room which was now full of locked file storage cabinets. He went to the table to wait as the doctor went to the cabinets, opened one, and extracted a thickish file.

The doctor brought it to the table. "The *Standartenführer's* records, sir. Just press this button when you're finished." He pointed to a white button in the middle of the table. "From the time of the former owner. We find it useful."

Schelberg nodded, selected a chair, and sat down.

"If you'd like some refreshment," the doctor went on, "I can arrange it. Coffee, French of course."

"I don't suppose you could manage something a little more...robust. I feel I need it."

The doctor gave a tiny smile. "We...er...liberated an interesting wine stock. If you asked me to suggest..."

"Please do."

"A '33 Clos de Vougeot."

"The date of the new Reich. Appropriate. I'll have that."

"I'll send it in."

"Thank you, Doctor."

The doctor gave a slight nod of respect. "*Standartenführer.*" Then left the room, closing the door softly.

Schelberg drew the file towards him. "Now let's see what secrets you contain." He was reading the third document, when a polite knock sounded.

"In!"

He was surprised when a haughty young woman in civilian clothes entered, carrying a silver tray with the opened bottle, and an exquisite glass. She did not look friendly.

He shut the file as she approached.

She placed the tray before him, and turned to go.

"Wait," he said.

She paused, but did not turn round.

"What is your rank?" he demanded in German.

"I am not German," she replied in French. "I hope you enjoy my family's wine."

Astonished, Schelberg said in the same language, "*Your* family?"

She still did not turn round. "Yes. Our wine, our home, our grounds."

"Isn't it polite in your family to face someone when talking..."

"That would denote respect." Still without turning round, she went out.

Schelberg almost gaped. "Either very brave," he said to himself as the door closed, rather more firmly than when the doctor had left. "Or suicidal. Or both," he added.

Thoughtfully, he poured out some wine, and tasted it. An expression of approval crossed his features.

"If it's poisoned, I'll soon find out."

He continued reading the file. Halfway through, he saw nothing about Bock's toes. He ploughed on. He studied the file in detail. There was no record whatsoever of a broken toe.

Schelberg closed the file, leaned back in his chair, and had a swallow of wine. "Either someone's been at Bock's records...or Brödl's doctor got it wrong,"

Schelberg said to himself.

But he did not believe the medical *Sturmbannführer* would have made up the story.

"I need Bock's childhood records."

He finished the entire bottle, before pressing the white button.

The doctor returned. So did the young woman. She picked up the tray with the empty bottle and glass, without either looking at Schelberg, or saying anything.

Schelberg watched in detached amusement as she went out, closing the door just short of a slam.

He looked at the doctor. "What the devil?"

"It amuses the *Brigadeführer* to keep her here."

"*What?*"

"She's the granddaughter of the former owner."

"Who is now...where, exactly?"

"Dead. He...resisted. He was in the first war. Probably thought he still was. Anyway, he attacked with his pistol."

"A *pistol?*"

"He never got off a shot. The girl, who was with him at the time, picked it up."

"She must have been mad."

The doctor gave another tiny smile, "It must have seemed like it to the soldiers. She would have shot too."

"How did she survive?"

"The lieutenant in command of the assault in that particular part of the château stopped his men. She still had the pistol, pointing at them. You won't get off a shot, he said to her. Why waste your life, like the old man? It took a whole minute before she lowered that gun. 'I'm staying here', she said. 'You'll be leaving soon'. The lieutenant laughed at her. We'll be staying forever, he said. 'You'll be leaving soon', she insisted. Those who stay forever will be dead. When the *Brigadeführer* heard of the incident, he ordered that she be left here. The rest of the family and staff—those who survived—were relocated. It amuses the *Brigadeführer* to keep her around as a servant. She thinks she's the custodian of her former home."

"And he keeps her around to humiliate her. And one day, when he's bored with the situation, he'll have her shot."

The doctor's eyes were guarded. "I did not say that, sir."

"No. You did not."

The doctor glanced at the file. "Found what you were looking for?"

"I'm afraid not. I'll have to look elsewhere. But thank you for showing it to me."

"Sorry I could not be of more help."

"You got me a fine wine, and I met the custodian of the castle. The time was not wasted."

As he walked back to his quarters in the main house, Schelberg murmured, "'You'll be leaving soon'. Hope that's not a prophesy."

He did not see her again that day.

Château Eloise had been renamed in a fit of grandfatherly love, after its youngest possible heir—Eloise Louise Claire de la Cointe. She was just eighteen.

She looked down from her room at the very top of the main house, as Schelberg made his way across from the medical research center.

Her mouth turned down. "*Salaud Gestapo!*" she whispered in contempt. But for propriety's sake, and survival, she would have spat out of the window.

He did not see her, and even if he had looked up, it was doubtful he would have spotted her in the half-light. She usually stood well within the room, whenever she looked out.

The room was the same one she'd had since childhood. It was not her bedroom, which was now occupied by one of her unwanted "guests". This had been her special playroom which as a child, had seemed huge to her and which even now looked almost as big and as spacious, despite the approach of adulthood.

She was under no illusions about the SS commander, Forst. She fully realized he was toying with her, even to the point of allowing her to keep her own room. She expected that one day he would tire of his little game, and have her shot. She was not afraid. She had gone beyond fear. The only thing she hoped was that the SS would not torture her first, or use her as a sexual plaything before shooting her. If she were able to judge when that terrible day was likely to be, she had promised herself she would jump out the window first. Her room was high enough for her not to survive the fall. So she lived in her strange twilight, waiting for the day when she would have to make that jump.

She had no idea what had happened to her family. She was allowed no contact with an outside world that was not that of the occupiers. Yet oddly, she was allowed almost complete freedom within the grounds. There were also certain buildings she was not allowed to go into, and certain areas that were totally out of bounds. But as long as she remained within her flexible cage, she was left alone. Making her play the role of servant, seemed to amuse the SS general; for the time being.

She was finished for the day, and knew she would not be disturbed until morning when she would have to be downstairs, promptly at eight o'clock.

However, there was something she did that if Forst knew, would most unlikely cause him to end his game very swiftly, and put an end to her life.

She was writing a diary.

It was a very detailed chronicling of everything she had witnessed since the day the invaders had come to her home. It also described in equal detail, how they had transformed the place, even to the last gun emplacement. There was even a precise description of the chateau—inside and out—and its grounds. It was an intelligence treasure trove.

She used the blank pages of her old schoolbooks, and little diaries she had been given as presents since a childhood that now seemed very far away. She had barely written in those and they had lain, unwanted, for years; but now, she had found valuable use for them. She hid her writings in the secret place her grandfather had had constructed for her, when she was six years old. It was at the back of a built-in wardrobe, within the solid structure of the château. The back of the wardrobe was fully paneled, but a section could be pushed slightly and slid to betray the hiding place. She could hide there when she was smaller, pretending to have become invisible. Now, it hid the diary, and no amount of searching by someone who did not know of its existence, would lead to its discovery.

She had written about the Gestapo man, and the wine she had served him. But there was something she had written in the diary, for which she had no proof. She had written that she had heard the voices of children.

But she had never seen them.

Juif had not taken Odile Laurent's advice completely. He had indeed decided to pass on Annette; for the moment. But he had other plans that would have made Odile blench.

Once safely out of St. Sauveur, he had gone to a wood where he had stashed his weapons—a sniper rifle, an MP 40, a Browning Hi-Power pistol, and a vicious-looking knife. He also retrieved the pouch in which he kept the yellow stars, removed some to put into a pocket, then secured the pouch inside his decrepit, greenish black cotton jacket. Carrying all those weapons and their required ammunition should have weighed him down; but they did not seem to. He appeared to have received an almost superhuman strength from his burning hatred.

Juif was going SS hunting...and he had decided to do the hunting within the area of his old home, St. Jean-Bocage.

Contrary to what both Schelberg and Brödl believed, Juif had been close on many occasions, but he had not done any killing. They had all been dangerous reconnaissance probes; with a singular purpose: to sniff out the enemy. Brödl would have been shocked to know how well Juif knew his defensive positions. Many were the times he'd had members of Brödl's unit within the sights of his scope. He had spent days lying in wait, stalking them, even following them, without once being detected. For someone who had once been a cultured schoolmaster, the man who had become Juif now had more in common with a predator. Schelberg's instincts were accurate. The wounded wolf was prepared to hunt the fiercest of them, even in his own lair. But he had been planning his attack pattern for a long time; and he was going to do so before Brödl was ready for him.

Juif was now lying atop a big, vegetation-rich hedgerow, looking from secure cover at two well-camouflaged SS men. He had planned the attack well, having previously watched that position through his scope at different times that had spanned weeks. He even knew when the manning of the position was rotated. He had decided on the day because he knew when those two would be relieved. Eager to return to base, they would have grown just a little relaxed; and in relaxing, careless.

Juif did not intend to be greedy. Those two would be sufficient for now. Once he had killed them and left the stars, he would leave the area and would not be back for a while. But he would return to strike again; when it suited him. Meanwhile, there were other targets in other locations to attend to.

Juif had spent a considerable time perfecting his method of execution. He could reload so swiftly, the bolt-action rifle might well have been semi-automatic. He knew he had to be quick. Even relaxed, the SS men would react with speed. The second one would get over the shock of watching his comrade die within a split second; but that would be enough.

Even in the gloom of the bocage, there was still enough of the summer light to enable him to see his targets clearly. Within the shadows, his own position was virtually invisible.

He had the head of the first squarely in the scope. He centered the open T on the bridge of the nose, just beneath the rim of the man's helmet. He drew a breath softly. He could see the eyes in the camouflaged face. It was almost as if the man were looking directly at him. It was uncanny. His mouth was moving, obviously in conversation with his comrade.

Juif fired. He did not waste time checking. He knew he had scored a kill. He shifted to the second man, who was already bringing up his weapon, an MP 40. Even though the second soldier had no idea where he was, the SS man would fire a long burst. This would sound the alarm, and bring others running. The first shot of the sniper rifle would also sound a warning, but the others in the widely spaced positions would wait to hear if any of the positions were under threat before moving to reinforce. An MP 40 burst would galvanize them.

Juif knew he would have just about enough time to leave the stars and get out. This was a very close-in kill. Even so, the bark of a sniper shot was different. Someone would wonder.

He got the second man before the submachine gun could be fired.

Now came the moment of greatest risk. He had to get off the hedgerow, reach the position, leave the stars, then get away before their comrades came looking. The two single shots were not as alarming as a burst from an MP 40, and he had planned his route out. He had enough time.

Even as he thought this through he was already moving, scrambling off the hedgerow. He raced to the position, yellow stars already in hand. The two men lay unmoving. One shot, one kill. He did not waste time pausing to stare at them.

He put a star on each, then hurried away.

In the next position closest to the dead men, one of two soldiers said, "Two shots, so close, they were almost one."

They were alerted, but not anxious.

"Holz and Etting pissing about, trying to see who's fastest?"

"They wouldn't dare. Old Skull Face would have their balls. They would not enjoy the experience. Anyway, Holz has an MP 40."

"No burst. So they're not under attack. Wasn't Holz one of those who did the Jew woman?"

"Yes. There were six of them, taking turns. I wouldn't have touched it, myself. Some people will fuck anything."

"Oh I don't know. It's not as if he was going to marry her." He laughed at his own joke.

But the other did not join in the laughter. He remained thoughtful. "Call base. Just in case. I think those could have been sniper shots..."

"Why call base? If it's a false alarm..."

"Alright. Check with them first."

"They'll take the piss, our breaking radio silence to check up on them."

"If something's wrong, do you want to explain to Skull Face?"

The one with the radio made the call. There was no reply.

"Shit!" he said, and called base.

But Juif was long gone.

Brödl gripped the two yellow stars in his right hand and squeezed as if he wanted to strangle the life out of them.

"He was right *here!* Within my screen! *We* are the hunters...*not* the hunted, *damn it!*"

He thumped at the schoolmaster's desk with the edge of his tightly closed fist. The blow was of sufficient force to make the desk jump slightly, and its contents rattle.

When the stars had been brought to him after the bodies of Holz and Etting had been recovered, he had stared at them balefully, before summoning his deputy commander *Hauptsturmführer* Erwin Halser. Halser was also responsible for the unit's Intelligence gathering.

He stood respectfully to one side, while Brödl continued to rage.

"How can this be? How can we pay such a price for *one stinking Jewess? One* of them for how many of us so far? It is usually the *other* way round!" He pounded the desk again.

Halser remained silent.

"Erwin," Brödl began in a less enraged voice, "do you believe it is the schoolmaster?" He did not turn to look at his subordinate.

"All the information I have to date, sir, indicates that he was not such a man."

"But?"

"What happened to his wife could have pushed him over the edge."

"He married a Jew! His own fault. Even so...could this schoolmaster, this supposedly mild-mannered man become so driven, that he could transform himself into a hunter that can outwit the best in this unit?"

"I find that difficult to accept as well, sir. However, no amount of Intelligence can account for what might happen if someone does go over the edge. His behavior becomes unpredictable..."

"Not that much. There must be something about this man that we do not as yet know. I want that woman brought here. Tonight. The one who betrayed the Jew-lover. They had been friends since childhood. There must be something she knows about him, that even she does not realize."

"I'll see to it." Halser glanced at Brödl's still-closed fist. "Are you going to tell *Standartenführer* Schelberg about them?"

"I don't have to answer to the fucking Gestapo!" Brödl snarled. "But some of the things he said may make sense. No. I won't tell him about these. For now."

"Yes, sir."

It was just after eleven p.m. when Halser returned with a terrified Annette.

There was a Milice guard with her.

"You can wait outside," Brödl said in perfect French to the man, at the entrance to his office in the schoolmaster's home.

"She is a French citizen..." the officer began, then paused as Brödl's eyes became their most hooded.

"Let's get some things straight," Brödl said. "You are here, because I have allowed you to be. I can order any of my men to shoot you dead and he'll do so without pausing for breath, and dump your body on the road somewhere. I don't give a shit about your collaborationist government, and any objections they might raise. You'd still be very dead. So be a good little Frenchman and *stay out of my sight!*"

He slammed the door in the Milice's face, and turned to look at Annette, who was visibly shaking with fear. Once, she had been a vibrant woman. Now, she seemed far older than her mid-twenties. The bitter marriage, the festering jealousy, the betrayal of her closest friends, and the suicide of the man who in the end had despised her, had all taken their toll. She appeared shrunken.

Brödl turned, went to a chair, picked it up, and brought it to her.

"Please sit down, *Madame* Lariviere," he said to her in conversational tones, continuing in French.

Staring at him as she would a dangerous snake, Annette sat down. "I...I told you everything I know. Why have I been brought..."

"Let me be the judge of that," Brödl said, still sounding as if he were having a chat with someone he considered an equal.

He went to the desk, leaned against it, and put one gleaming jackbooted foot over the other.

Annette followed the movement, looking at the boots as if they were instruments of torture.

Halser, as before, was standing to one side.

Brödl took out his cigarette case, opened it, and leaned forward, offering her one. "American," he said.

Annette looked at the neat row of cigarettes. Her tongue passed briefly over her lips. It was very clear she would have liked one; but she shook her head in a nervous jerk.

"As you wish."

Brödl leaned away, relaxed in his position, selected a cigarette, went through the tapping routine, snapped the case shut and put it away, then lit up. He drew on it strongly, and blew out a stream of smoke.

"And so...to business, *Madame* Lariviere." Brödl held his left arm across his chest, rested his right elbow upon it, held that arm upright with the cigarette in a two-fingered grip in his hand, which he kept close to his right cheek. He brought the cigarette to his lips for a brief puff, before holding it away again.

"We are very grateful to you for showing us where the Jew was hiding," he continued. "But now, we seem to have a problem. That Jew is becoming expensive. I am losing men, *Madame* Lariviere. I hate losing men at any time; but most of all, I hate losing men to someone who was sick enough to *marry* a Jew. I cannot begin to tell you what effect this has upon me." The sunken eyes glared at Annette, terrifying her to her very soul. "So if there is anything you know about that man..."

"I...I said everything I knew...!"

"*Madame* Lariviere," Brödl said, voice still conversational, "if there is one thing I hate more than losing men, it is being interrupted. You will speak when I have clearly indicated that I wish you to. Are we agreed?"

She gave a quick jerk of a nod.

"Good. We understand each other. I like understanding between two sensible people. Now tell me...is Hubert LaSalle given to violence?"

She shook her head. "Not even since childhood."

"Are you certain?"

"Yes. I remember when we were about eight, some bigger boys surrounded him and began to tease him because he liked to read. They pushed him around, but he would not fight back."

"A committed pacifist," Brödl said with distaste, "even that young. He never even defended himself?"

"No. He said fighting was barbaric. He got bruised very often."

Brödl puffed at his cigarette, almost spat out the smoke, mouth turning down. "Remarkable. A pacifist at any price. I find that hard to believe."

"It's true. That really did happen."

"I've no doubt it happened as you have said. But there is something missing. Would he have defended you, if those boys had attacked you?"

Annette shrugged. "Probably not." There were years on bitterness in those words.

Brödl glanced at Halser. "But?" he urged Annette.

It was not long in coming. "He would have protected Sarah, though. Even then."

Brödl again shot Halser another glance. "And did that ever happen, *Madame* Lariviere?"

"I never saw it, so I cannot say for sure."

"But?"

"When he was about fifteen, I heard that some boy had called her a dirty Jew. She was very pretty, and I think he and his gang just hated that everybody liked her."

"And you liked her too. After all, she was your friend. You, your husband, and Sarah and Hubert were the...top circle, and you were proud to be part of it. Am I right?"

She nodded, digging the thumb of one hand into the palm of the other. "So what happened in that incident you did not see, but heard about?"

"It could be just a story. Hubert and Sarah never talked about it."

"You let me judge," Brödl said again. "What did you hear?"

"That Hubert grabbed the boy and smashed his head against a wall."

"*Ah!* Not pacifism at any price. What happened after that?"

"They said the police were called."

"It was serious enough?"

"They said the boy had to be taken to hospital...but I don't remember Hubert having to go to the court or anything. So maybe it was just people talking. We never discussed it. It was never mentioned between us. Not even Guillaume talked to me about it."

"Guillaume, your future husband."

"Yes."

"Thank you, *Madame* Lariviere. You have been very helpful."

"I have? I'm not even sure that story is true..."

"True or not, you have certainly helped us again. Now we know who we are dealing with."

"*Hubert?* You have *seen* him?"

"No. But we shall...soon enough."

Suddenly, Annette began to cry. She did so quietly, but without reservation. Brödl looked on with open disgust. "My God, You still *love* him!" He looked at Halser. "Take her out of here and hand her to the Frenchman, then come back."

Halser nodded. "Come, *Madame*." He helped Annette up, and took her out.

"If I wanted to waste a bullet," Brödl said when Halser had returned, "I'd personally put that wretch out of her misery."

"Somewhere in her mind," Halser said, "she probably thinks getting rid of the wife would make him love her."

"I almost feel sorry for the bastard." Halser looked at him.

"Not *that* sorry," Brödl said.

"Shall I see if I can find any old village documents that might have that incident recorded? Just to confirm he is our man. If that story is just a rumor that grew out of proportion, we could be looking for the wrong person."

"It's a good idea and yes, we could be chasing the wrong person. I can't stand betrayal," Brödl went on. "From any quarter. If any member of this unit, for example, betrayed the Führer's ideal, I would shoot him myself. In a strange way, I feel a kind of respect for the *Untermensch* Jew that man married. She *fought*, even though she knew she was lost. She expected no quarter, and gave none, and now that man—if it is he—is avenging her. Like his dead woman, he is following the warrior ideal. Like *us*, Erwin. Like us. A true warrior. I find that exciting. That creature who betrayed them is not fit to walk in their shadow." He glanced at his subordinate. "Do you find that contradictory, Erwin?"

"I find it understandable."

"Exactly! She was still an *Untermensch*...can't change that; but she *fought!* My God. How she *fought*." Brödl's sunken eyes looked distant. "Yes...we may well be hunting the wrong man; but somehow, I don't think so. A wounded wolf, taking on the fiercest."

"Sir?"
"Something Schelberg said."

Outskirts of Macon, Georgia. July 2006.
Haines came back from wherever he'd been in his mind.
"Brödl. Now there was an enigma. A killer, pure and simple. A monster. No question. Yet…he respected those who fought back; even those he saw as the *Untermensch*. A screw loose…somewhere. There were a lot of screws loose back then. He was not the only one…"

Château Eloise, Normandy, France. The next morning, July 1941, 0800 local.
Alistair James would have been stunned if someone had told him that he would one day receive an SS funeral, with full honors. Massed ranks of SS, resplendent in black uniforms and gleaming boots, badges of rank appearing to shine, stood rigidly to attention as Forst delivered the eulogy.

Standing with Forst, Schelberg stared at the coffin. *Who were you?* he thought over Forst's barked delivery.

In her eyrie, Eloise had a perfect view of the ceremony. She had gone down as usual, only to be told that Forst had left strict orders that she should remain in her room until told she could return. She had been allowed to take something up for breakfast.

She now watched the ceremony with disgust. Not knowing the true identity of the man being buried, she considered that the SS were polluting the family grounds with their dead comrade. She vowed if she survived the war, she would have the remains dug up, taken to some desolate wood well away from the château grounds, and burnt and scattered like so much rubbish.

She wrote about the ceremony in great detail, pinpointing the exact spot where the body was interred. She also wrote about what she intended to have done to it, after the war.

* * *

Cambridge Boys squadron, Normandy, France. July 1941. 1100 local.

Stroeme looked up in surprise as an unexpected visitor entered his office. "*Herr* Schelberg! What a surprise."

"A good one, I hope," Schelberg, in civilian attire, said without shame. He beamed at Stroeme.

"Needing another Storch?" Stroeme remained seated, and waved Schelberg to a chair.

"Thank you, Major," Schelberg said as he sat down. "As for the Storch, I think the experience of that flight is seared into my brain...as are your quite astonishing flying abilities."

"Thank *you*, *Herr* Schelberg. A little accolade now and then does not go amiss. Coffee?"

"Genuine praise where it's due," Schelberg remarked with one of his fleeting smiles. "No coffee for now. I had a rather full breakfast at the château." Schelberg paused, then went on, "I would, however, ask a favor."

"Ask away."

"Will there be a transport aircraft coming this way within the next few days? I need a flight back to the Reich."

"Berlin?"

"No. I need to go to Rendsburg."

"Well, you're partially in luck," Stroeme said. "We've got a Ju-52 bringing mail, among other things, late this afternoon. It leaves tomorrow morning at 0700. Can you make it?"

"I certainly can. This is excellent."

"It won't take you to Rendsburg, however. It is returning to Berlin, via Cologne. You can get off there, and perhaps find another lift to Rendsburg."

"I am certain I shall be able to."

"It will be making another trip in three days, again via Cologne. If you want to catch it, you'll have to be there at 1200 sharp. It won't wait."

"I'll be there." Schelberg gave Stroeme a speculative look. "Don't you wish to know why I am making this flight?"

"I know better, *Herr* Schelberg, than to inquire about Gestapo business."

Schelberg gave another tiny smile. "Very prudent. I am reporting the death of a son to his family," he added.

This made Stroeme curious, but he said neutrally, "Isn't that a little odd?"

"Do you mean that I am delivering the sad news, when someone up there could have been detailed to do it?"

"Well...frankly, yes."

"Understandable. There is a mystery to his death that I need to clear up."

"I see. Who was it?"

"One of our brightest. You and I were searching for him in your Storch. *Standartenführer* Bock."

Stroeme's eyes widened. His surprise was genuine. "*What?* When did this happen?"

"Yesterday. To be precise, we found him and his driver in the bocage, during the previous night. As you know, given the incident with the Storch, our search was fruitless. But he had managed to escape the attempt, and had returned to the château. He decided not to be intimidated—courageous, but ultimately fatal—went out, and the French kidnapped him again, this time adding the driver to their catch. The French then shot them. Bock was dead when we found him, but the driver managed to survive, despite being severely wounded. He is still unconscious. He was lucky. A vanity case—probably belonging to his girlfriend—was in a breast pocket. It contained her picture, and a thick letter from her. It prevented the bullet from going deep. One could say his girlfriend saved his life."

"Remarkable."

"I thought so too. Bock was buried at the château this morning. He was born in Rendsburg."

"I see," Stroeme repeated. "I am amazed that the French were so foolish. They must know what will happen next, because of this."

"One of the reasons I need to look further into the incident. It does indeed seem a suicidal thing to do, even for them. There is another...let us say...odd situation, at the château. A young French woman—a member of the family who owned it—is living there as, it would seem, a servant."

Stroeme stared at him. "And how did *this* come about?"

"It would appear that when the place was taken, the then owner, her grandfather, tried to defend his castle with a pistol from the Great War..."

"A *pistol?*"

"The French," Schelberg said, as if that explained everything. "He was shot dead, of course. Then this young woman, this granddaughter, who was with him at the time—child, really... Even now, she can't be more than eighteen. She picked up the pistol, and was ready to continue where the old man had left off. The lieutenant in command of the troopers in that part of the building told her to put it down. She faced him for a full minute, before finally allowing commonsense to take over. Then she said—according to one of the doctors at the château—and I quote 'I'm staying here. You'll be leaving soon'. The lieutenant of course laughed at her, saying we—that's you, me, and the rest of us—would be staying forever."

Schelberg paused, and looked at Stroeme with a strange smile. "Her reply was recklessly brave, foolish, and hopefully, not prophetic. I quote her words again, according to the doctor. She repeated her first warning: 'You'll be leaving soon. Those who stay forever will be dead.'"

Stroeme's eyes widened briefly. "Your own Cassandra."

Schelberg gave a sharp chuckle. "Let us hope not."

"What happened to the family?"

"The rest of the family and staff, were taken away; but *Brigadeführer* Forst decided to let her stay...as a servant. I think the situation amuses him."

Stroeme continued to stare at Schelberg. "Why?"

"*She* thinks, it's because he likes to humiliate her. I doubt that he has succeeded. She is a very proud young woman."

"You *talked* to her?"

"I never knew she was there. I had never seen her, until yesterday. I needed to check some documents."

Schelberg related the incident with the wine.

"She certainly does not sound like someone who has been humiliated," Stroeme agreed.

"She has spirit. Pretty young thing, too."

"You surprise me, *Herr* Schelberg. If I did not know better, I would say this sounds suspiciously like admiration."

"I am first and foremost, Major, a policeman. I am also SS, yes. I am not a barbarian. I can admire courage. Do you not admire the *Tommi* you shoot down, if he has shown courage in the fight?"

Stroeme gave a slow nod. "Yes," he admitted.

"There you are. This young woman has not got a chance in hell. Yet, she keeps her dignity. You cannot conquer, or control, those who do not fear you."

"Isn't that dangerous thinking from a member of the Gestapo?"

"Not at all. Underestimating an enemy can be as fatal as getting shot; because he will surprise you. Would you, Major, ever go into combat underestimating the man you face?"

"No."

Schelberg nodded at him. "Then we are not so far apart." He got to his feet. "Thank you for the flight. I shall be here at 0700."

Stroeme had also risen. "I'll be aloft when you arrive for the Ju-52. Have a good flight. And don't become meat for any marauding *Tommi*."

"Let us hope not," Schelberg repeated. "See you in a few days."

"Yes. And thank you again, Major."

They did not shake hands. Schelberg went back to his waiting car.

"What's really going on behind those pebbled eyes of yours, *Herr* Schelberg?" Stroeme said to himself, as the vehicle moved off. "And are you becoming attracted to that girl?"

Rendsburg, Schleswig-Holstein, Nazi Germany. Next day, July, 1941. 1400 local.

Seven hours, Schelberg thought. *It took* seven *hours to get here*.

The car moved slowly along a canal-side street. The local Gestapo had put one at his disposal.

Framed by two stretches of water—one a river, the other a canal—Rendsburg was virtually an island. The Eider flowed past its north-western shore, the Northsea-Baltic Canal, its south-east.

The driver wanted to talk. "The *Nord-Ostsee Kanal*," he began, almost like a tour guide. "Good target for the *Tommis*, I think, *Standartenführer*. The shipyard is not far along here. But so far, most of the attacks are on Hamburg, Kiel, and Raisdorf. Sometimes, the bombers pass overhead, on their way to Kiel. The fault of the Jews, of course. Without them, none of this would be happening. But our fighters have shot down many planes. The flak too. Once, I was in Raisdorf, and I saw one go down like a huge flaming candle."

"That is good."

"That is very good. I imagined all those *Tommis* burning inside it, and felt very happy to see that. No one asked them to fight for the Jews," the driver added, warming to his pet theme.

Schelberg did not comment.

"I have a brother who is a fighter pilot," the driver said into the silence.

"Really? Is he stationed up here?"

"No, *Standartenführer*. He is in France. Lucky bastard. All that wine and coffee!"

"Yes. He must be enjoying life."

"They say you have come from France, *Standartenführer*. I hope you don't mind me speaking."

"You may speak, but do not speak of my travels again...to anyone."

"Yes...I mean no, *Standartenführer!*"

"And whoever mentioned this to you was breaching security."

"Yes, *Standartenführer!*"

"However, I shall let that pass. This time only."

"Yes, *Standartenführer!*"

Having made the point, Schelberg continued, "Now about your brother..."

The driver almost turned round in his anxiety. "*Standartenführer!* Please. Do not punish..."

"I am not going to punish him, man, because of your oversight. The Reich needs good fighter pilots. I merely intend to tell him I met you, in case I run into him."

The driver was almost weeping with relief. "Oh thank you, *Standartenführer!*"

"His name?"

"Fritz, *Standartenführer*," the driver replied. "He's a *Lieutenant*. I am Johann, and he is Jürgen."

"You are twins?"

The driver gave a laugh that was a little too tinged by his relief. "No, *Standartenführer*. I am four years older."

"You sound proud of him."

"I am! I hope he gets many *Tommis*, to make the Führer as proud as I am!"

"I'm sure he will."

"He is also a true Party member."

"That is always good to hear. Ah," Schelberg went on. "This looks like the address. That house there."

The car stopped and Schelberg, not waiting for the driver to open the door, got out. The man looked chagrined.

Two S-boats, in perfect formation, powered up the canal, heading for Kiel. A submarine was berthed, some distance away.

Schelberg glanced up at the sky. The submarine was a nice target for any marauding enemy aircraft: but he doubted there would be a daylight attack.

"Don't worry," Schelberg said to the driver. "I know how to open doors. Now let's see if we have come to the right place. Wait here."

The driver, caught in the middle of getting out, stared at him uncertainly as he crossed the road to walk over to the house in question, before getting back behind the wheel.

The house was L-shaped, and more substantial than Schelberg had expected it to be. The shorter leg faced the canal. It was four-storied, with a steeply pitched roof that went down to ceiling level of the ground floor, its windows decreasing in number with each upper floor. The rest of the building extended to the right, and housed a small shop whose awning displayed the legend "Bock" in gothic letters.

"Well," Schelberg murmured, "it's the right place."

He entered the shop.

There were no customers. A woman with greying hair and a tired face, was behind the counter. She looked up as he entered, a smile of welcome creasing the worn expression.

"Can I..." She stopped, smiled fading. "Gestapo. Have I done something?" She did not look afraid.

"It is that obvious?"

"There is a manner. So what is it, *Herr Gestapo*?" Her voice bordered on truculence.

"That's a hostile attitude. What are you? A communist?"

"Just a true German. What do you want? There are no Jews hiding here and anyway, I have nothing against Jews. They are humans, like the rest of us."

"What makes you so angry, *Frau* Bock?" Schelberg countered. He decided to ignore her outburst about Jews.

"Stay the night, and you'll hear."

"Ah. You mean the bombers."

"And the reason they keep coming."

"I think we should get off the route this conversation is taking. It could lead into dangerous areas..."

"And then what? You'll shoot me?"

"*Frau* Bock, please. Let us stop this. I have come here on another matter." Schelberg removed his hat.

She looked at him, eyes widening slightly, face becoming older. "Is it...is it my son?"

Schelberg nodded.

Marina Bock gave a low moan, and gripped the counter for support.

Schelberg went quickly forward to help, but she shook her head vehemently. He stood back, idly fussing with his hat.

She looked down at the counter. "He did what I did not want him to...but a mother cannot hate her son."

"He served the Reich..."

Her head snapped up, eyes suddenly blazing. "The *Reich!* What do I care about your stinking *Reich?* What have you brought? *War!* Listen to it tonight. Tell the people of Hamburg, and Kiel!"

"*Frau* Bock! I will excuse this language because of your distress..."

"Distress! What do you know about distress? *Look* at me! I am not yet fifty, but I look twenty years older. My hair is grey. The Kaiser took my Otto. He never saw his son grow up. I had to make ends meet by taking people into my home, and to give my boy some education. This shop is dying a slow death. And things will get worse. As for the bombs...it is only the beginning." She paused, and drew a heavy breath. "He is smart, you know, my Heinrich. A scientist. Now your...*Führer* has taken him too. I wanted him to use his learning to help others, but what does he do? *He joins the SS!* To 'serve' the Reich!"

If only you knew how he served, Schelberg thought.

"What do I care about your *Reich*," Marina Bock repeated. "It will die soon. Germany will die; just like my shop, my Otto and now, my Heinrich. What more can you take from me? My life? It would be a favor!"

For a senior member of the Gestapo, Schelberg had listened to her tirade with astonishing tolerance. He did not yet know it, but something was already changing within him; but it would take him a very long time to discover what it was.

"You are very fortunate, *Frau* Bock," he said, "that I am the one listening to this, and not one of my colleagues. I have a young colleague, ambitious, dedicated to the Reich. He would have arrested you by now. Despite the fact that you are the mother of a most valued *Standartenführer*, this could have got you into very serious trouble."

"*Herr Gestapo*..."

"My name is Schelberg."

"*Herr Gestapo*," she insisted, "what serious trouble do you think I can be got into? The whole of *Germany* is in serious trouble!"

"That is defeatist..."

"Only to a fool! Are *you* a fool, *Herr Gestapo?* Somehow, I don't think so. You should start thinking of what will happen to people like you, when the Reich comes crashing down!"

Schelberg stared at her, astonished by her apparent recklessness.

Then she changed tack with a sudden abruptness, her voice softened as she said, "Where...where...did he die?"

"In France."

"And his body?"

"We...retrieved it. He was buried with honor...yesterday, in a very pleasant place. The grounds of a beautiful château."

"Was he...in pieces?"

"No. No disfigurement."

She was silent for a while. Then she said, going back into a memory. "He was so worried, you know, going into the SS. Not about the SS, or course, but whether they would take him because of his disfigurement..."

Schelberg forced himself not to overreact. "Disfigurement? There was no disfigurement."

"Not everyone would see it; but an SS inspection would discover it. It was a small thing, but he was very worried they would reject him."

"Why?"

"He used to love football as a boy. One day, he broke his toe. It never healed properly, and was a little crooked. There was a friend of his who also went into the SS medical branch. They used to play together."

And there it was.

Schelberg barely heard the rest of what she was saying. The British, he realized, had managed to successfully infiltrate the research center, with God knew what potential damage.

They did the job well, he thought, *even to falsifying the medical records.*

The records were on genuine official forms. Department stamps were also genuine; relevant dates all correct. It had been a very thorough job, with nothing left to chance. Had it not been for the medical officer at Brödl's unit—Bock's football-playing, childhood friend—no one would have been the wiser. And had it not been for the fake Bock's untimely death, the entire impersonation would have gone unnoticed. It had been beautifully planned, and executed. But it could not have worked without inside help.

Schelberg wondered where the real Heinrich Bock had met his own death, and in what manner. Certainly, not in the way he had described to the mother. Her son's body, he felt certain, would never be found.

"*Frau* Bock," Schelberg said, putting his hat back on. "I am truly sorry."

She did not look up as he paused on his way out, to look back at her. She was leaning over the counter, head resting upon her arms, weeping.

Schelberg walked out, feeling strangely chastened.

"Three women," he said quietly as he took his time walking back to the car. "A Jew in a village in France, a girl in a château, and a German mother who has lost everything. Fearless. You cannot conquer or control, those who do not fear you."

CHAPTER TEN

Cambridge Boys squadron. Normandy, Occupied France. July 1941. 1100 local.

Stroeme was in his squadron office. The patrol had been routine, with no excitements. He had gone up with Fritz who, as usual, had been eager for some combat, and had been openly disappointed when they had landed again without once sighting the enemy.

"You're right, Hans," he now said to his deputy. "He's going to get himself killed."

"He wants many kills to offer to his beloved *Führer*," Dasinger commented, trying hard not to sound dry and failing. "We've got ourselves an Iron Cross chaser."

"The only cross he'll get, if he's not careful, is the one that will be planted in his memory. If I had my way, I'd have him off the squadron."

"He idolizes you."

"Only because he thinks I'll lead him to the Iron Cross treasure chest."

"He's a good pilot."

"He's a damned good pilot. It's not his flying that worries me." Stroeme gave a tired sigh.

"We were that young once," Dasinger said.

"Really? How long ago was that?"

"Oh...just under two years."

"That long." They laughed.

Stroeme rose to his feet. "I'd better get going to the

commandant's office, to let him know I'm going off the base. Sooner I'm gone, sooner I'll be back."

Dasinger looked rueful. "Lucky you. Ask her if she has a sister."

"Shame on you, Hans. You're married."

"I'm not so sure."

Stroeme paused. "What are you telling me?"

"I almost wish that Ju-52 had not come."

"The mail? You looked happy when you got yours."

"That was before I'd read them."

Stroeme stared at him. "It's over?"

"Not in so many words. But reading between the lines..." Dasinger paused. "One senses these things. She's been doing a lot of partying. Meeting the 'right' people, as she describes it. She's been talking to 'someone' whom she believes can get me posted to Berlin, where I'll be 'safer'. I wonder what price she paid for that 'promise'. This is so humiliating. I'd rather be shot down by a *Tommi*..."

"Don't say things like that, Hans. If one of the pilots were to say this to you, what would tell him?"

"To pull himself together."

"Take your own advice. Are you sure you can handle this? I can postpone..."

"Now don't you make things worse." Dasinger grinned. "Or I'll start thinking my squadron CO is losing confidence in me. Then where would I be?"

"Nowhere you'd want to be," they said together.

"I won't be long," Stroeme said.

"Don't be ridiculous. Take your time. The airspace is clear. Enjoy the lady. Now get out of here, squadron commander, sir, while I warm your chair. And don't let the wrong kind of French get you." Dasinger gave a jokey salute.

Stroeme arrived at Marie du Vaillion's mansion one hour later, hoping she had no German visitors.

She was waiting for him, having long seen his car approaching. She looked very happy to see him, and hurried to the car as he stopped.

"No visitors I hope," he began, climbing out.

She gave him a quick, welcoming kiss, then linked arms as they walked to the house. "None at the moment. But a couple of generals are coming for dinner." She gave his arm a brief stroke. "We can spend the afternoon in bed. And you can stay, if you'd like. We'll have the night to ourselves, after they've gone."

"Better not. Anyway, just imagine it. Two generals sitting at your table, watching this lowly major, and probably knowing we were impatient for them to leave..."

She giggled. "Like two fathers refusing to leave so we couldn't get up to what they knew we wanted to."

"Worse than two fathers, I think Fathers can't remove you from your command. Besides, I'm really here to tell you something."

"Then we'd better go up to my room."

"Living up to our reputation?"

"What better way to hide what we do?"

They lay back in the opulent bed, exhausted by a bout of fierce lovemaking.

"Leave me some strength so that I can still fly," he pleaded.

She lay her body partially on top of him, one leg between his. "You're strong enough. So? What's the urgency?"

"First, let them know that all the squadron aircraft now sport blue tails. My own has a new distinguishing mark; a gothic double S. just beneath the left side of the cockpit. I'll explain further when I next go over."

She nodded. "Okay."

"Do you remember the night I returned?"

"There were those roadblocks. The SS had lost a colonel." She gave another giggle at the thought.

"When you hear what happened next, you won't feel like laughing. He managed to escape, but was kidnapped again..."

"Is he mad? Are *they?*"

"Was."

"What?"

"He's past tense. They killed him. He was buried yesterday, at the

Château Eloise."

She sat up. "My God! The SS will really go crazy."

"Perhaps."

"What do you mean?"

"They put a Gestapo man in charge. He was sent specially from Berlin; but he seems to be playing the softly-softly game. His name is Schelberg. 'I'm not a barbarian' he said to me. Says who, I thought. The Gestapo and barbarity are intimate bedfellows. Apart from their more unsavory habits, they also spy on their own comrades, irrespective of rank. No honor among the thieves. Watch out for him. He is a cunning bastard. One has the feeling he's watching everybody. I took the opportunity to come here to warn you because he's gone back to Berlin for a few days. He knows all about you—well, not about what you really do—but he mentioned you to me in a way that carried a veiled threat. A sort of warning, that if he became suspicious of me for any reason...you can guess the rest. He's bound to come here one of these days. Be very much on your guard. Don't trust him."

"Don't worry. I won't." She said this with great feeling.

"One other piece of information. This one's very strange. It seems that one of the members of the de la Cointe family is still there."

She stared at him. "How is this possible?"

"It's a very odd business. Schelberg told me, so if you ever do meet him, you know nothing about it. If he introduces the subject, be very careful how you react. He'll be watching you."

"I'll be careful. And who is the de la Cointe?"

"Schelberg did not give a name, but he did say it was a young girl, about eighteen."

"Oh no! It's Eloise! It must be. They renamed the Château when she was born. She was the apple of her grandfather's eye."

"Well, the SS commander is keeping her there, as a servant."

Marie was shocked. "These animals! What are they doing to that poor child?"

"According to what Schelberg said, *she* refused to leave. After they had shot her grandfather, she picked up the pistol, ready to fire at them..."

"Good for her!"

"She was lucky not to have been shot immediately. For whatever reason, the SS lieutenant in charge must have found some humanity. He persuaded her to put the gun down. But instead, she told him the SS and the rest of us, would be leaving soon, and that those who did stay would be the dead ones. Brave girl. In the end, she did put the gun down. The SS general decided to keep her there. He seems amused by the situation."

"It's sick!"

"Of course it is."

"We must get her out."

"Not if she does not want to leave. And besides, the chance of doing so is nil. Getting into that establishment is very difficult, if not impossible, if you are not SS. As for getting out again..." Stroeme's look spoke volumes. "I have never been there. Not even our Commandant has been; not that he wants to. It is a very tightly controlled area. They would shoot people who don't belong there; including, I suspect, even those from other SS units."

"So what do we do?"

"For now, we just pass the information on. Let them decide across the channel, how best to make use of it."

Berlin. July, 1941. 1645 local.

Schelberg had some luck. He'd got a flight to Berlin, on another supply Ju-52. He went straight to his office, and began making arrangements to see Bock's original SS records, but hid the true target of interest by requesting a selection of files which he had not the slightest intention of studying. Bock's records would therefore appear to be just one of a general lot. He had a day or two within which to have a good scrutiny of them, to see if he could find some answers. He planned to work in a way that would arouse no suspicions in whoever had made the switch. The British may well have embedded a spy long before the war. Schelberg intended to catch him, or her, no matter how long it took.

He had just finished making the arrangements, when there was a soft knock, and a man in the uniform of an SS major poked his head through. He grinned at Schelberg, clearly happy to see him.

"Heinrich! I heard you were back. So how was France, you lucky dog? Still in one piece, too."

"Good to see you too, Emil. Only here for a day or so." Schelberg got to his feet, and they shook hands warmly. They were good friends, and on the personal level, they dispensed with rank protocol.

Emil Jorlach, the young colleague Schelberg had talked to Marina Bock about, looked disappointed. "Shame! Secretly, I'm jealous. You get an interesting investigation in France, I get to hunt out Jews. In October, we'll start really moving them out in serious numbers. Are you sure you can't use an assistant down there?"

Schelberg quickly thought about this. On one hand, he thought Jorlach could be useful; but after a second thought, he decided against it. The case was far too sensitive. He wanted to handle this alone.

"To begin with, Emil, I can't discuss it with anyone. But I will say this, if I feel I may need you, I'll send word. Anyway, I know you enjoy your work."

"I do. I do! But it would still be nice to be in France." Jorlach brightened. "I'll be on the very next plane immediately after I hear from you."

"I'm not promising anything; but I'll keep it in mind."

"Good enough for me."

"Besides," Schelberg said, "rumor has it you're one of the best Jew-hunters around. I believe even the *Reichsführer* himself is watching from afar. You could do very well indeed, Emil."

"*He* is taking notice?"

"According to what I've heard. But don't broadcast it. It could go against you."

"I won't," Jorlach vowed. "But that, is something." He was hugely pleased.

"Keep it up," Schelberg encouraged.

"Oh I will. I will!" Jorlach's cold eyes held a promised terror for his prospective victims. A slim man in his smart uniform, humanity was something that had long left him; and it was fortunate for Marina Bock that she had been spared his tender mercies. "Well I'd better leave you to your work," he went on. He grinned again. "Jews to catch. And don't forget, if you need me..."

"I'll call," Schelberg promised.

Jorlach gave him a Himmler version of the Hitler salute, and swaggered away, fired by the thought that the man himself had taken an interest in him.

Schelberg looked on without expression.

When the day came for him to catch the plane that would take him back, he was none the wiser. Not one of Bock's documents had a record of the broken toe. If it had not been for Marina Bock's own words, he would have begun to doubt the veracity of the comments made by the doctor in Brödl's unit.

The job had indeed been well done. Someone had carried out detailed research on Bock; or had been given the information that had subsequently been put to use.

Who had supplied it? Schelberg wondered as the aircraft headed west towards Cologne. This was a conspiracy with far-reaching impact. He was certain he had barely touched its surface.

But why would the French kill an Allied agent? Had it been a monumental screw-up? Perhaps the operation, whatever it was, had been so secret, the French had been kept well out of it. They had seen a senior SS officer, and following their own agenda, had acted independently, and had kidnapped him.

Schelberg paused. To what purpose? Information? A prisoner exchange? Then why kill him?

"That can't be it;" he said aloud.

"I beg your pardon?"

Schelberg looked at the young Luftwaffe pilot who had grabbed a lift back, and was sitting across the aisle from him. When configured for passengers the aircraft had two single rows of seats on either side, giving a view out of the square windows. There were just four seats fitted. No one occupied them. The rest of the cabin space of the triple-engined Ju-52 was taken up with various types of cargo, including mail.

"Sorry," Schelberg said. "Thinking aloud." He did not introduce himself. Instead, he looked at the bright new ribbon of the Iron Cross. "Just got that?"

The pilot nodded. "From the *Führer* himself!"

"Congratulations!"

The pilot smiled. "Thank you."

"You must have got a few."

"Five bombers, four fighters." The pilot did not hide his pride. The he added, hesitantly, "in two days."

Schelberg's eyebrows did a brief, upwards dance. "Most impressive. Well done."

The pilot nodded again, and looked out of the window.

Schelberg glanced down. The pilot's hands were tightly clasped, as if to prevent them from shaking.

It could not be a terror of flying, Schelberg decided. Not after scoring nine kills in just two days. He knew other *experten* had higher scores, but this diffident pilot seemed almost surprised by his prowess. Some fearless pilots known to be bad passengers. It was all about not being in control. It could also not be because of a possible fighter attack on the defenseless plane. Though the ubiquitous made-of-all-work Ju-52 could be fitted with light machine guns for defense, this one was not so equipped. Fighters this far inland would have to traverse heavily defended territory, and would need the range. There was more likelihood of being downed by a stray bomb. But enemy bombers at that time of day were conspicuous by their absence.

The time when day and night bombing would become a terrible part of daily life had not yet come and the possibility this happening was not something either contemplated upon.

He's scared, Schelberg thought in surprise. *Scared of returning to the cauldron. He's putting a brave face on it; because he has no choice.*

"Where did you get them?" Schelberg asked.

The pilot turned to look at him blankly. "The Eastern Front."

Schelberg nodded with approval. "Things are going very well out there."

"They are. Easy pickings."

"Earned a home visit too?"

The pilot looked at him guardedly, then shook his head. He turned back to the window.

"I understand," Schelberg said. "No talking about such things."

Schelberg glanced down at the hands again. They were still tightly clasped. He looked away and out of his own window, not wanting to let the pilot see he had looked in on his secret.

He found himself again thinking about the three women who were worlds apart, yet who in a disturbing way, had the uncanny feel of being messengers of foreboding: the French wife and mother—a Jew—who had fought the SS to the death; the teenaged chatelaine, whose words might turn out to be prophetic; and the German mother and wife who had lost everything, and who in her grieving despair, had sounded a warning that could have easily got her executed for disloyalty and defeatism, for daring to say so.

All Cassandras? he wondered.

It did not bear thinking about.

He stole another glance at the pilot. The hands were still holding each other tightly, now and then whitening at the knuckles as the young lieutenant squeezed them together.

A defender of the Reich? Or a wasteful sacrifice?

I'm not supposed to think like this, Schelberg thought. *I am a high-ranking member of the world's most feared police, belonging to the world's most fearsome power. Germans and non-Germans alike, are terrified of us.* He again thought of the three women. *But what of the exceptions?*

The Ju-52 made an unmolested flight to its first stop at a Luftwaffe airfield just outside Cologne. The lieutenant got off without saying goodbye, almost before the aircraft had come to a halt, and with Schelberg still seated. The aircraft had three crew—two pilots, and an engineer who had gone aft to open the exit door.

He now came up to Schelberg. "You've got just under an hour, sir, while we off-load, take on some new cargo, and refuel for the next leg. Time for calls of nature, and so on. We take-off at 1200. We won't wait. Not allowed."

"I've been told," Schelberg said with a fleeting smile, "I'll be in time."

He returned with five minutes to spare, and had not seen the Iron Cross pilot again. Then he climbed aboard, and stared.

The pilot was back in his seat, and he too was staring at Schelberg in surprise.

"So," Schelberg began as he regained his own seat. "It appears we are going the same way. Or are you continuing on from there?"

The pilot shook his head. "That's my destination."

"Remarkable. You must be going to join the squadron down

there. I know the commander personally."

"Oh?"

The engineer shut the door and went to join his crew members as Schelberg said, "Major Stroeme. Excellent pilot, as I had reason to find out, and to be thankful. His skill saved my life when we were shot down in the Storch he was flying."

"*Shot* down? Where?"

One of the Ju-52's three engines was started.

"Not so far from the airfield. Alas, it was by one of our own—a halftrack whose crew had poor recognition skills."

The pilot stared at him. "What happened to them?"

"They were killed by the real enemy—in four all-black Hurricanes from what I could see of them—who came looking for trouble. Rather poetic, I thought at the time."

"Ah," the pilot commented with some uncertainty. "*Black* Hurricanes?" he added.

"Yes. That grabbed my interest too. I've been wondering about what unit they belong to, ever since. They were very fast, and very heavily armed. They ripped the halftrack apart. It would be interesting to know about that unit, and its purpose. Perhaps you will shoot one down for us over land, for us to study; and hopefully its pilot, if he survives."

"Perhaps," the pilot said, giving Schelberg a look that clearly said he was wondering who the hell Schelberg was.

Schelberg finally decided to introduce himself. "Schelberg," he said, with a slight nod.

The pilot hesitated.

"Gestapo," Schelberg continued, and added for good measure. "*Standartenführer* SS."

The lieutenant went faintly pale.

"Yes. We do have that effect on people." Schelberg was dry about it.

All three BMW engines going, the Ju-52 began to taxi.

Schelberg had a sudden thought. "You are not Jürgen Fritz, by any chance, are you?"

The pilot shook his head, giving Schelberg a wary look. "Hagen...sir. Michael."

"You're going to an extremely professional squadron, *Lieutenant* Hagen. I am certain they will be pleased to have you."

"Thank you...sir."

Hagen again retreated into his thoughts, and looked out of the window.

Office, Intelligence unit, Whitehall, London. July 1941. 1140 local.

The brigadier looked up with a smile as Haines was ushered in "There you are, Haines. Sorry to drag you back so soon."

He had been sitting on the edge of his desk He heaved himself off, and came forward to shake Haines warmly by the hand.

"Truly sorry, old boy," he repeated, "but you're the only man immediately available; plus, of course, you're being reasonably familiar with the territory. Pity about that rest you should have had." The brigadier gave him a close look. "Are you up to it? If not, just say the word."

"I'm here, sir."

"What? Oh! Yes. Good show. Good show! You'll be taking the radio with you. Sooner than expected, eh?"

"Why the hurry, sir?"

The brigadier paused, as if wondering whether to tell Haines anything. "Reluctant to send you back so soon to that area, especially after what happened to Alistair. But there's no baulking. Got to be done."

"Yes, sir."

The brigadier nodded, and went back to leaning on his desk. He folded his arms across his chest. "We've received some quite peculiar news. It would seem that the Hun has given Alistair a rather spectacular burial."

"*What?*"

"Yes. Odd, isn't it? They kill the lad, then bury him with full SS honors. In the château grounds, of all places. Mad, the Hun. Who knows about his peculiarities? The question is, why do that, if they were wise to the idea that he was not the real Bock?"

"Perhaps," Haines began without batting an eye, "they do not want it known that they'd had a British spy deep inside one of their most secret establishments. Heads would roll, if that was known."

"My thoughts exactly. None so vicious as the Hun against his own kind if he suspects he's been had. You're going back to find out the truth of the matter. You're happy with continuing to play that Waffen-SS Major?"

"I'm fine, sir."

The brigadier nodded again. "There is one other thing, rather peculiar, if you ask me...and this may prove extremely difficult, not to say dangerous. We have also heard that the SS at the château have got in there, a young gel belonging to the family who actually own it."

"A prisoner?"

"There's the thing...she apparently remained of her own free will. Well may you stare, Haines," the brigadier continued, "but those are the facts we've got. First, she took a pistol to Jerry when he came to take her home off her, survived that folly, then decided to remain until the day that the château returns to its rightful ownership. Brave, foolish, and fantastically optimistic, all at the same time. And do you know what, Haines? We must not disappoint her. One day, we *shall* wrest France from the Hun's grip; and with it, Europe and everywhere else he's set foot."

"How come they let her live?"

"Seems it amuses the head Hun over there to keep her as a servant. Needs to massage his ego, one supposes. But this gives us an opportunity. That girl will be a mine of information. She will have perhaps seen and heard much of what goes on; at least, enough to be of value to us when the time comes to bomb the place to smithereens."

Haines' eyes widened. "You're going to *destroy* it?"

"Always on the cards, Haines. Had Alistair managed to make it back with the goods, the place would have been attacked. Put a stop to whatever they're up to. But without Alistair's valuable information..."

"Didn't he get anything to you while he was out there?"

"That was not the idea. He had to remain deep, until he had got what he went there for. The pity was the real Bock never spilled the beans until our little charade. Torture would not have got anything out of a fanatic like that. We had to go slowly. Besides, I don't personally abide by torture, even on the wretched Hun. The slow way worked, as you know; but alas, Alistair was killed, after finally getting what he went for."

The brigadier had been somewhat less than honest, but Haines would not realize that for some considerable time.

"Could they have found it out there...wherever it might have fallen when he was killed?"

"We need to know that as well."

"Yes, sir. Sir," Haines went on, "may I ask what makes it so important."

"You may not, Lieutenant Haines. There's a good chap."

"Sir."

"Back to the young lady. Yes?" The brigadier paused, seeing that Haines clearly wanted to ask another question.

"Are we rescuing her?"

"Good God, no! Stir up a hornet's nest. We're not ready for that as yet. That day *will* come, as the Hun will find out, to his considerable cost."

"If we're not rescuing her..."

"You're going to find a way to get to her, and give her that radio. We'll find another one for you in due course." The brigadier paused, waiting for the inevitable reaction.

"Give her... That's a death sentence! If I could ever get that in, the first time she uses it—if she ever manages to use it properly..."

"There are full instructions—in English, and French—under the false bottom. She sounds like a very smart young gel. She'll get the hang of it. And having lived in that château all her life, I am certain she has many hiding places for the radio that the Hun will not even think of. She will not be required to make regular contact; only if something truly momentous occurs, or if we specifically make contact. All she has to do is listen out for one minute at set times. Details in the instructions. If we need something from her, we'll make contact, with instructions for timing of a report. Apart from that, life for her goes on as normal; or what passes for normal where she is."

"Sir, it's impossible! That place is a fortress. When I took Bock—I mean Colonel James back, it was like..."

"I know. I've read your report of that event. You're supposed to be Waffen-SS, Haines. Hitler's elite. You're resourceful. You'll find a way. I'm certain of it."

Haines stared at his superior for some moments, dumbfounded. "What about the Gestapo man Colonel James warned about?" he at last continued. "*He* could be a darned big problem."

"Schelberg. Gestapo. Yes. We have some documentation on him, including a psychological profile. Written by the Hun, no less. As your German's excellent, I'll make it available for you to study here. You might find it useful, if you ever have a run-in with him. We'll give you as much detail as we've got about the château and its environs. The girl, Eloise de la Cointe, will naturally have an owner's knowledge of it; which will be of great use to you, should you succeed in getting to her. Perhaps you will get to know what's going on in there. Until then, it's best if you know nothing."

"In case I'm captured, you mean, sir."

"It's a risk," the brigadier conceded. "I'll not lie to you."

But he already had.

Later, Haines was walking along Piccadilly. The same man as before, matched steps with him.

"I'm going back," Haines said.

"When?"

"In a few days,"

"Perfect. You can bring the merchandise this time."

"'Merchandise'?" Haines said in a sharp hiss. "Do you think I'm doing this for *money?*"

"I see. It's the power it might bring. Is that it?"

But the man was talking to himself. Haines had crossed the road, and was walking in the opposite direction.

He stared at Haines' receding figure. "Careful how you choose to play this," he murmured. "It could be a long war, buddy. Anything can happen."

Galen Private Archives, New York. Tuesday, July 2006. 1100 local.

"Listen to this!" Tad Duchamps said, and began to read. "'When I left..."' Ellen's mobile rang. She picked it up from the low table in front of her desk, at which they were sitting.

She looked at the display. "Daphne," she said in some surprise.

"*Daphne?* When did she get your cell number?"

"I gave it to her last night, when you were on the roof."

"When the world gets me down, I head for the roof," he joked.

She gave him a pained look, then said into the phone, "Hi, Daphne."

"I'm coming over," Daphne said, and hung up.

Ellen stared at the phone. "She's coming over, and she hung up."

"Smart. People hack phones. She's coming now?"

"I guess."

"Then we'd better put the senator's confessions back in the hiding place, before she gets here."

"What were you beginning to read? There's time before she arrives."

"Not if she's right outside..."

"Come on, read it. She can't surprise us. She's got to go through security, who will call me, then I've got to open up for her. So read."

Duchamps looked uncertain. "Okay. '*When I left the brigadier that day*'," he read, "'*I had no idea then, that he had left out a lot of details. Was he lying to me? He sure as hell was. And all that British thing about if I did not want to go I just had to sing out, was a load of bull. If I'd said no, a look would have come into his eyes. A subtle British put-down that would have told me he thought I had lost the guts for it. Poor old Haines, he would have said to his fellow generals. LMF, don't you know. LMF means lack of moral fiber. Coldly polite way to call a man a coward. But I did not go back because of the brigadier. I went back because of the people I really worked for, and for the miniature camera with which Alistair James had photographed those so important documents. I had no concept at the time, of just how important...*'" The office phone rang.

"Right," Ellen said. "She's here. Back they go." She went to her desk and grabbed the phone. "This is Ellen."

"Miss Haines," the security man said, "I have Miss Daphne Howe for you."

"Send her up."

"Yes, Miss Haines."

"Thank you." She put the phone down, and looked at Duchamps. "Done?"

"All back in the valise." He picked it up.

"I can carry it," she said. "I brought it here all the way from Macon, Georgia. And if Eloise de la Cointe could carry it around when it was a radio..."

He let her do so with a look of amusement. "You're the boss."

She picked it up. "Damn. Forgot how heavy it was."

But pride prevented her from asking him to take it to the strong room with her. And he did not offer to do so.

"You could offer," she accused.

"Nope." He grinned. "Done so already. Was rejected."

By the time she had safely locked the senator's secrets away, Daphne was at the outer door, and she had no time for a suitable retort. She gave him a look that could have meant anything, and went to let Daphne in. Discussion about what the senator could have meant by "important", would have to wait for now.

Daphne entered the inner office ahead of Ellen. "This is nice," she said looking around. "Big, roomy, a haven of peace. Not like my hen house of an office. Modern, open plan, *noisy*. This is like what they call a gentleman's study. I almost expected to see a yachting cap somewhere."

"Well it is a classic old building," Ellen said.

"But modernized with taste. " Daphne looked at Duchamps. "Hi, Tad. Haven't seen you in a while."

"Hi, Daphne. When was it? Last year?"

"A year since this morning? Time does fly..."

"Daphne!" Ellen cut in. "It had better be good."

"It is," Daphne said, looking at Duchamps. "What happened to your interview?"

"I dumped it. The guy was a sleaze. He wanted to get his best-dressed pants into my pants. Five minutes into the interview, he had his hand on my knee. I told him to quit it. He did not. I told him he had the wrong interviewer, and left." All the while, Daphne kept looking at Duchamps.

Ellen was not sure she liked that. "So what brings you..."

"Here?" Daphne addressed Duchamps. "What hornet's nest *have* you been poking into, Tad?"

Slightly puzzled by this, Duchamps said, "You know what."

She shook her head. "Either you don't know, or you're not telling." She took a chair close to him, and sat down.

Seeing this, Ellen performed an almost exact imitation of the brigadier, back in 1941. She folded her arms, and leaned against her desk, a watchful and almost territorial expression upon her face.

"When I dumped that piece of sleaze," Daphne continued to Duchamps, "I called a guy I knew who used to work at the Pentagon. I said nothing to him on the phone. Just that I was in town, and it would be nice to meet. He was one of Wiley's buddies. When Wiley...died, he was more like a brother to me than Dean ever could be. We met for a late brunch—or very early lunch—and after a while, I asked him if he'd heard of an Air Force pilot called Duchamps. You should have seen his face then." She looked at Ellen. "You should have *seen* his face," she repeated.

Duchamps was staring at her, but said nothing.

She turned back to him. "'Daphne', he said to me, '"you don't want to go there. If you're researching an article. Take some good advice from a guy who looked on Wiley as a brother, and looks on you as a loved sister. Drop it'. Would Wiley have said that? I asked him. 'He would have used stronger words', Wiley's pal said. 'He would have known the kind of danger you're getting into. I understand it. Wiley would have been more...forceful.'" Daphne looked from one to the other. "Then he closed up completely."

"Is he one of the guys you said would watch your back?" Duchamps asked.

She nodded. "I was counting on him."

"Can you still count on him after this?"

"To be honest? Right now, I don't know. These guys are not wimps, you know."

"They're anything but. Did he look scared?"

Again, Daphne looked from one to the other. "Not for himself. For me."

Duchamps glanced at Ellen. "Now's the time to back off, Daphne. I don't know what the guy means; but if he was Wiley's Special

Forces buddy, and he knows the Pentagon, he may have good reason to give you that warning. Perhaps he heard, or knows something that makes him feel he should warn you. It may not be anything *in* the Pentagon."

"There's something else."

The looked at her, and waited.

"Right after that article on you was pulled, an Air Force major decided on his own initiative, to see if there was anything in what you said. Well..." Daphne paused.

"What?" they said together.

"Seems he liked to hunt. There was an accident."

"What have we here?" Duchamps remarked. "The ducks shooting back?"

"Wiley's buddy did not use the same words, but he suggested just about the same thing, and believed the 'accident' thing as much as you do."

"Scratch one major who got too nosey. And no one investigates an accident." Duchamps shot Ellen another glance. "I guess they wanted to make sure the major never got the time to make contact with me, if he found anything. Did he give you the major's name?"

"No."

"Then take the advice, Daphne. You're not dealing with a best-dressed sleaze who thinks he's too sexy for his mirror. You're dealing with guys who shoot old veterans, and who would take you out without breaking sweat."

"They don't scare me."

"They scare *me*."

"And me," Ellen added for good measure.

"I'm doing this for the reasons you already know," Duchamps said to Daphne. "You don't have that excuse."

"I hear what you're saying. But I am a journalist, fashion mag or not. I want to do this."

"You want to be dead?" Ellen suggested.

"You two are going after this," Daphne protested.

"I'm just helping Tad with archive research, *if* we can find any documents here that might be of use. That's not the same as doing reporter stuff. "

"Wiley's buddy gave you good advice," Duchamps repeated. "Take it. We appreciate your wanting to help; but *we* don't even know where we're headed. We've all seen the movie where the guy says to the girl, stay there. *Don't* move. What does she do as soon as his back's turned? She *moves*..."

"Sometimes, moving saves her life."

Duchamps looked at Ellen. "*You* tell her."

"Tad's right. Perhaps it was not a great idea to agree last night, Daphne. We don't want you getting hurt because of it. As Tad says...listen to Wiley's friend."

Daphne looked at each in turn. "Come *on*, kids! I want to help."

"And we want you to keep on breathing," Duchamps said.

"Your last word?"

"Yep."

"Okay," she said, getting to her feet.

"Daphne," Ellen said in warning. "Can we trust you on this?"

"Sure you can. Well...got a plane back to LA to catch. Nice meeting you, Tad." She gave him a quick kiss at the corner of his mouth. Even if I can't tell them at the office. Ellen..."

"I'll see you out."

"Okay,"

Ellen shot Duchamps an enigmatic glance, as she followed Daphne. He heard them talk briefly, say goodbye, then the outer door was opened, and shut.

"Do you buy that?" Ellen said as soon as she returned.

"Nope."

"Me, neither. We were crazy to tell her even what we did."

"There wasn't much choice once she'd come to your place. And it was a good thing she told us about Dean. But...she's looking to get herself killed."

"So what do we do?"

"Hope she takes the good advice from Wiley's pal."

"She seems to like kissing you." It sounded like an accusation.

Daphne went nowhere near the plane she was supposed to catch. Instead, she went to her father's office at the bank.

"Daphne," he began, rising from behind his huge desk in the vast inner sanctum when she was shown in. "I was surprised when they told me you were on your way," he continued as he came towards her. "After what happened last night, I expected you to be long gone."

"I'm taking a later flight."

"Did you look in on Dean on the way?"

"Why would I?"

Augustus Howe nodded. "That would have been a real surprise." He went over to a hung window, and looked down upon Manhattan. "I'm not going to be here forever. I'd hoped Dean..." He paused. "You've got more spirit than he has." He did not look at her.

"What's this? Peace offering?"

"Daphne, we've had our differences..."

"Hah! That's what you call them? '*Differences*'? You turned your back when I needed you. I used to admire you. I used to think if ever I needed someone in my corner, no matter what, Pops would be there. A rock."

"'Pops'. You used to call me that when..."

"I was a naïve child. A woman knows better."

"So the war goes on." he turned to look at her. "Why are you here?"

"Something Dean said last night does not make sense. Why would a Southern belle like Ellen have a black man—according to Dean—in her car? She comes from an old, good ol' boy family. Her granddad's the Senator Haines who thinks blacks are fine as long as they know their place. She grew up in that environment. Why would she take a black man *home*? According to Dean, that is."

Howe's eyes were neutral, but unblinking. "What are you getting at?"

"I'm a reporter. I get curious when things don't fit."

"So you come to me?"

"You're not the president of your own bank because you're a fool. I saw how you looked at Dean when he was letting his jealousy rule what brains he has. You were thinking about something. You had a speculative look."

"And you're letting your journalist's need for a story get the better of you. Dean was just letting what's in his pants cloud his judgement as usual. People look dark in shadows, or poor lighting. It's a non-story. I doubt your readers would want to read an article in your glossy magazine, about your wildly jealous brother. Why don't you join the bank?" Howe added with a suddenness that took Daphne by complete surprise.

"*Me?* In *this* bank?"

"Why not? You were always the smarter of the two."

"That's not what you said when I met Wiley."

"I never said at the time, that you were stupid. I said I thought you were headstrong."

"'Headstrong' people don't join the executive boards of banks; although jealous ones do, when they're the boss's son. You can't buy me off. I'm staying in LA."

"I'm not attempting to 'buy' you off. You would do a good job here. You have the skill..."

"I don't know anything about banking."

"What do you think your brother really knows?" Howe countered.

"No deal. I'm going back to LA."

Howe stared at her. "That's it?"

"I thought you might be able to explain Dean's bizarre little scene last night, but I see you can't. See you around."

She was nearly at the door, when Howe said, "Daphne."

The way he spoke, made her pause. She looked at him over a shoulder, and waited.

"There's nothing there for you."

She turned round. "What do you mean?"

"Forget Dean's outburst."

She gave him a long, searching look, shook her head slowly, then turned and walked out.

As the door shut behind her, Howe said quietly, "Don't let your curiosity get the better of you."

It sounded like a plea.

Although she did not hear her father's words, Daphne was frowning as she walked away from his office.

"My *father* knows something about this?" she said to herself. "How can that be?" She could only look upon what he had said, she decided, as a veiled warning of some kind. "How far does this thing go? And whom does it reach?"

CHAPTER ELEVEN

Galen Private Archives, New York. Tuesday, July 2006. 1245 local.

Duchamps had gone back to the particular diary with the passage he'd been reading, before Daphne's unexpected visit had interrupted him.

"Okay," he began. "Back to the senator's adventures. I stopped..." he sought out the section of the passage. "here. '*I had no concept at the time, of just how important. But I decided if whatever was on the film excited so many people, as long as I had it, I had insurance. Anything can happen in a war. I decided to leave the camera, in Alistair James's small portfolio bag, where I had hidden it in the bocage country. I knew exactly how to find it again. No one else knew of where it had been hidden, that it was still in the bocage country. If I did not survive the war, no one would find it. If I survived, it would still be my insurance. If by some twist of fate that particular hedgerow took devastating fire during combat, if anything were left of the camera, the film would be useless. Either way, I was covered. If in the fullness of time anyone found it accidentally, it's purpose would have been diminished by the passage of time. Or so I thought.*'"

Duchamps stopped, and looked at Ellen. "What the hell was in that camera? These diaries tell us plenty; but they can't give us the whole picture. We should start using that nice plane your grandpa put at your disposal."

"Yours too."

"I'm still wondering about his true reasons for being so kind to me."

"I can almost hear the acid sizzling."

"In my place, how would you feel?"

"My acid would be boiling. Don't forget I've got cause too."

"Well for me, the jury's going to be out on that old man for some time; and went it does return, it could be with a conviction. And we," Duchamps continued, "need to find some of those people he's mentioned—if they're still alive—or at least their families, who might be able to put some more pieces together."

"So we go to those locations?"

He nodded. "It's what your grandpa gave us that plane for. One of those places has got to be their old base in England. Even if it's been disused since that time, there could still be people around the area who remember it. And any squadron buddies still alive. Another important place I *must* see, is that airfield where my grandpa got shot. It's near Bourg-en-Bresse, France. It's still operating as a civilian field; but it also used to be a wartime forward field after D-Day."

"You think they spent some time there during the war?"

"I don't know for sure, but it's possible. My grandpa never mentioned it in the little he did say about his service. But why go there for a reunion, if it had no significance?"

"And the place where the senator hid the camera...perhaps it's still there." Ellen pointed to the valise, "somewhere in those books, he'll have put down exactly where."

"Or not. If so, how many Normandy hedgerows would you like to check?"

"How many years would that take?"

"More than we could live. Now if we had some nice Pentagon toys, a fancy imaging system from a satellite would spot it...if we could find someone to do it for us, and if we could keep those friendly people in the green SUVs, and their bosses, from finding out."

"And the chances are, of that happening?"

"Nil."

"So we do it the hard way."

"Not as if we had a choice," Duchamps said. "And speaking of cameras, we should take one. I've got..."

"And I've got four at my disposal, right here. Professional

models."

"Four?"

"This is an archive. We use cameras in our work. I've lost count of how many we've got here. My allocation is four."

"What are they?"

"A Minolta *Maxxum*—that's *Dynax*—9; analogue SLR. Then a Fujifilm S3 pro UVIR Digital SLR. The UVIR is one of our stars. It's a full spectrum camera, but we use it mainly for ultraviolet and infrared photography. It's perfect for our kind of work, dealing with documents that can sometimes be very old. We once had someone who's will had been tampered with. In normal light, you could not tell the difference. The UVIR shots showed that the will had been doctored. The man had died, leaving his daughter the house. His young, second wife said he'd changed the will in her favor. She'd cooked up the scheme with her lawyer, who was also her lover."

"Nice wife. Smarter daughter."

"The original will was kept here. We suggested using a UVIR to check the supposedly new one. The camera showed several attempts to fake the signature. They had practiced tracing it from an original."

"Who's the 'we'?"

"I suggested it. That was a couple of years ago."

"Smart Ellen."

"The third camera is..."

"I...think I'll leave my snapshot gizmo at home," Duchamps said.

"I doubt it's a snapshot camera, but why not take the pro cameras that are already right here? Less trouble."

"Why not," he said.

"Two should be enough. The Dynax, and the UVIR. I still like to have a good analogue camera around. People are going digital, digital. For me, nothing really beats a good analogue. That's a personal opinion. Others may not agree."

"Then we take them. You never know when they could be useful."

The phone on the desk rang. Ellen went over, and picked it up. The display showed it was again security.

"This is Ellen."

"Miss Haines. Miss Howe is back. She says it's very urgent."

"Send her right up," a very surprised Ellen said.

"Yes, Miss Haines."

Ellen turned to Duchamps as she put the phone down. "it's Daphne! She's back."

"What the..." Duchamps said, as he quickly began to put the diary he'd been reading, back into the valise.

By the time Daphne had turned up, there was no sign of it.

They were taken aback by her expression. Gone was the jokey, cynical journalist hunting out what could be a juicy story. Instead, she looked as if she were at last beginning to realize—despite the warning from Wiley's former team colleague, just how dangerous the situation could become for her. Not knowing what had happened, it seemed to them that the defining moment had caught up with her at some point during the time after they had last seen her; and had done so without warning.

"Daphne?" Ellen began. "You okay?"

But Daphne strode through, going straight to the inner office.

A puzzled Ellen followed. "Daphne?" she said again.

Duchamps looked up, waiting.

Daphne sat down heavily.

"Your plane to LA," Ellen said.

"I'm catching a later flight."

"Okay," Ellen said, as if she understood.

Daphne looked at Duchamps. "I think my father knows something about this."

"You're kidding me," he said.

"Don't stare at me like that. I haven't just grown two horns."

"Your *father?*" Ellen said.

"After I left you, I changed my flight to a later one, and went to the bank to see my father."

"Why?"

"I wanted to ask him something about this..."

"*Daphne!*" Ellen said in horror. "You promised!"

"No, no. You're misunderstanding. I said nothing about Tad. When Dean was having his jealous tantrum last night, I saw my father looking at him very steadily, but saying nothing. It was not because of Dean's jealous rage. It was because he seemed very interested that

Dean had seen you sneak someone into your apartment. I don't know...call it intuition. It's just the way my father stood. Alert, like a hunting dog scenting something. There was a look in his eyes that made me think he wanted to talk about that with Dean."

"And did he?" Duchamps asked.

"I did not see it happen. I'd left by then. When I saw my father, we talked a bit. Family business. He has no confidence in Dean, and he offered me a seat on the board..."

"Buying you off?" Ellen suggested.

Daphne shook her head. "We hadn't come to the matter of Dean's little fit. My father genuinely believes when he's gone, the bank will no longer be a family business. He believes Dean will sell out, and he feels if I'm on the board, that won't happen. Then I asked why Dean had made such a big thing about your taking a man home. I suggested that as you were from the kind of Southern family who would not entertain a black man, Dean must have been mistaken..."

"Well thanks!" Ellen cut in pointedly.

"Sorry. But I thought he'd expect that from me, and not feel there was anything else behind it; and he did rake it at face value. But when I was leaving, he said something strange to me, when I was at the door. He said I should forget Dean's outburst. When I asked what he meant by that, all he said was that there was nothing there for me. Meaning, don't play the reporter."

Ellen glanced at Duchamps, before saying to Daphne, "And then?"

"I left. On the way, I looked in on Dean. I asked him if Dad had spoken to him about what he'd seen. He answered yes. No hesitation. Said he couldn't understand why Dad was so interested. He even asked if the person Dean saw looked military."

"Shit!" Duchamps said. "You didn't say anything to Dean about..."

"Of course not! I just played the weirdo sister. He likes that. Makes him feel superior. I thought you two should know about this."

Duchamps nodded. "Thanks. It gives us some warning. Warnings can give you a small step ahead. If your father's in this as well..." He paused. "He can't be old enough to have been in that war."

"My grandfather was. Dad was in Vietnam."

"So handed down—whatever it is—to the son?"

"Why not? If Dad's really involved, that could have been the route in his case." A reflective look came into Daphne's eyes. "He's a big disappointment to me. He wasn't always like that. I used to admire him. When he was younger, he was a kind of hippy-rocker..."

"Come *on*," Duchamps said. "Your Mr. Banker dad?"

She nodded. "It's true. He's got all sorts of stuff in his den. Among his records, is a favorite, Country Joe..."

"You've got to be kidding me."

Daphne shook her head. "All true. He's got a picture right above his desk, from his days in Vietnam. There are six guys in it. Two officers, four non-coms. '*The Asskickers*', they called themselves. Dad, and the guy he once told me was like a brother to him, were the officers—lieutenants. Each led his own team, and they operated together. They were very successful, and they never got their men killed. Some wounded, but none ever died. Then the lieutenant my father called his brother, got killed...saving my dad. The thing that shocked me most when he behaved the way he did with Wiley, was that this guy, this lieutenant who died to save his ass, was black. I really believed *he*, of all people, would have understood about Wiley. Now this."

Duchamps glanced at Ellen, then intoned to no one in particular. "My fellow Americans, you're good enough to die, but keep your dark hands away from our daughters. What happened with your father," he went on to Daphne, "is not so strange. In war, people become buddies with other people they never would have had as friends back home. Sometimes, the decent guys remain buddies for life. Others go back to the way it was, as soon as they get back home. Maybe that's what happened with your father. He went back to being the guy who inherited the family bank. He could still have inherited the bank and kept his humanity. Perhaps he's just not the kind."

"I find it hard to believe. He was very different, especially after Vietnam, my mother once told me. The death of his friend in that way, really hit him."

"Did he ever go see the guy's family?" Ellen asked.

"Not that I know of."

"There you go," Duchamps said. "And in all those years since

Vietnam. Yep. He really cared for his 'brother' He doesn't know you've seen Ellen, does he?"

"No!" she replied, giving him a look that said how could he ask.

"Just finding out where we stand," Duchamps said, making a pacifying motion with a hand.

Daphne glanced at her watch. "This time, I must catch that plane." She stood up.

Duchamps rose to his feet.

"I'll take you out through the back," Ellen said. "Just in case. You never know."

Daphne nodded. "Sure." She looked at Duchamps. "I can still help, you know."

"How?"

"I can at least find out if my father's involved."

"You're in LA. He's here in New York."

"I'll find a way. There's a branch of the bank in LA. He visits it regularly. The magazine has an account there."

"Nothing like keeping it in the family. He gave you a warning."

"Yes," she said. "He did." She leaned forward to give him another of her quick kisses, while Ellen gave the ceiling a world-weary glance. "Look after yourself."

"You too."

"I will. Okay, Ellen. Show me the way."

"Don't tempt me," Ellen mouthed at Daphne's back. She shot Duchamps another of those glances that could have meant anything, as they went out.

"Lucky for you she's really going back to LA this time," Ellen said as soon as she returned.

"What do you mean?"

"Nothing. And are we going travelling?" she went on before Duchamps could respond.

He gave her a tolerant smile. "We've got the plane. All we need to do is warn Mary, and I go to my apartment to get my passport."

"How are you going to do that, with those people watching your place?"

"I'll go in openly. Let them see me. I'll meet you here. They don't know we're together. My car's still at the airport. But as they saw me in town yesterday, they'll not expect me to leave the country, and definitely not by private jet. I'll come out again, but they won't see me leave. I'm taking nothing but my passport, and the credit cards I've got with me."

"Don't use them unless it's a real emergency. We'll use mine."

"Hey..."

"The senator's paying, remember? Using yours will make it easier for them to track you by the withdrawals. They're watching you. Not me."

"What about the plane? Mary's got to file flight plans, and give passenger details. Once they place us together, they'll know the senator's bankrolling us and more to the point, they'll know why."

"Okay...so they'll go for him."

"But we'll be long gone. I think the senator's already thought this through. They won't know about the diaries. Killing him won't save their asses."

Ellen gave him a steady look. "But killing us could."

"Perhaps the senator's using us to flush some heavyweight people out into the open, even using his own granddaughter as bait."

"Why would he turn on his old pals?"

"As I said...maybe his conscience is finally troubling him. He's had a nice, long life; longer than my grandpa's; longer than the people he killed along the way. We're being bankrolled by a monster."

"We need the monster When do you think we should leave?"

"As soon a possible. We don't travel with the diaries. They'll really be safe here?"

She nodded. "Of course. No one gets into this strong-room without me. If I'm not here, I'm not here. People must wait till I get back."

Duchamps had a thoughtful look in his eyes. "Got an idea. I've said that the diaries might not give us everything we need; but this place, your archives, could also have some answers. A lot of people from the war years must have left some interesting documents with you."

"They have. Many who escaped from Europe at the time have

done so—"

"Ah!"

"Not 'ah'. The primary function of this place is to safeguard *private* documents, including photographs. This means, *they* own the rights to those documents. No one gets to look at them without their permission."

"No one?"

"*No* one. That includes me, and my other colleagues. This isn't a public library. But, we do have a public department, with open access. These are documents in the public domain. And before you say 'ah' again, I don't think anything of use to you would be in those."

"Maybe. But even little items that seem uninteresting, could give away something. An article in a local paper..."

"Which, as we agreed before, would not have been allowed."

"Sometimes, things escape."

"True. But we might have a better chance in Europe, of finding stuff like that. Our public department does have some restricted stuff. What this means is that we give access only to genuine researchers, mainly scientists of different disciplines, who have to sign for the access. They can't take anything away, or copy them. We also have the art department—private and public. Some stored works of art belong to the Archives. Some of those have restricted access. Others are open. We've got a wide selection—from paintings to drawings, even to scribbles from concentration camp survivors, to soldiers from all sides. Many people have donated those."

"Plenty to look at then. Those wartime scribbles especially. As for your confidential department, the *staff*—which means *you*—can have access. Right?"

"Right. I can pick up a box, and bring it here to look through."

"Photos in these too?"

She nodded. "Yes."

"Do you have to sign these boxes out?"

"Sure. It's standard procedure."

"And anyone looking there would see your signature."

She nodded again, dark eyes looking at him steadily. "I don't think we should leave tracks like that if we can help it."

"You're right. Perhaps we really should head off to Europe first, while they still expect me to be hitting brick walls on this side of the ocean."

"And head back here, when they think we're in Europe."

"If we're still alive."

"So..." Ellen said, "...when do we leave? We can do so whenever you want. My colleagues can cover the other stuff that does not need use of my office, or this strong-room."

"You've got it all figured."

"As you've just said, the senator has. Remember he first arranged for me to be in this job. He's been programming my life for years. Now, he's programming yours too."

"He's been programming lives for longer than you or I have been alive; and terminating them, when he felt like it."

Cambridge Boys squadron. Normandy, Occupied France. July, 1941. 1430 local.

The Ju-52 landed, and taxied to its designated spot on the flightline. To avoid possible interception, it had taken a customary route that was well inland. In the event, the flight had been without incident.

A car had come for Schelberg who stood by when he had climbed out, waiting for Hagen to collect his personal belongings. He had offered to take the pilot to squadron headquarters.

"Help him," Schelberg ordered the driver as Hagen appeared with his kit.

"Yes, sir." The driver hurried forward to take the holdall and stow it.

Schelberg and Hagen got into the back, and the car set off for the squadron buildings.

"Your new home," Schelberg said as the car drew to a halt. He climbed out, followed by Hagen, who looked about him with great interest.

"This is almost like being on holiday," Hagen remarked softly. "So quiet after the Eastern Front."

"Don't be fooled," a voice said behind them. "You're very close to the *Tommis* here. They'll be much harder to take down than the

Russians."

They turned to see a faintly amused Dasinger staring back at them.

"You must be *Lieutenant* Hagen," Dasinger said to the pilot who snapped to attention and saluted.

"Yes, sir!"

Dasinger returned the salute with a casual response, and extended his hand.

"Welcome," Dasinger said, as they shook hands. "I'm Dasinger, deputy commander. We've been expecting you. Impressive record. You might find the kills a little harder to get out here. We don't go looking for trouble. We let it come to us. Our orders are to defend..." Dasinger paused deliberately. "...at all costs." He glanced at Schelberg. "Is that not so, *Herr* Schelberg?"

"It is indeed."

"Thank you for bringing the *Lieutenant* over."

"A pleasure. We discovered ourselves to have been unexpected travelling companions."

"The CO—Major Stroeme—is up with Fritzi," Dasinger went on to Hagen. "Fritzi's our youngest, and keen. Perhaps a little too keen to get killed. The major's teaching him a few lessons that might prolong his life, while enabling him to do some of his own killing before that happens. He'll take you up too for a trial, despite your own kills." Dasinger smiled. "Don't take it personally. He does that to everyone: even me."

"Yes, sir."

"Did you say 'Fritzi'?," Schelberg said to Dasinger.

Dasinger looked at him. "You *know* him, *Herr* Schelberg?"

"Not personally. No. I met his brother, Johann, recently. That is, if he *is* Jürgen Fritz. I mistook *Lieutenant* Hagen for him.

"Yes," Dasinger said. "He is Jürgen Fritz."

"Then tell him his brother sends his regards, and expects many kills from him."

"I'll tell him." Then Dasinger turned, looking west. "Ah. Here they come. Might as well stay for the show, *Herr* Schelberg."

"Where? I can't see anything."

"I can," Hagen said, following Dasinger's gaze.

It was some moments before Schelberg spotted the fast-moving, distant specks. "Ah, yes. I can see them now. Eyes of eagles, you two. No wonder I am not a pilot, eh?"

Any further comment would have been drowned by the uneven beat of the powerful, characteristic high-pitched scream of the Daimler-Benz inverted V-12 engines, the searing whistle of their superchargers an integral part of the sound. The two 109s came low, racing just above the runway to pull up in the break, banking steeply, curving tightly to position themselves neatly for the landing, throttling back, speed dropping rapidly as the automatic leading-edge slats deployed. Then flaps and the narrow-track landing gear were lowered. That landing gear arrangement was a nightmare for novice pilots. Landing and take-off accidents sometimes took a heavy toll of pilots and aircraft. Even the Cambridge Boys had suffered at least two such.

But Stroeme and Fritzi landed very smoothly.

Schelberg had cast surreptitious glances at Hagen during this display. The new pilot's eyes had been riveted upon the aircraft, head turning to follow their maneuver's. Schelberg noticed a shine in Hagen eyes, and realized the pilot was looking at the aircraft with something akin to love.

And this puzzled Schelberg. If not the flying, what was Hagen afraid of?

Noting the look in Hagen's eyes, Dasinger said, "You'll be up there soon enough."

"They are beautiful!" Hagen said. "Where are the others?"

"Dispersed about the airfield, under cover. No need to leave them out like sitting ducks in case the *Tommis* come looking. We seldom have them neatly lined up, as if for inspection. The active aircraft always have their pilots next to them."

"Impressive," Schelberg said.

"What, *Herr* Schelberg?" Dasinger asked. "The approach? Or the way we disperse the aircraft?"

"Both." Schelberg looked at Hagen. "I can see it will not take you long to settle in, Lieutenant Hagen. Good hunting."

"Thank you, sir." Hagen saluted.

Schelberg gave a brief nod in response, and looked at Dasinger. "See you around, Captain."

Dasinger waved a hand at his high-peaked cap. "*Herr* Schelberg."

Schelberg again nodded, and went back to his car.

Dasinger and Hagen watched silently as it drove away. Then Hagen asked, "What's the Gestapo doing here?"

"You know the Gestapo," Dasinger replied neutrally. "They're everywhere. Now let's introduce you to the boss. I've got the *Kübelwagen* just over there. Bring your kit."

Dasinger halted the vehicle close to the dispersal location of the two aircraft, which were now taxiing towards them.

As he looked about him, Hagen was now able to see where the other aircraft were parked, beneath their camouflaged netting. He then turned his attention to the taxiing aircraft as he and Dasinger got out of the *Kübelwagen*. He studied them with anticipation.

The aircraft turned broadside-on a safe distance away, showing their left flanks, and came to an almost choreographed halt. Engines were cut in unison. Immediately, the dispersal crews swarmed about them, as the canopies were slid back and the pilots, yellow lifejackets over their uniforms, began to climb out.

Hagen noted the big gothic double-S on beneath the cockpit of the lead aircraft. He watched as Stroeme got down jauntily. Then he saw the youthful Fritz come round the tail of the lead aircraft. He drew himself to attention as the two men approached, Fritz slightly behind.

Hagen saluted smartly as Stroeme stopped before him, searching eyes appearing to smile a welcome.

"*Lieutenant* Hagen, sir! Reporting."

Stroeme grabbed the saluting hand, and shook it warmly. "Welcome to our little piece of Normandy. A bit quieter than where you've been."

"Yes, sir!"

"This young reprobate staring at your Iron Cross is Fritzi. You will be paired with him. You have the lead. Are you fine with that? I've already warned him. I think he's happy with it."

Hagen looked at Fritzi, who was grinning hugely.

"Yes, sir." Hagen extended a hand to Fritz, who shook it with enthusiasm. "Michael."

"Jürgen," Fritz introduced himself, "but everyone calls me Fritzi."
"Alright, Fritzi."
"Message from your brother, Fritzi," Dasinger said.
"Johann?" Fritzi said in surprise, looking at the captain. "He's *here?* He's supposed to be in Rendsburg. He's Gestapo, you know."
"I see. Well no. He's not here. The message was relayed. He sends his regards, and expects you to do some good hunting."
Another huge grin pasted itself upon Fritz's face, and he gave Hagen's Iron Cross a second look. "I aim to do so! Who brought the message, sir?"
"None other than *Standartenführer* Schelberg himself," Dasinger replied with a straight face.
Fritz was suitably impressed. "I've never met him, although I have heard he's here. He does me a great honor to bring me a family message."
"I'm sure he does," Dasinger glanced at Stroeme, who remained suitably expressionless.
"Now that's all over," Stroeme began, "Michael, Hans Dasinger will take you to our quarters. Rather more opulent perhaps than what you've been used to on the Eastern Front. Get settled in, and be ready to fly at 1630. You'll be going up with me."
"Yes, sir."
"Your allocated aircraft will be waiting. Your kills have already been put on the tail."
"Thank you, sir."
"Alright. Fritzi and I are walking. I'll see you in my office before we fly. When we land, I'll take you to meet the Commandant."
"Yes, sir."
"And Michael..."
"Sir?"
"Not so many sirs out here. I'm certain you understand when protocol is necessary."
"Yes, s..." Hagen smiled. "Alright."
Stroeme gave Hagen a pat on the shoulder. "Good to have you with us." He looked at Fritz. "Come on. Let's discuss that mistake you made up there."
As Stroeme and Fritz walked on, Hagen said to Dasinger, "He's

very casual."

"Don't let that fool you. Make a mistake in the air, and you'll discover just how uncasual he can be. It does not bear thinking about. Get in."

RAF Shawbridge. July, 1941. About the same moment in time.

Hamilton, with Murchison standing by, was giving his pilots a very special briefing.

"Alright, everyone. Settle down. I have some news to concentrate your minds. It would seem that Jerry has decided to confuse us. *All* of Major Stroeme's squadron aircraft are now sporting the blue tail."

A collective groan went up.

"Well might you groan, but there it is. However, all is not lost. The major's aircraft can still be identified. It carries a damned big, gothic double-S beneath the left cockpit rim. If you have the time in a melee—debatable—try and spot that double-S before popping off at the target. While he will try to avoid attacking you, do not take this for granted. Remember where he will be. His own pilots might wonder at this uncharacteristic reluctance to engage, which might not be a good thing for him."

"So he really *will* be *shooting* at us?" someone asked.

"He'll try to miss."

"That's a big help," Pew said.

"Thank you, Pew," Hamilton said with a stern look in Pew's direction.

"Sir."

The others smirked at Pew.

"We've got some other news," Hamilton went on, "from other sources. There has been a new addition to the major's squadron—an ace from the recently opened Eastern Front. He supposedly scored nine victories within two days, in just two sorties." Hamilton paused, waiting for the inevitable groans.

Silence greeted him.

"What? No groans?"

"It's called shock, sir," Pew offered. "But I'm certain Tad, or Jamie, will sort him out in rapid order."

"What about you?"

"Me, sir?"

"You, sir."

"As I'm a gentleman, I think I'll give them first shot. Stand back to watch the fun, as it were."

Subdued titters followed this.

"Thank you, gentlemen. To continue—just as we are able to find out about Jerry's activities, so will he keep trying to find out about us; who we are, and what is our purpose. As yet, he has no idea; but he *will* keep trying. So remember, *always*, that walls do have some very interested ears. And that sweet young lady you may meet at the pub, may well be interested in more than your shiny wings."

"I hope so!" someone quipped.

Hamilton gave a tight smile. "Don't let your sap run away with you. That's it, gentlemen. Thank you. Messrs. Duchamps, Fernando, and Farley-Wyatt. A moment, please."

The other pilots looked curiously at the three as they filed out, but no one said anything.

Hamilton waited until the other pilots had gone, before saying, "Gather around."

They went forward to stand in a gaggle with Hamilton and Murchison. "Tomorrow at 0400 hours," Hamilton continued, "you three will be in your Hurricanes, ready for take-off. Tad will lead. You will be escorting me, in our brand new PR Mosquito. This type of aircraft, like the other variants of Mosquito you will see arriving on squadron strength during this summer, is not yet officially operational. We are the only unit to make operational use of the type so far, and this will not be officially acknowledged. The mission is a reconnaissance of the highest importance. My navigator will be a civilian with Mosquito experience. His identity does not concern you. The films will not be developed here when we land. He will take them back with him.

"I cannot sufficiently impress upon you the need to ensure that we are not shot down. Neither he, nor the aircraft, can be allowed to fall into enemy hands. The Mosquito is designed to be well nigh impossible to intercept; but let us not ignore the vagaries of chance. Jerry has not yet seen anything like the Mosquito. When he does get to know of it, it will be his nightmare. Now, gentlemen, are you up to it?"

"Yes, sir," they replied together.

"Good show."

"Can you tell us where we're going, sir?" Pew asked.

"Full briefing at 0310 hours, Mr. Farley-Wyatt."

"Sir."

"And that's it, gentlemen. No late-night, NAAFI carousing. See you at briefing."

Showing no emotion, Hamilton and Murchison watched them leave.

Then Hamilton said, "Are they up to it?"

"I'd bet my shirt on it."

"Well let's hope Jerry does not collect one highly special aircraft, one highly important civilian...and me."

"You wouldn't have selected them, if you did not believe they could do it."

"On your recommendation."

"Which I would not have done, if I did not believe they could."

Hamilton removed his cap, passed a hand through his hair, and put the cap back on. "About that ace from the Eastern Front—Hagen. Your sources given you any more on him?"

"He's a lieutenant. Could be psychologically damaged."

"How so?"

"Seems he had a brother out there with him. Younger. Fresh kid. The brother got shot down almost as soon as he entered combat, not by some Russian hotshot pilot, but by German flak."

"Uh-oh."

"The cockpit was jammed by the hit. The kid went down in flames. Hagen heard him screaming all the way down."

"Dear God. I know he was the enemy, but even so. Hell of a fate."

"You and I and every other pilot knows the pilot's worst nightmare is being trapped alive, in a flaming cockpit."

"And for Hagen, that nightmare has an extra, vivid quality because of what happened."

"Exactly. It is believed that's why he was rotated west after Hitler himself decorated him for those kills. My sources' opinion is that he'll have a real, sick fear of fire."

"Could be of use to us. A few incendiaries his way..."

"Could spook him. We have plenty of incendiary ammo."

"Then let's not be sparing with it. Let us ensure Lieutenant Hagen joins his brother as soon as possible."

Murchison gave Hamilton a mildly surprised look.

Hamilton knew why. "You are surprised by my apparent cold-heartedness. Make no mistake, I will hunt down Jerry to the last of his days, or mine. But that does not prevent me from having sympathy for a fellow pilot who dies like that, even if I were responsible for sending him that way. It changes nothing about what I feel for him as an enemy, in combat. I am here to remove him from the arena. Permanently."

"You'll get no argument from me," Murchison said.

Cambridge Boys squadron. Normandy, Occupied France. July, 1941. 1615 local.

Hagen was sitting in Stroeme's office, life jacket and helmet on his lap.

"Sorry about your brother," Stroeme was saying. "Terrible accident."

Hagen nodded. "I wanted to shoot up that flak battery. Incompetent fools."

"I don't blame you. A halftrack crew did the same to me. If I'd been in my 109 and it was still able to fly, who knows what might have happened."

"I heard about that."

"From Schelberg?"

Hagen gave another brief nod. "He sang your praises."

"He's just glad to have survived," Stroeme said with a reminiscent smile. He gave Hagen a pat on the shoulder as he got to his feet. "Come on. Let's see what you can do."

They took off on time, and in tight formation.

"I'll not give you warning," Stroeme reminded Hagen as they climbed away.

Still in the climb, Stroeme broke away suddenly. Hagen did not waste time looking to see where Stroeme had disappeared to. He reacted immediately, broke in the opposite direction, and headed earthwards, rolled in the dive, levelling out almost skimming the ground, before leaping skywards again.

"Where am I?" he heard.

Hagen flicked left, continued the roll through to the right, pulling into a tight turn as he did so, almost pivoting on his tail.

"Where am I?" he heard again.

Scheisse! he thought.

He pushed the stick briefly forward. Unlike the Merlin-engined Spitfires and Hurricanes, the fuel-injected engine of the 109 did not temporarily starve itself of fuel during such a maneuver, leading to a brief, and sometimes fatal cut-out, if an enemy were within gun range. The smart pilots of those aircraft utilized the aesthetically pleasing maneuver of flipping onto their backs into the dive, to maintain positive forces on the fuel system.

Directly after the push-down, Hagen had rolled 180, and pulled fluidly back.

The 109, engine screaming hungrily, had nimbly reversed its direction.

"Good!" he heard. "You evaded well, but that would not have given you a chance to shoot. Try again."

Stroeme forced Hagen to work harder than the Iron Cross ace ever thought was possible. Never once did he acquire a gun solution. On the single occasion that he'd thought he was getting close, Stroeme's aircraft had vanished even before it had reached the outer edge of the gunsight.

At last, Stroeme called a halt.

"That was good work," Hagen heard.

"*Good?*" Hagen was disgusted with himself. "I never got close!"

"You made me work hard. That says plenty to me."

They landed, and Hagen taxied to his dispersal point, next to Fritzi's aircraft, while Stroeme taxied on to the squadron commander's position. They met up for the walk back.

"The important thing to remember," Stroeme said, "is that this is not the Eastern Front. There are no easy pickings. The *Tommi* pilots are highly motivated, well trained, are ferocious, and they fly excellent aircraft. In short, they are everything your Eastern Front opponents at the time, were not...except perhaps for the motivation in some cases. The Spitfire is a magnificent aircraft, agile, and deadly. Remember that famous—or infamous, depending on your point of view—comment to the *Reichsmarschall* during *Adlertag*, about wanting a squadron of Spitfires.

"The Hurricane, which does not have the glamour, is not to be underestimated. It has sent too many of our comrades to an early grave; in greater numbers than the Spitfire. It is a superb gun platform, can take more punishment than a Spitfire, and at low level, in the hands of a good pilot, can hang on to your tail with the tenacity of a bull terrier. Assume they are all good pilots; because if you're unlucky enough to have one on your tail and you mistakenly believe he is not a match for you, it may be the last mistake you ever make."

Stroeme glanced at Hagen as he said this. "I am not belittling your Iron Cross, Michael. I am giving you the benefit of my own experience. I once made the mistake of underestimating a Hurricane pilot. The only reason I am still here to give you this piece of advice, is because he ran out of ammunition."

Hagen stared at him. "He was *better?*"

"Very much so. I had just been promoted to captain. It was very nearly the shortest promotion, if not on record, then very close to being so. At one point, he flew *between* two trees, to cut into my circle. I, on the other hand, had gained some height to clear the trees. This widened my own circle, and he was able to cut through it, rising to chew off my tail. But his ammunition had gone. Another lesson— you don't carry unlimited ammunition, or fuel. Despite the fact that this unknown person had intended to kill me, I had to admire his tenacity, and skill. We fly the *hundert-neun Friedrich*, a great aircraft. But it still has a higher wing loading than the Hurricane, which maneuvers excellently at low levels. It also has a very high speed in the dive. Our controls stiffen at speed. Remember all these things."

"When you knew his guns were dead, couldn't you have turned the tables on him?"

Stroeme shook his head. "I was already very low on fuel. He had tied me up, keeping me from escaping. All the time, my fuel was going. He knew that sooner or later, I would have to leave the aircraft if that went on for much longer. It would be a 'kill' for him. He was out of ammunition, and I was running out of fuel. We decided to go our separate ways."

Hagen couldn't know that Stroeme was talking about Hamilton who at that time, could not have known that Stroeme was a member of a highly secret anti-Hitler group within the armed forces, already in tentative contact with the Allies. It was only when Raven Squadron was at the beginning of the planning stage, that he and the initially intensely suspicious Hamilton had met; and it was during a guarded conversation when Stroeme had mentioned the tree-flying episode, that both men suddenly realized that they had tried to kill each other that day.

Stroeme glanced at Hagen. *If only you knew*, he thought.

"Perhaps you'll meet him again up there, one day."

"Who knows?" Stroeme said. "Our combat area," he continued, "is within a radius of 50 kilometers from here. We receive warning of any intruder approaching the edge of this circle from another 50 kilometers beyond that. He is tracked and if he does not alter course, we go on the alert. Although we sometimes send a patrol aloft, we do not keep regular standing patrols to conserve fuel, and to save wear and tear on the aircraft."

"So you keep aircraft at readiness, for quick take-off. *Alarmstart*."

"Exactly. To use a *Tommi* term, we scramble. As an element leader, you have the additional responsibility to discipline your wingman. You've got Fritzi at the moment. One of his good, as well as his bad points, is his eagerness. This can sometimes get the better of him. We *never* go beyond our designated area. Our primary function, as you now know, is to *defend* this place, not to go hunting. Other units will take care of that. When you're in the lead, you are to ensure that your wingman, whoever he happens to be—and irrespective of rank—*never* strays, no matter what the provocation. An apparent easy kill, could be a trap. I shall hold you personally responsible for the safety of your wingman, and the integrity of your intercept. I don't want dead wingmen."

Hagen received this with a sober, "Yes, sir."

"Good."

* * *

RAF Shawbridge flightline. Pre-dawn. July, 1941. 0330 local.
Murchison took the briefing. There were just the four of them in the room. The three young pilots looked at him expectantly.

Murchison noted that Pews's expression had an extra edge to it.

"Something straining your mind, Mr. Farley-Wyatt?" he asked.

Duchamps and Fernando glanced at Pew with amused smiles.

"Nicknames, sir," Pew replied, an almost beatific look upon his face.

Murchison's eyebrows seemed to do a startled dance. *"Nicknames?"*

Pew was unabashed. "Well, sir, everyone calls me Pew. And Jamie here's got 'Choo-Choo', because there's a song about a train with his name in it..."

"My name's only part of it," Fernando whispered to Pew. "There's a 'San' in the song, before Fernando."

Murchison shot a glance at Fernando, who shut up quickly.

"'Choo-Choo'." Murchison said to Pew.

"Yes, sir. And when he starts killing a few Jerry trains, the name will be apt. Even Major Stroeme has one. You call him 'Cagey', from his initials K-G for Karl-Gustav."

"Is this going somewhere, Mr. Farley-Wyatt?"

"Well, sir. Tad hasn't got one."

"And you've got an idea."

"I have indeed. First, I thought of Icarus..."

"Who crashed and burned. Not good."

"No, sir. But Tad's partially descended from a pirate."

"So you thought, why not 'Jolly Roger'," Murchison said with a straight face.

Pew was pleasantly surprised. "Yes, sir!"

Murchison looked at Duchamps. "Mr. Duchamps?"

Duchamps looked pained.

"I'll make a suggestion," Murchison said, surprising them all. "After your exploits with those flak guns, Mr. Duchamps, I suggest 'Guns'. Guns Duchamps has a ring to it. And Mr. Farley-Wyatt, as no self-respecting Louisiana pirate would get very far without a well-gunned ship, the skull and crossbones, on the tail of Mr. Duchamps'

Hurricane should do it. Anyone against?"

Neither Pew, nor Fernando were.

"There you go, Mr. Duchamps," Murchison said, "You are now Guns Duchamps. Fun over, gentlemen. Briefing. The wing commander is seeing to his Mosquito, and making sure his civilian navigator's requirements are met. He will join us later, to close this briefing."

Murchison went over to a large map of Normandy. An area was encircled in bright red. Next to that was another, this time of a south-eastern chunk of England from Shawbridge to the Isle of Wight, and Normandy. On this map, a thick blue line dog-legged inland from Shawbridge to a point on the southeast coast, where it crossed the Channel to France, with a slightly different return route.

"In the center of that circle, is a high-value target. You will not be attacking it. The Mosquito is a PR aircraft, so there will also be no attack by the wing commander. The area within that circle, is the defense responsibility of Cagey Stroeme's outfit. You are *not* to enter that circle under *any* circumstances. You can engage any enemy aircraft outside that circle. Major Stroeme's boys are under strict orders from Berlin, *never* to go beyond that boundary. Their primary function is to defend the area within it. Anything outside is the responsibility of other air units in Normandy. So unless you are very bad at navigation, there is no chance that you will have a bust-up with his boys."

"How big is that radius, sir?" Tad asked.

"50 kilometers. That's about 30 miles and a bit. You'll be going in low, to avoid detection. If you are spotted, they will be warned when you are 30 miles from the edge of that circle. Cagey will have some of his boys scrambled, but they will not cross that line. See that you do the same.

"You will approach the enemy coast in tight formation with the Mosquito. The low level will give you low visibility against the backdrop of the Channel at that time of day. Your route has been chosen to keep you clear of enemy sea patrols. So hopefully, none will see you pass. Other squadrons will be keeping Jerry's attention diverted. As will operations by small groups of commandos carrying out raiding forays into enemy territory. These commandos will form the basis of an as yet unnamed group, and will be of great distraction benefit to us in the future. They are part of the Special Operations Executive and as such, are closer to us than you might at first think. Today's raids will be of sufficient disruption to keep Jerry even further occupied. They will be using fast motor torpedo boats, so if you spot one, *don't* mistake it for a Jerry E-boat, and let rip.

"Before reaching the circle, your formation will veer north, then split. The Mosquito will carry on alone. Its high speed at low level will make it virtually impossible to catch by the enemy. It will go inland, then turn to enter the circle at a particular point from the east, heading generally westwards again. You need not concern yourselves about that. It will do what it is supposed to, then rendezvous with you at this point."

Murchison jabbed at a name on the map, near Fécamp.

"The Mosquito will rendezvous at speed...here—Eletot. This is a little over 3 kilometers north of Fécamp, and right on the coast. Be ready. Or it will leave you in its wake. It will throttle back once over water. When it is too late for any neighboring fighters to scramble, hoping to intercept, it will gain altitude. You will follow, and keep an eye out for enemy aircraft returning from our side of the Channel. If you do encounter the enemy, the Mosquito will head for the heavens and keep going. The enemy will be short of fuel and won't engage for long. Make him regret being there. Mr. Duchamps, as escort leader, it is your responsibility to ensure all goes well. I want to see all four aircraft safely back."

"Yes, sir."

"Now...questions?"

"And if all does not go swimmingly, sir?" Pew asked.

"You've got a Hurricane with great big teeth, Pew. Take a bite of something."

Duchamps and Fernando shook their heads slowly, and chuckled at Pew.

"That's it, gentlemen," Murchison said. "You've already got the weather for this mission. Check your maps for accuracy and timings. The wing commander will be here in..." He glanced at his watch. "...five minutes."

The wing commander was.

Duchamps, Fernando, and Pew began to rise smartly to their feet.

"At ease, gentlemen," Hamilton told them, waving them back down. "This won't take long. Wing Commander Murchison has already briefed you, so all I've got to say is good luck, and see you all back safely." He raised his left wrist to check his watch. "Synchronize watches. The time is 0335...*now*."

They set their watches to his time.

So far, it was going well. The four, black aircraft were so low over the water, they seemed to be skimming it. They were a full 60 feet lower than the high ground at the top of the 100-foot Fécamp cliffs. There was no radio chatter. Strict radio silence—which would only be broken for warnings, or combat—was in force.

They had landed briefly at a coastal airfield to take on fuel and had taken off again, with barely a word to the airfield personnel; discreet personnel who were themselves well versed in the swift, and quiet art of servicing aircraft passing through, on their way to clandestine missions.

Despite the fact that the Mosquito had nearly more than four times the range of the Hurricanes, it had also landed at the fuel-stop airfield, but had not taken on fuel. Planning for the mission had deliberately allowed for the stop, to avoid the need for the Hurricanes to carry drop tanks. The primary requirements were combat endurance coupled with speed, and the fuel stop removed the need for the drag-inducing external tanks.

They were flying in trail formation, seemingly glued to the Mosquito, and giving the appearance of being the long tail of the twin-engined aircraft. Like some primeval, winged predator, the black formation hurtled just above the surface of the water. They were now approaching the outer boundary before the imaginary red circle that marked Stroeme's defense area, and began their turn to port, to avoid straying into it.

They had passed no E-boats along the way and as yet, no one seemed to have detected them.

CHAPTER TWELVE

Cambridge Boys squadron. Normandy, Occupied France. July, 1941. 0610 local.

Stroeme was just about to leave his quarters to go to the dining room for breakfast in the commandeered mansion that served as the officers' Mess, when the phone rang.

He grabbed at it. "Stroeme."

It was Dasinger. "We've got an intruder alarm."

"How far? And how many?"

"Outside our area at 20 kilometers. Numbers are uncertain. At the moment, we've been advised of two. Moving fast."

"Approaching?"

"No. Turning north."

"Keep an eye on this. Hagen and Fritz are on alert, aren't they?"

"Yes," Dasinger confirmed.

"Send them up."

"Already done. Stolzer and Krumm are sitting in their aircraft, just in case."

"Good. Send Stolzer and Krumm aloft. They are to patrol the eastern sector, north and south. Hagen and Fritz the western sector, north and south."

"Will do."

"Put two more pairs on standby, ready for scramble. All serviceable aircraft are to be made ready, including yours, and mine."

"You expect them to be headed our way?"

"A precaution. If everyone's alert, the reaction time will be shorter. I'm about to grab breakfast. Get back to me the moment it looks as if we are the likely point of interest. I'll come to the squadron as soon as I'm done, if the situation does not escalate."

"Will do." Dasinger repeated.

"And warn Hagen to keep an eye on Fritz. We don't want our eager eagle to stray."

"He's been duly warned."

"Thank you, Hans. I won't be long."

The "eager eagle" was chomping at the bit.

"Black One," Fritz called. "Where are they?"

"Don't be in too much of a hurry," Hagen warned.

They were at medium altitude, cruising, looking for prey.

"Ach," Fritz commented dismissively. "A *Tommi?* I want to get a few for the *Führer*."

"Black Two," Hagen began in a firm voice, knowing what Fritz might be crazy enough to do. "You do *not* take *any* action without my orders. Got it?"

"But..."

"*Got it?*"

"Got it," Fritz acknowledged with palpable reluctance.

I'm going to have trouble with this one, Hagen thought. *Dasinger was right. He wants to die young.*

Far below, the Mosquito was heading eastwards at almost treetop height, and at high speed.

Duchamps meanwhile, was leading his formation, now spread out, slightly out to sea, still at low level. There was no fire coming from any of the coastal batteries.

They must be asleep, he thought.

The mission called for him to keep out to sea, until time approached for the rendezvous with the returning Mosquito. It would not take long. Fifteen minutes at most.

"A lot can happen in fifteen minutes," he said to himself, listening to the powerful drone of the Hurricane's Merlin XX engine. It sounded sweet, not missing a single beat.

He glanced at the water. He did not fancy a ditching, if something went wrong; and certainly, not so close to enemy territory. He scanned sea and sky, looking out for possible trouble.

Nothing. No patrol boats, no prowling aircraft.

"They must be zizzing," he murmured. "Or the war's over, and nobody's told us."

But the war was not over.

It was Fritz's eagle eyes that spotted them.

"*Tommis!*" he yelled. "*There! Over the water!*" He began to leave formation.

"*Black Two!*" Hagen shouted. "Rejoin formation at once! That's an order!" He scanned below, looking for what Fritz had supposedly seen. Then he saw them. "*Black Two!* They are out of area! Rejoin! Rejoin!*"

But Fritz had become fixated, and was diving to attack.

"*Scheisse!*" Hagen raged. "*Cambridge!*" he called back to base. "Fritz has gone crazy and is attacking out of area. Repeat. *Out of area!* I'm going to try and get the fool back before he gets into trouble. Warn other units there are *Tommis* out to sea."

"Acknowledged," he heard in confirmation.

On the ground, Dasinger picked up his phone. "It's *Lieutenant* Fritz, sir," a controller from the tower said in his ear. "He has broken formation and is attacking outside the area. *Lieutenant* Hagen has gone to try and bring him back."

"Are they *Tommi* aircraft?"

"Yes, sir, but out to sea. We are warning other fighter units."

"Thank you," he said, and hung up. "*Scheisse!*" he swore, emulating Hagen's own sense of frustration. He called Stroeme who was in his office, ready to fly if need be.

Stroeme swore as well, when he heard. "How many *Tommis?*" he asked. "Unknown at this time. Two, maybe."

"If Fritz survives and Hagen dies, I'll ground him the moment he lands, and throw him out of the squadron for good measure! The young idiot!"

"My feelings exactly."
"So it's not a raid."
"Does not look like it."
"*The idiot!*" Stroeme said again.
"That he is. He wants an Iron Cross."
"He'll get a mouthful of Channel instead!"

That was Fritz's most likely prospect.

Pew had glanced upwards, and had seen the Messerschmitt descending. "*Bandit!*" he called. "Three o'clock! Coming down!"

The three black Hurricanes went into a well-choreographed break, splitting in different directions and altitudes, now that they had been spotted.

"*Food!*" Pew shouted in glee. "I'm going to bite something!"

Duchamps had been looking for more, and saw Hagen's aircraft coming down.

"His buddy's on the way down," Duchamps called. "You two handle that eager beaver. I'm going up after his buddy. Do it quick before more join the party. Time soon for the rendezvous."

"Roger," Fernando acknowledged.

Hagen had a moment's pause when he saw the black aircraft. What were they? He wondered. No markings. He recognized the unmistakable shape of the Hurricane; and with those four protruding guns, what type? And to what kind of unit did they belong?

But there was no time for speculation. Fritz was in serious trouble, and the third Hurricane was effectively blocking his path, preventing him from going to Fritz's aid. Then it vanished. He realized what he was about to face, when a blaze of cannon fire seared past him.

The 109 rocked.

My God! Hagen thought. *Where is he? I never saw him.*

He could not see Fritz or the other two Hurricanes, having his hands full with trying to avoid being hit again. Luckily, the damage—such as it was—did not seem to affect the aircraft. And he was not wounded. He thought he could see holes in his left wing, but the aircraft continued to handle normally.

Damn you, Fritz! he raged in his mind.

Then suddenly, a thumping sound, and half his left wing disappeared. He just barely made it out of the dying aircraft, before its frantic gyrations made this impossible.

He did not see Fritz again.

"Everybody ok?" Duchamps called.

"Raven Four," Pew responded. "I shared a bite with Choo-Choo."

"Raven Three," came Fernando. "True. But the bastard was able to bail out. Hope he can't swim, the sod."

"Good work, guys. Time to head for the rendezvous."

"Saw that efficient dispatch, Guns," Pew said. "My word! You did chew into him."

"Had to do it fast. Had the feeling if I gave him the chance, he'd be all over me."

"They were blue tails. Did you see? They were not supposed to be out here."

"Yep. Saw the blue tail. They must have been at the wrong briefing."

Pew chuckled. "Perhaps you got the new ace!"

"If he was the ace, he hit the silk just in time. I hope he drowns! I might not get so lucky next time."

By now, the Mosquito, still low, was racing westwards. It crossed the imaginary red line, and into Stroeme's airspace, its current course taking it directly towards the Château Eloise and the research complex.

"Cameras set, Mr. Rourke?" Hamilton asked his civilian navigator.

"All ready to roll, Wing Commander. Three vertical, and one oblique, ready to tell us some things about what Jerry's up to down there, and other incidentals."

Rourke did not explain about the "incidentals". He spoke with a soft Irish accent; but his name was not Rourke, and he was not just "a civilian".

"We're nearly there," Hamilton warned.

"Rolling," Rourke said.

On the ground, there was consternation. Everyone had been caught napping. They saw the fleeting black shape, heard the mighty roar of Merlins at full chat, then it was gone. People poured out of buildings. Not a single anti-aircraft gun had fired.

Schelberg had not yet gone to breakfast. Both he and Forst had rushed out of the château, just in time to see the speeding shape.

"It came from the east," Forst said to Schelberg. "Perhaps one of our secret aircraft on a trial flight to France. I've never seen anything like it before. It was beautiful."

Schelberg had been looking in the direction the strange aircraft had gone. He could still see its graceful black shape in his mind's eye.

"What do you think it was?" Forst asked Schelberg.

The Gestapo man took a while before he replied. "Nemesis," he finally said in a thoughtful voice.

Forst stared at him.

But Schelberg was remembering Marina Bock's words and for the first time, began to give serious thought to his future.

In her room, Eloise had heard the approach of the tearing sound. She had leapt out of bed to rush to a window, just in time to see the black aeroplane hurtle past. It was so low, she felt that from her eyrie, she could have almost touched it.

A huge wave of elation made her quiver with excitement. Despite the fact that she had seen no distinguishing markings, she felt certain the aircraft was British.

If they already had aircraft which could do this now; which could fly so fast the gunners were totally surprised. Who knew when they would come back to free France?

She gave a sigh that was full of hope. It was a beginning.

"One day," she said, "our château will belong to us again."

It was the happiest she had felt for a long time; and it was something she would set down in her diary.

THE RAVEN CONSPIRACY – CODE NAME: ICARUS

* * *

"Here they come!" Duchamps warned. "Gawd! She's beautiful!"

The Mosquito appeared bang on time, and dropped close to the water. "Glad to see you, Raven One!" he called to Hamilton.

"Glad you're there to welcome us. Let's go home. Radio silence."

The Hurricanes moved smoothly into position, and the quartet continued westwards.

No other fighters came their way.

Stroeme and Dasinger were in the control tower.

"*Black One! Black Two!*" one of the controllers called. He'd been doing so without success, for some time. "Respond!"

The controller looked at his superiors, and shook his head slowly.

Grim-faced, Stroeme and Dasinger glanced at each other.

Somewhere, a phone rang.

"*Sir!*" the person who had picked it up shouted. Stroeme and Dasinger hurried over.

"What is it?" Stroeme asked.

Wordlessly, the man handed the phone over.

"Stroeme."

"Ah, Major. I've been trying to reach you."

"You've got me, *Herr* Schelberg. What is it? We're rather busy. Trying to find out what's happened to two of my pilots."

"Ah," Schelberg said again.

The way the Gestapo man had spoken made Stroeme say, "You *know* something about it?"

"Not that I know about it exactly...but I may have a clue."

"Which is?"

"We had an early morning visit. A beautiful, black plane. No markings. Came like the wind, without warning and low down, and was gone. Definitely not one of ours."

"Are you saying it may be responsible for my missing pilots?"

"I have no idea, but its brief presence may have something to do with it."

"*Herr* Schelberg, perhaps..."

Another phone rang. "*Sir!*"

"*Herr* Schelberg..." Stroeme began.

"I understand, Major. Perhaps later."

"Yes. Thank you." Stroeme turned to the person who had called to him as he handed the phone back. "Yes?"

"They've *found* them, sir! A *Schnellboot's* picked them up. They're alive!"

There was a cheer in the control tower. But Stroeme and Dasinger did not lose their grim expressions.

"I want those two," Stroeme said as they left the control tower, "*in* my office, the moment they get here. No matter what time it is."

"If I have to drag them in myself," Dasinger promised.

"They'll wish the *Tommis* had sent them to their Maker, or the Channel had finished the job. And Fritz is out. It's no thanks to him that Hagen is still alive."

"*Bandits!*" Pew called. "Eleven o'clock! Descending. Three!"

"I see them," came Hamilton's calm voice. "I'm for altitude. Raven Two, you're now Raven One."

"Roger," Duchamps acknowledge. "Ravens, let's go get 'em."

As the Mosquito accelerated towards the upper reaches, the three Hurricanes moved onto an intercept course, effectively preventing the enemy fighters from getting close to the climbing Mosquito.

The returning fighters—Me-109s—had no option but to turn towards the threat. "Remember they're low on fuel," Duchamps reminded his flight. "Make them waste more."

The Hurricanes split in the climb. Pew went low, Fernando went high. Duchamps held a head-on course towards the lead 109. Then at the last moment, he broke right, and went down, gaining speed as the Hurricane fell towards the sea. The 109 had put its nose down, and was curving to follow. But Duchamps was already rising with speed in hand, now going left.

The 109 was forced to make a harsh correction. It wobbled slightly.

Duchamps knew its pilot would be worrying about his fuel.

"Raven Two," he called. "Where's your bandit?"

"Your 3 o'clock," Pew replied. "Low."

"I see him. Let's swap. My bandit is at my 7 o'clock. His heart's not in it. He's wallowing a bit. Take him. He'll never expect it. I'll have your bandit."

"Roger. Swapping."

Duchamps flicked the Hurricane onto its back, and plunged after Pew's erstwhile bandit.

The 109 that had been following him, oblivious of Pew's approach, turned to follow. That was when Pew crept up behind and opened up with the Hurricane's quadruple 20mm cannon.

"Oh my Lor'!" Duchamps heard Pew exclaim. "What a bonfire!"

Duchamps thought something vivid had flashed somewhere behind him, as he drew closer to the 109 that was intent on stalking Pew.

The enemy pilot, perhaps too fixated and also worried about his own fuel, was concentrating on Pew, unaware of the falling black shape curving behind him.

Then some instinct must have made him glance behind, and he began to roll away from his intended victim. It was too late. Duchamps was close enough. He fired a two-second burst. A mixed load of twenty high explosive and solid steel rounds slammed into the same spot on the spine of the enemy aircraft. The 109 seemed to come to a halt in mid-air; then the complete tail section simply fell off. The aircraft whirled crazily towards the water. It hit with a violent splash that cascaded in a brief, rising curtain, before collapsing outwards, and upon itself. The pilot was still in the cockpit as the aircraft sank.

"Raven Three," Duchamps called. "Your bandit?"

"Gone," Fernando answered.

"Gone where?"

"Down, man! What do you think?"

Duchamps smiled. "Okay guys. Join up. Last man to breakfast is a sucker."

"You're on," Pew said.

In close formation, the three Hurricanes headed home.

"What a morning!" Pew said.

When they landed at Shawbridge, the found the Mosquito safely parked on the flightline, and Murchison waiting.

Pew jumped down from his aircraft, grinning. "What a morning!" he repeated in exhilaration as Duchamps and Fernando joined him. "My word," he went on to Duchamps. "What did you do to that poor Hun whose wing you shot off? It seemed to come apart with no further attention from you."

"I was aiming for his cockpit," Duchamps said. "He moved! So the full shot landed on his wing. I guess I hit something vital."

"I'll say you did! That wing came off as if you'd taken a saw to it."

Murchison joined them. "I can see by your faces you had an early breakfast out there. Good work, Mr. Duchamps. You took four aircraft out, and you brought four back safely. Report your adventures to the spy, then see the CO for a debrief. After that, a real breakfast in the Mess."

"What a morning!" Pew said for a third time.

"We never heard that before, Pew," Duchamps said, straight-faced, with a glance at Fernando.

Murchison watched with faint amusement as they went off to report their kills to the "spy", the unit's Intelligence Officer. Harry McNair was a pre-war Flight Lieutenant. Older than any of them, including both wing commanders. He had seen service in the Middle East., flying Hawker Hind biplanes. McNair was no longer fit for flying duties. A crash landing had damaged his right leg and while not severely, had left him with a permanent limp. Sometimes, it gave him trouble and he would whack at it with a swagger stick, to counter twitches of pain, and mild itching. It was sometimes disconcerting to hear a sudden loud thwack, while in conversation with him. The experienced barely noticed. The Raven pilots had gradually become accustomed to McNair's idiosyncrasy.

"And what have we here," he greeted the three as they entered his domain. *Whack.* "Terrors of the Jerries, eh?" *Whack, whack.* He grinned at them beneath his luxurious handlebar moustache. "Heard from the Navy. They've hauled two Jerry bodies out of the drink. Seems the third may still be in his cockpit, talking to Davy Jones. And, according to some monitored, frantic conversation, it also seems as if two more Jerries went for an enforced swim. Even got their names...Hagen, and Fritz. Imagine having the surname Fritz." McNair had a rich Scottish accent.

"Hagen!" Pew exclaimed. He turned to Duchamps, eyes wide. "You got that new ace!"

McNair looked at Duchamps with interest. "So...*you* got him, lad. Good shooting. Five Jerries on a morn, to you three. Good bag."

"Hagen is still alive," Duchamps said. "That could mean a second round, one day."

"Aye. Well let's hope you survive it, lad, if you do meet up again. Now, let's be having your tales. And no exaggerating, mind." He grinned at them once more. "Or the spy will sniff you out." *Whack, whack.* "Eh?" *Whack.* "Damned leg."

Murchison had joined Hamilton in the briefing room.

"Home are the hunters," Hamilton said as they entered. "A job well done, gentlemen."

"Thank you, sir," they said.

"And Mr. Duchamps, impressive leadership."

"I didn't do much, sir."

"On the contrary. By not doing 'much', as you put it, you did do rather a lot. Good leadership comes from not having to stand on the hair of those under your command. And to all three of you, excellent work. Five Jerries down for no loss is always excellent, in my book."

"Two of them had blue tails, sir," Pew said.

"Yes. Pity, that. But they did stray beyond their boundary. That broke the...'agreement', and made them fair game. And they did attack you. Your response was, understandably, appropriate. Perhaps we'll know further, how that situation managed to come about."

"Tad got that new ace you told us about, sir," Pew said.

"Yes," Hamilton said. "Superb shooting, Tad."

"Beginner's luck."

"I very much doubt that. No beginner catches an ace so completely off-guard. To continue—thanks to you three, the mission was highly successful. We got what we went there for; even more than was expected. In the fullness of time, what you helped us achieve today, might well help shorten the war. Well done! Now I'm certain you're all eager for breakfast."

"Rather!" Pew said. "I could eat a pig farm."

"Very er...colorful, Mr. Farley-Wyatt."

"Duchamps is turning into a real gunfighter," Murchison observed after they had gone. "According to Pew, he got Hagen with just a few moves, and economical shooting. No waste of ammo."

"De-winged the blighter," Hamilton said with approval. "He's certainly got the makings."

"I think he's earned his pirate ancestor's skull and crossbones."

"Of course he shall have them. What a romantic Yankee you are."

"Not a yankee. My genes come from the South. Hell, maybe I've even got some pirate blood, like Duchamps."

"My parents always said we've got blood from all over the country—English, Scottish, Irish, and Welsh. My mother's family are half Morgans. Perhaps there's some of old Sir Henry in me. That do?"

Murchison grinned. "It'll have to. There must be more like Duchamps in the States," he continued, grin vanishing. "I can't believe the thinking of the folks who turn their backs on that potential source of good fighter pilots. It's crazy."

"I'm going to be selfish. If they had, we would not have got the likes of Duchamps for Raven Squadron. Your lot would have had him."

"One way of looking at it."

Cambridge Boys squadron, Normandy, Occupied France. July, 1941. 1000 local.

To describe Stroeme as being furious, would have been massive understatement. He was livid. He glared at the hapless Fritz with cold, angry eyes.

Though dried-out after his involuntary dunking, Fritz looked bedraggled. He stood to attention before Stroeme, eyes fixed upon a far distance.

"You are, *Lieutenant* Fritz, a disgrace to this unit!" Though he did not shout, the coldness in Stroeme's voice was implacable. "You willfully disobeyed the standing orders of the squadron, and the unit in general. This means, you disobeyed the *Commandant!* You disobeyed the commander *himself* and in so doing, the *Führer!* Are you *insane...?*"

"Sir, I..."

"*Do not interrupt me, Lieutenant!*"

Fritz fell rigidly silent.

"Not content with disobeying the *Führer*, the *Commandant*, and the commander of the squadron—myself—you then proceeded to disobey the explicit orders of your section leader, *Lieutenant* Hagen. He ordered you not to engage the enemy outside the clearly defined airspace of this squadron. That limit is there for a purpose! In refusing his direct order more than once, you placed not only yourself at risk, but your section leader as well, and the security of the establishment we are sworn to protect! Your stupidity nearly cost him his life! Further, you cost the Reich two valuable aircraft, and for no loss to the enemy! *I should have you shot!*" Still glaring, Stroeme paused. "I want you *out* of this squadron! I have recommended to the *Commandant*, and he has approved, that you be transferred from this unit, to one on the Eastern Front. Meanwhile, you are grounded while you remain on this unit. That is all. Ask *Lieutenant* Hagen to come in. Now *get out!*"

Face stiff with humiliation and not a little anger, Fritz opened the door and marched out like a clockwork toy. He shut the door behind him.

"Your turn," he said to Hagen, who had heard most of the conversation through the closed door.

Hagen looked less haggard than Fritz, despite his unscheduled swim.

"To think I respected that man," Fritz hissed.

Hagen looked at him with merciless eyes. "Shut up!" he hissed back sharply. Then he went to the door, opened it, and entered without looking back at Fritz.

He shut the door quietly, coming to attention as he turned to face Stroeme.

"I take full responsibility, sir!"

Stroeme looked at him for long moments. "For what?"

"As you told me not so long ago, you would hold me responsible for Fritz's actions. I have no excuse."

Stroeme gave a world weary sigh. He waved to a chair. "Relax, and sit down, Michael."

Hagen looked uncertain.

"Come on. Sit down."

Hagen at last did so, perching himself on the edge of the hard chair.

"Fritz disobeyed explicit orders," Stroeme began. "He disobeyed everyone. You just happened to be at the end of that particular chain. You were heard ordering him to return."

"It was still my responsibility."

"Yes, it was. And you acted upon it. Had you not gone to his aid, the *Tommis* would not just have shot him down. He'd be dead. You could not have left him to them."

"I wasn't much help. I ended up in the drink as well."

"That's the part that intrigues me. What happened, exactly?"

"It was Fritz who first spotted them," Hagen began. "They were clearly out of area, and it seemed to me they had no intention of coming in. They stayed out to sea. But Fritz could not resist. It was three to one. I had to go in."

Stroeme nodded. "You had no option, once he'd broken ranks. Go on."

"As I went in, I saw their unusual paint scheme more clearly. They were all black—well, not a uniform black. There seemed to be various shades of black, all flowing into each other. It gave them a very indistinct shape that was also menacing. I never thought a Hurricane could look so fearsome. They were like black birds of prey. True predators.

"As I fell towards them, one which was a little away from the others, turned towards me, climbing, completely blocking me, preventing me from being of any help to Fritz. He was going for a head-to-head, I thought. Well, let's see how he liked the *Friedrich's* cannon barrage. But before I could fire, he rolled away in the climb, and was suddenly gone. Instinct made me break immediately. I was rolling when I heard his cannon shells striking. My wing was hit, but the *Friedrich* seemed fine. No control problems. Then I heard another thumping. I thought he'd got another shot in. Then my left wing just fell off. I just made it out of the cockpit in time."

"You did not underestimate him?"

Hagen gave a short, bitter laugh. "Underestimate! The way he turned towards me...there was no mistaking it. I knew at that moment that if I was not very, very careful, this man was going to kill me. No underestimating that."

"And he only shot *once?*"

Hagen nodded. "It was incredible. It was as if he knew exactly where my wing would be when I rolled. Looking back, I realize he was firing just before I began to roll. I literally fed my wing into his fire. It was as if he positioned his fire, and just waited for me to fly into it. Perhaps I met up with that *Tommi* of yours—the ace who flew between the trees."

"Perhaps. When I met him, he was not flying a black Hurricane; but you never know."

"He's efficient. I'll say that. He wastes no time, and no ammunition."

"There's admiration in your voice."

"You can't help admiring someone who flies, and shoots, like that. Like your *Tommi*. If I hadn't got out, I'd be dead. Up there, he's a killer."

Again, Stroeme nodded. "You're back in one piece. That's what matters." He paused. "I'm throwing Fritz off the squadron."

"I heard, sir."

"I was a little loud, I know. Alright, Michael. Thank you. Go and get into some fresh clothes, and something to eat."

"Yes, sir."

About an hour later, Stroeme had a visitor. Schelberg had returned.

"*Herr* Schelberg," Stroeme said as the Gestapo man entered his office. "I'm beginning to think you want to become a pilot."

"I'm afraid I have not got the necessary qualifies," Schelberg remarked with mild deprecation. "I could not handle one of those things, and I am far too old, even if I could."

"I doubt that you are too old, *Herr* Schelberg," Stroeme said with no hint of flattery.

Schelberg responded to this with the tiniest of smiles. "You are kind."

"*Herr* Schelberg," Stroeme continued, "I appreciate the visit but as I am certain you know by now, I lost two valuable planes this morning."

"Yes. It has been quite a morning. I am glad your pilots were recovered safely."

"No thanks to *Lieutenant* Fritz, who disobeyed unequivocal orders and cost us those planes."

"I can understand your annoyance."

"It is rather more than 'annoyance'."

"I quite understand. In your place, I might well have shot him on the spot. You are far more patient than I am."

Stroeme wondered what was really behind that oddly frank admission; and the visit; but before he could react, Schelberg was speaking again.

"We also had an...interesting morning," Schelberg went on smoothly. "We were visited by a remarkable aircraft. Not one we had ever seen before; very fast, very low, with twin engines, and all in black. No unit markings. Even the *Brigaderführer* thought it to be one of our secret projects. But of course, it was no such thing."

Already aware of the Mosquito, Stroeme stared at him. "You were *attacked?*"

Schelberg shook his head. "Not an attack. Just a visit. I believe the British were letting us know they have something virtually proof to interception. And not a single flak gun fired, so complete was the surprise. When the *Brigadeführer* wondered aloud what it was, I told him Nemesis."

"'*Nemesis*'?"

"Indeed. I think we had a privileged look at the first of many. A word of warning, Major. I believe the *Brigadeführer* may attempt to lay blame on you for the incursion; but of course, that would be nonsense. No one could have stopped that aircraft. He has just not got round to seeing that humbling truth as yet. The machines which tempted *Lieutenant* Fritz into rashly disobeying his orders, were an obvious decoy. It focused attention upon them, while our visitor sneaked in from the east."

"It had occurred to me. I have long warned my pilots of such an eventuality. Fritz is the only one not to have understood that."

"Ah, yes. Fritz."

Here it comes, Stroeme thought. *The real reason why you're here.*

Schelberg had paused, with theatrical timing. Then with seeming reluctance, said, "Major, there is something I must tell you. It is about *Lieutenant* Fritz."

Knowing he was not going to like it, Stroeme waited.

"Word has come from Berlin," Schelberg began, "that *Lieutenant* Fritz must be reinstated."

Stroeme was on his feet with outrage. "*What?* Are they insane?"

Schelberg seemed undisturbed by Stroeme's reaction. "Because of our recently shared...adventures, I shall overlook that comment." Though the familiar little smile lived briefly on his lips, there was no smile behind the glasses.

"*Herr* Schelberg, even the most incompetent senior commander would know that to reinstate someone like Fritz after being grounded for such gross and willful disobedience, not to mention insubordination, is in itself an undermining of the authority of the commander on the ground. It is a disaster for discipline! A squadron like ours is a close-knit organization. We depend upon discipline, trust, and respect. Losing any one of these components can result in someone's death...as nearly happened today. Countermanding my order adds something no unit wants to suffer, a blow to morale. How is it going to look to my pilots if the man I have grounded, a man they can no longer trust in the air, is reinstated by orders from Berlin? Is Berlin prepared to sacrifice the efficiency of an entire squadron—the very squadron tasked with the defense of the airspace above an establishment of great important to the Reich—for the sake of one junior pilot incapable of obeying orders? Is Berlin prepared to put all this in jeopardy for him?"

"You underestimate yourself, Major. Berlin has every confidence in your ability to ensure *Lieutenant* Fritz knows his place in the scheme of things."

"What is so special about him?"

"Nothing particularly special. But he has got—shall we say—friends in high places. He is a valued member of the Party. Many kills are expected of him."

You mean they want their little Nazi to remain on my squadron, Stroeme thought with contempt. He made certain his thoughts were not mirrored by his expression.

"I understand how you must feel, Major. In your place, I would not like it at all. However, I would also consider my options. Suppose I was in command of a pilot who had given me justifiable cause not only to ground him, but to have him posted to another unit, say on the Eastern Front. And suppose the interests of those greatly superior to me were not served by the dismissal of this pilot—I would consider whether I would not find myself in the pilot's place, heading for the Eastern Front. I would be leaving my pilots—who respect me—to the commander who replaced me, and who might not command the squadron at all well. I would also be leaving a valued…friend, to who knows what possible fate, this being war. I would ask myself whether I would wish to jeopardize all that, for one relatively insignificant pilot. I would ask myself whether I would sacrifice so much for what is…relatively speaking, so little. I really would."

"You are suggesting that I undermine my own command?"

"I suggest nothing. I am merely giving some friendly advice. I would not jeopardize all that, for the sake of pride."

Stroeme stared at the Gestapo man. "You believe this to be about *pride?*"

Schelberg got to his feet with slow deliberation. "You're right. You are much smarter than that." He paused again and looked about him, as if he were the one who would be forced to relinquish command. "Rommel and Guderian disobeyed explicit orders during our invasion. Today, we hold France."

"Inspired initiative—even when risky—is one thing. Terminal stupidity is quite another. Rommel was lucky. If the enemy had been organized enough to launch a counter-attack when his rush left him exposed for lack of fuel reserves, we would well *not* be holding France. What Fritz did was not inspired initiative. It was, as I've said, terminal stupidity, which barely escaped being fatal; while leaving two almost brand new *Friedrichs* at the bottom of the *Armel*. I do not find that particularly inspiring."

"Indeed. But the fact is, we *did* succeed. We *are* here."

"The war is not yet over, *Herr* Schelberg, as you yourself are well aware. Your comment to *Brigadeführer* Forst about Nemesis, tells me you are thinking beyond Party propaganda. It was a bold thing to say to him, under the circumstances."

Schelberg's eyes gave nothing away. "I am a man of many facets, Colonel."

"I am still a Major."

"Perhaps not for long," Schelberg said. "You see...I also have it on good authority that this squadron deserves a commander and deputy commander of suitable rank." Another pause. "I have been told that the ranks of Lieutenant-Colonel, and Major, have been mentioned. The *Commandant* has already been advised. I believe he raised no objection." Throughout, Schelberg had kept his hat firmly upon his head. He now raised it briefly, in salute. "I'll leave you to your duties, Colonel. I know you have much to think about."

He went out, leaving Stroeme to stare at the closing door.

For several seconds, Stroeme did not move. Then he picked up the phone, and called Dasinger. "Hans, in my office. In your own time."

Dasinger turned up quickly. "When you put it like that," he began, "my curiosity about what's really between the lines works every time. You know me too well."

"That being so, take a seat. You'll need it."

Dasinger listened in complete silence as Stroeme told him about Schelberg's repeat visit. When he was finished, Stroeme sat back and watched his deputy for reactions.

For several seconds, Dasinger said nothing: but his face had clouded over. Then he got to his feet. "Those *stupid* bastards in Berlin!"

"Careful, Hans. Like me, you've got people you care about. They have many methods of exerting pressure. Schelberg was very good at hinting just how many."

"How can they do that to us? How can they do this to you? It is bad for discipline! Do they want a fighter unit? Or a Party flying club?"

"They are sweetening the pill."

"You can't be bought with rank, and neither can I. Taking back the little shit is not worth it! We treated him as just another eager kid, even though we considered his 'true believer' attitude a joke. But now, it's no longer a joke. It is threatening squadron cohesion."

"How old's your sister, Hans?"

The unexpected question made Dasinger pause. "Just turned fifteen. Why?"

"How would you like her to be a chosen vessel for an SS man or two, or three?"

Dasinger paled. "They wouldn't...!"

"You've heard Schelberg's words. Not specific threats. But many 'facets', as he put it. The fact is, Hans, they have got our country by the throat. They can do what they want. Ever since we failed to knock out the Royal Air Force, we are...'suspect' in some quarters. Perhaps they feel they need to 'strengthen' our resolve with selected 'true believers'."

"Like Fritz."

"Like Fritz. They want him to score victories, so that he gets decorations, is rapidly promoted...you can guess the rest."

"Perhaps he'll meet some more *Tommis* like the ones he was introduced to today."

"Perhaps. In the meantime, I'm going to do what every good subordinate does. See my superior officer. If the *Commandant* is prepared to allow Fritz back, I can hardly go against his decision. I will not let him pay for my refusal to bend. They would take their revenge, and all three of us might end up on the Eastern Front, where a convenient accident might happen. You've got a young sister and the rest of your family to worry about; and I've got Marie, and my own family. As I've said, many points of pressure. Hold the fort while I see the *Commandant*."

"Readiness state the same as before Fritz and Hagen went in?"

"The same. Thank God we do not have a second Fritz."

The *Commandant* was standing in the same pose, and at the same window when Stroeme had last seen him in his office. It was almost as if he had never moved from the spot.

"Ah, Karl," Feldbruch said without turning from his scrutiny of the world beyond his window as Stroeme was shown in. "You've no doubt come about *Lieutenant* Fritz."

"Yes, sir. I had another visit from our friendly man from the Gestapo."

Feldbruch nodded to himself. "Schelberg," Feldbruch sounded as if someone had just passed a very bad smell beneath his nose. At last, he turned round. "Do I approve of Fritz's reinstatement? Most emphatically, *no*. Will I sign the order for his reinstatement? I have already done so. I am sorry, Karl. As I'm certain you have already found out, we have little choice in the matter. I'm making it difficult for you to maintain your perfectly correct stance on this matter. I hope I have perhaps saved you plenty of trouble from quarters you certainly do not want hounding you. In approving your promotion, and Hans Dasinger's to Lieutenant-Colonel, and Major, I am at least doing something I most certainly approve of. You both deserve it, without the crass ploy of the carrot these people believe they're offering."

Feldbruch turned back to the window. "The 1000-year Reich." He gave a bitter chuckle. "We are in July, 1941. If it lasts another four years—at the most—I shall be very surprised. Unfortunately, the nation's back will be broken by then, and it will have become a pariah nation whose name will be a bad word for decades, perhaps centuries. I wish there were a shortcut from now to then, to spare the suffering and humiliation. But like doomed actors, we must play the part to the bitter end, going through the motions until the full horrors of the corporal's ludicrous '*Endsieg*' is upon us."

Stroeme stood there, listening to his colonel.

"Whatever happens, I doubt I shall last out the war. If it does not take me, our friends in the Gestapo, and the SS, surely will. Don't worry, I am not going to lock myself in my quarters one day, and blow my head off. I would not give them the satisfaction."

Stroeme said nothing.

"My family live in Hamburg. When the time comes, try to see them for me."

"Yes, sir. I promise. But I am certain you'll be doing that yourself."

Feldbruch turned round again, with a tired smile. "Ever the optimist. Germany will need people like you; when those dark souls now feeding upon it are gone."

Stroeme realized that the colonel had repeated almost exactly what he had said previously, after that first visit by Schelberg and Forst. Obsessed by the path down which his country was being led, Feldbruch could see no way out.

"It's like being on a runaway train," Feldbruch said. "It is far too late to divert and subdue the maniacs in control. You know the train is going to crash; and all you can hope for is that this will not be too severe. Unfortunately—for us—it will be the worst of all crashes. Hold on to your humanity, Karl, if you can. You'll need it."

"Yes, sir." There was not much more he could have said, Stroeme decided. "What do you make of Schelberg, sir?" he added.

"What do *you?*" Feldbruch countered.

"I find him something of an enigma," Stroeme admitted. "I would feel safer tied to an angry cobra; but there is something else about him. He gives the impression of being a dedicated Nazi, in love with his horrible job. Yet...I get the feeling it's all on the outside."

"In it for the power?"

Stroeme nodded. "There is that aspect."

"He's not unique. The corporal has put power into the hands of people who should never have it. The results are plain to see; and Germany will pay savagely for that, for a long time to come."

"Something he said also intrigues. When that aircraft made its low pass over the château grounds, Forst wondered what type, believing it to be one of our secret projects. Schelberg answered 'Nemesis'."

Feldbruch said nothing for a few moments. "Perhaps he is more perceptive, than we believe."

"I would still choose the cobra."

"So would I. Whether he is dedicated to his *Führer* or not, he is probably more dedicated to himself. One other thing," Feldbruch went on. "Berlin wants that unit with the black aircraft found, and destroyed; or at least prevented from operating."

"Are we to do this?" Stroeme asked in surprise.

Feldbruch shook his head. "Our task remains the same. However, a second squadron, with more aircraft and dedicated to that task, will be coming here."

"Under your command?"

"No. You and I will have nothing to do with it. It will be a separate command, under Forst's direct authority."

"Are they mad? The *SS* in command of a Luftwaffe unit?"

"Forst will not have command in the accepted sense. But as the senior officer in our specific area he does—as you already know—have overall *administrative* command. However, in their wisdom, Berlin have taken the bizarre step of making the new squadron answerable only to him, bypassing me."

"I'm sorry..."

"Don't be. I am relieved, as a matter of fact. When it all goes wrong, as it will, it will be Forst's head; not mine. They have learned nothing from *Adler Tag*. The same fuel constraints apply. And the British will be waiting to trap them over land and chew them to pieces."

"For all they know, that unit, wherever it might be, could be well inland..."

"And costly in fuel. I suspect few will return from there. I told them it was not feasible. They did not openly call me defeatist; but it was there in their attitude to my comments. They simply do not want to know."

"What aircraft will this squadron be using?"

"*Friedrichs*. Half will be fitted with a mix of high-explosive, high-incendiary bombs. The other half will act as escorts. The idea is that once the bombs are gone, those aircraft will once again revert to being fighters, and be able to fight their way back home."

"They'll be sitting ducks on the way in."

"I warned them of that too. They chose not to listen. The destruction of that unit takes precedence."

"And the pilots who've got to do this?"

"All. Including their commander, hand-picked for political 'soundness'. From various units."

"Perhaps we should offer Fritz to them," Stroeme said with some bite.

This actually got a brief smile out of Feldbruch. "That would be the perfect solution to our little problem. But I believe they would refuse the suggestion. They want him to remain with us. They're at war with us, Karl. They're at war with anyone who does not follow their tune; German, and non-German."

"And when do these wonder boys arrive?"

"In August, which is just a week away. But their advance guard will be arriving any day. Forst sat here and practically gloated. The pilots, and other personnel, he said, could easily be members of the SS. He also remarked that your Cambridge Blue tails have given him an idea. To make certain there will be no mistaking the difference between the squadrons, he's considering having SS runes painted on the tails."

"An SS squadron in Luftwaffe uniform. Wonderful. I can see many of them taking up that one-way ticket to Britain the *Tommis* offered us last year. Those tails will draw their attention like magnets, accompanied by cannon shells."

"'Come to Britain and stay'," Feldbruch quoted with a low chuckle. "Bizarre sense of humor, these *Tommis*. You ought to be familiar with it, Karl, having been to Cambridge."

"It does take some getting used to," Stroeme admitted.

CHAPTER THIRTEEN

Raven Squadron flightline, Shawbridge. July 1941, 1255 local.
Duchamps was walking slowly round the black Mosquito. Like the Hurricanes, its paint scheme was a mixture of varying shades of black, giving it the unreal presence that Hagen had observed on the Hurricanes he had so briefly encountered. The RAF roundels were there, on the wings and fuselage; but they too were silhouettes of themselves, marked out just slightly more prominently than the overall color scheme. It was very easy to miss them.

He now stood just in front of the left wing, admiring the lines of the port engine nacelle.

"Want one of those for Christmas?" a voice said from somewhere to his left.

Recognizing the voice, he whirled to see Hamilton standing a short distance away, legs slightly apart, hands behind his back.

"Er...sir! Er..." Duchamps paused in slight confusion. "Well, sir, I love my Hurricane."

"But you'd like to have a go in one of these."

"When she's got some teeth...yes, sir."

"Well as we'll be having some with teeth at some stage, I'll keep that in mind."

Duchamps' grin of pleasure was unrestrained. "Yes, sir!"

"And...I'm recommending you for a gong. The DFC."

Duchamps was astonished. Uncertain of how to react, his gave a slightly stuttered response. "Th...thank you, sir!"

"Don't thank me. You deserve it."

"And the others, sir?"

Hamilton gave a tolerant smile. "Thinking about your men. Good show. Don't worry. They won't go hungry, if your flight keeps performing like this."

Duchamps nodded.

"Mr. Duchamps."

"Sir?"

"After her foray into enemy airspace earlier today, I plan to take the Mossie up for an air test. I was hoping to persuade our Yank from the South, Wing Commander Murchison, to fill the spare seat. But it occurred to me that if something went wrong, the brass hats at His Majesty's Air Ministry might not take too kindly to losing both wing commanders in an air test. As you happen to be another Yank from the South and clearly have a certain liking for..."

"*Yes, sir!*" the eager Duchamps said.

"Well. Interrupting a wing commander in full flow is not the done thing, but as you have volunteered so smartly, perhaps you should hurry up and get your kit."

"I'm a dot," Duchamps said.

Hamilton watched him go, with a ghost of a smile.

By the time Duchamps returned, Hamilton had his gear on, and was waiting.

"Commendably quick, Mr. Duchamps. As a PR Mossie, she of course has only single controls, so if you do not mind the navigator's perch..."

"Don't mind at all, sir."

"Good show. You'll still have a sense of what she can do. And you've got a silly grin on, Mr. Duchamps."

"Yes, sir."

Duchamps watched with interest as Hamilton went through the final take-off checks, following the wing commander's swift motions.

Elevator trim—slightly nose heavy; rudder—slightly right; ailerons—neutral; props at max RPM: fuel cocks—fully on; flaps at 25 degrees; radiators open.

"Raven Zero-One," he called, "ready for takeoff."

"Raven Zero-One," the tower said. "Clear takeoff."

"Roger," Hamilton responded. "Zero-One clear takeoff."

In the right hand seat, Duchamps watched as Hamilton moved the throttles forward. The Mosquito gathered speed rapidly, twin Merlins on sweet song. He glanced to his left and right, as if checking. They looked beautiful, he thought.

Within moments, the Mosquito was airborne. Hamilton kept it low, as the speed built and the flaps and wheels were raised.

"I almost always keep the superchargers on auto," Hamilton said. "One less thing to worry about." He banked the aircraft steeply as the speed continued to build. "Let's go and say hello to the Welsh mountains. She's in her element at high, or low altitudes. How are you enjoying it so far?"

"Wow!" Duchamps exclaimed. "She handles like a fighter!"

"She does. And she will be used as such. Among other things. When she has teeth, one of her fits will be four cannon in the belly, and four machine guns in the nose. Eight-gunned teeth."

"I like the sound of that!"

In the mountains, Hamilton treated Duchamps to the kind of low-flying that had once astonished Stroeme. The Mosquito was threaded between peaks, along valleys, river courses, and sent hurtling up steep slopes in a manner that was breath-robbing. At all tunes, the Merlin engines sang their sweet song.

As they returned to Shawbridge and Hamilton went through the landing checks, Duchamps noted that full flaps was 45 degrees, though the gauge went up to 70 degrees.

Hamilton caught the gaze. "Well spotted," he said. "One of her idiosyncrasies. Full flaps are *always* at 45."

Hamilton landed with panache, and taxied back.

"Well, Mr. Duchamps," he said as they climbed out. "You've got that silly grin on. I take you liked the ride. Do you still want one with teeth when it becomes available?"

"I still love my Hurricane, sir. But yes, I want a Mossie with teeth as well!"

"I'm certain that can be arranged. On this unit, we expect Ravens to be able to do many things." There was an expression of approval on Hamilton's face.

Duchamps gave the wing of the aircraft a gentle stroke.

"Mr. Duchamps," Hamilton said. "I nearly forgot." He fished into a pocket, and took out a small square envelope. "This came for you, via routes unknown. A carrier pigeon with Danish nationality, most likely." He hand it over with a fleeting smile.

"Thank you, sir."

Duchamps opened it with barely restrained eagerness.

I hope we survive this war, he read silently. *I want to have your baby. Helle.*

He made a kind of strangled sound that was an expressive mixture of delight, astonishment, and scarcely believing his luck.

"Everything alright, Mr. Duchamps?" Hamilton seemed to have a smile on.

"Sir...er...yes, sir! Er...may I...?"

"On your way, Mr. Duchamps. Enjoy your letter."

Duchamps nodded and went off, head down, re-reading the few words as if wanting to be ensure they would not vanish off the paper.

Hamilton was still watching the receding figure of Duchamps roughly a minute later, when Murchison came round the aircraft.

"It's a bitch having to read other people's mail first," he said.

"It isn't a pleasant task; I'll grant you; but the war demands censoring. I'd rather read my own aircrew's letters, than have some faceless bod in some office somewhere doing it. He must have re-read those few lines ten times in as many paces. I hope they make it."

"No one said life was fair," Murchison said. "But I hope they do. So?" he continued. "How did it go?"

"He loves the Mossie."

"And does he have what it takes?"

"Oh yes. He was itching to have a go. Had this been the twin-control trainer, I'd have let him."

"And I suppose you gave him that crap about the Air Ministry not wanting to lose two wingcos at one go."

"I did."

"You're a devious bastard, you know that?"

"I'm a wing commander. I'm supposed to be devious. And so are you."

Murchison gave a gruff chuckle. "Speaking of devious...we'll need to be at our most. Got the word from my people about some news from Berlin. Seems the Ravens have poked a hornet's nest. They're setting up a specialist squadron, dedicated to taking us out...if they can find us."

Hamilton stared at him. "Really? Any more on that?"

"Only that the squadron—which is to be based, of all places—at Cagey's airfield, are made up of people our sources describe as SS in Luftwaffe uniform; hardcase, true believers. That's about all that came through. Should make it a pleasure to kill the bastards. Kind of ironic. We give Tad the skull and crossbones on his tail, and these guys seem to be the type who would wear the death's head on their caps, if they had a different uniform."

"Interesting, *and* fitting, I would say. Perhaps Karl will be able to get more details to us."

"And meanwhile?"

"We plan. Deviously."

Intelligence Unit, Whitehall. Photo Interpretation section. July, 1941. 1300 local.

The films from the PR Mosquito had all been developed, and some photographs were spread out on a wide table. An RAF corporal was fiddling with two prints, maneuvering them into position. Then he picked up something that looked like a child's idea of a pair of glasses, and flipped down a pair of spindly legs at each end. He placed this on the photographs, and peered through it.

A 3D image appeared.

He studied it for some time, frowning slightly. Then he straightened, and leaving the "glasses" in place, went to a young female officer who was looking through a similar set at another table.

"'scuse, me ma'am."

She looked up at him. "Yes?"

"Have a look through my stereoscope, ma'am. I'd like your permission to have that part of the photo enlarged."

She followed him to his table, and looked through the scope. She said nothing for a while, studying what she saw.

At last, she straightened. "Plenty of flak guns," she said.

"Not what I meant, ma'am. There's something by those trees, next to one of the flak guns."

"The section you want enlarged."

"Yes, ma'am."

"I trust your judgement, John," she said. At times, when no one else was near, she addressed him by his first name. "Have it done. Priority. Then I'll have another look."

"Thank you, ma'am."

It did not take long. When the prints of the section in question had arrived, he quickly set them up, and looked again.

He gasped. "My God!" He hurried over to the officer. "Ma'am. You should see this."

She came to look and as with him. a gasp escaped her. Near the flak gun, and being hurried under cover by two men in SS uniform as the aircraft had passed, was a small group of people. Some of them, being naturally curious, were looking up at the unseen camera. Small faces were looking up at her.

"*Children*," she breathed. "What are children doing in that place? How many do you think are down there?" she asked the corporal.

"I've counted ten. At least. Others are probably already under cover."

She nodded, and began to gather up the new enlargements. "I'll take these through. Good work, John. Borrow your 'scope?"

"Of course, ma'am."

Brigadier's office. Intelligence Unit, Whitehall. July, 1941. 1415, local.

"*Children?*" the Brigadier exclaimed. "Are you certain?"

"Take a look for yourself, sir," the officer said. "John Graham, my corporal, is one of the best interpreters we've got. He spotted something on the main print, and asked for that section to be enlarged. What you'll see, is what that section was hiding."

She had laid the photographs on the general's desk. She placed the scope over them, and stood back as he went forward to lean over for a look.

"My God," he said. "You're right! What the devil are *children* doing there? To put them out into the open so that we can't bomb the place?"

"I don't think so, sir. It's a medical research center..." She let her words hang, but their meaning was clear. "It fits in with some of the rumors we've been getting," she added.

He nodded slowly. "It does tally with something Alistair James hinted at. Great pity about him. Great pity we did not get the proof. Good work, Babs."

"Good work, John Graham," she corrected. "I would have missed it completely."

He pointed to the photographs. "Keep these, shall I?"

She nodded. "We can have more copies made if you need them." She picked up the 'scope. "Have to take this back."

"I'm sure I can find one somewhere." The general's eyes seemed to have a twinkle in them. As she was about to leave, he said, "Not sweet on that young man, are you? But for the war, you two would never have met."

"The war is changing many things, Daddy."

"You from an old Army family. Joining the RAF. Nothing short of scandalous." But he smiled as he said that. "Natural class barriers dropping..."

"Nothing natural about those barriers, Daddy. You can always talk to your friends and have him commissioned...or have me demoted to corporal." She went out before he could say more.

"Humph," he said. "Damned youth of today." But he gave another smile, which vanished as he stared at the photographs. "One for Haines, I think."

Outskirts of Macon, Georgia. July, 2006. 1425 hours, local.

"Yep. One for me, on top of the others. Called me back, just before I was about to go over, to give me the glad news."

Haines was still in his study, looking out upon a world he knew he would soon be leaving.

"By now, the black Icarus was approaching ace status. *Big goddamned hero!* A nigger with a gun is bad enough; but here was a goddamned nigger with a goddamned potent aeroplane, killing white folk." Haines gave a sudden cackle. "Boy. That would have had some people back home back then, all worked up. Nigger officer from the South, in the British air force, *and* well on his way to becoming a goddamned ace. And Helle...*my* Helle..."

Haines stopped, mind switched back in time, to the war years.

"God *damn* you, Duchamps! Why'd you take her from me? *Why?*"

In all those decades, Haines could still not bring himself to accept that Helle was never his, and never would have been, even if she had never met Duchamps. For over sixty years, the fantasy of Duchamps' "theft" had gnawed at him.

Downstairs, Martha watched from one of the salons with heightened curiosity, as a dark green SUV pulled up before the colonnaded entrance of the old mansion. Three men in suits got out, one of them black. He hung back slightly, as they approached in a gaggle.

"Smell like government to me," she murmured, leaving the room to go to the tall double door.

She opened it at the first ring. "Can I help you?" Her eyes raked them, and did not like what they saw.

The one apparently in command smiled at her. His own eyes, however, bore a strange chill. It put Martha instantly on her guard, though she gave no outward indication of this.

"Beautiful old house," the man began as his opening gambit.

"It's old," she said, looking at him with an unwavering stare. "Can I help you?" she repeated.

"We're here to see Senator Haines."

"Do you have an appointment? He's kind of old, and we need to arrange these things. Usually, he gets his daytime sleep about this time."

"We won't be long."

"Who is it, Martha?" came Emma-Mae's voice as she approached.

Martha waited until she had joined her. "These...gentleman say they want to see the senator."

Emma-Mae was apology itself. "I'm so sorry," she said to them. "The senator's up in his study, and he usually has his sleep..."

"We won't disturb him for long, Mrs. Haines. I promise. It's matter of national importance."

"What would he have to do with national security? The senator retired a long time ago. He's just an old man who sleeps most of the day."

"You know how it is, Mrs. Haines. Once in, never out." The man smiled, as if to a confidante. Again, his eyes held the cold stillness of a dead pond.

"Why don't you let them in?" Martha suggested, her look probing at them. "The senator won't mind. I guess. If it's national security..."

"I didn't say..." the man began to protest.

"You said 'national importance'," Martha interrupted. "That's just another way of saying national security."

The man did not like being interrupted, but he let it pass. "You're a smart lady."

"I'm smart," she said. "I bet you've got some ID." She waited until they began fishing into their suits for some form of identification.

With obvious exasperation, they showed her their ID's.

"I've never heard of your people," she said. "You could be anyone. It's all alphabet soup."

The man was getting impatient. "Lady, we've showed you our ID's. Now can we please see the senator?"

"Miss Emma," Martha said, eyes still on the men, "why don't you show these...gentlemen up to the senator, while I make them all something to drink?"

"What? Oh! Yes. Alright. Come with me, please, gentlemen."

She turned, nodding back at them to follow.

As they filed in, the black one hung back slightly, to whisper at Martha, "You give the orders around here?"

"You taking them like a good boy?" she snapped.

Her glared at her, and walked stiffly on.

She watched them go, then hurried to a room that was not the kitchen. It was the downstairs gunroom, for which she had the key.

She went to the enclosed gun rack. She had the key for that too.

She took a pump shotgun from the many guns there, and loaded it. She took some spare ammunition.

Led by Emma-Mae, the three men in suits entered Haines' study.

"Would you leave us for a moment, please, Mrs. Haines?" the man in command said.

Haines seemed to have roused himself, and was staring at the men. "Leave us, Emma-Mae," he said, in an unexpectedly firm voice. He kept his eyes on the men. "I know your type," he continued to them when the door had closed behind his wife. "I used to be like you, once. Why are you here? To shoot me?" He cackled at them.

"You have some people worried, Senator." The man who seemed to be doing all the talking began.

"Do I?"

"Your granddaughter flew down to see you. According to the airline records, she did not fly back. Yet she is in New York."

"Last I heard there were buses, trains, cars, motorbikes, bicycles, horses, feet..."

"This isn't funny, Senator."

"Damned right it isn't!" Haines snarled in a sudden shout. "You bust into my house uninvited! What the hell right have you got, coming here questioning me? *Me!* I've done more for this country than you can ever imagine. Or you ever will! Get out! Get the hell out!"

"Senator..."

"You heard the man!" a voice said from the doorway.

The three suits snapped round to look. Martha, with the shotgun.

"This thing in my hands makes a Godawful mess at close range. I can use it."

Haines gave another cackle. "And she can. Best goddamned shot in this house, after me. *And I'm good.* Even now. A nigger with a gun. Your nightmare."

The black suit snapped his head round at Haines with a look of contempt. "You let him talk about you like that?" He said to Martha, still looking at Haines.

"Talk about me like what?" she countered. "What you should be asking yourself is if I'll use this. Easy answer. I will. You're intruders..."

"Lady," the one in command began.

"Stop calling me that. You know you don't mean it. Now, like the senator says...*get the hell out!*" She emphasized the command with a short jerk of the gun.

"You're making a bad mistake."

"Not as bad as someone who's going to get a great big shotgun hole in his belly. I can get all three of you before you can reach any gun you've got on you. So. Are you moving? Or do you need some encouragement? There's one round already in."

Haines, eyes lively, was looking from Martha to the men and back again, a tiny smile hovering about the corners of his mouth.

"Move it!" Martha snapped.

After some stubborn hesitation, the men began to leave. Standing back to let them through, Martha followed. A puzzled Emma-Mae, worry and fear of the unknown creasing her forehead, trailed at a safe distance.

When they were back downstairs and at the front door, the man paused. "Lady..."

"You call me that one more time and I swear I'll shoot you where you stand. My name's *Martha!*"

"Look. Martha...we're on the wrong foot here..."

"The only foot you're on, is the one that takes you and your robot friends, out of here! Now move!"

"We're government..."

"Tell you what, Mr. 'Government'—when you're gone, I'll call the sheriff, have him check you out. If you're really 'government', he's sure to find out. Then he can come back with you, to talk with the senator. But I got the feeling that won't happen."

"This is way above the sheriff."

"I'll bet it is, Mr. 'Government'. Say goodbye."

The man gave her a cold stare. "You're making a big mistake."

"Life's full of mistakes. See that you don't make one with me. *Out!*" The men filed out.

* * *

Up in the study, Haines had already gone back to his memories.

"Word came." he reminisced, "that a new enemy squadron, hand-picked pilots, and planes with SS tails, was being formed with one objective in mind...to destroy the Raven unit. But they had to find it first. Hamilton and Murchison began planning its defense. But although the anti-aircraft defenses were beefed up until they could plaster the air with shells all across our airspace, the two wing commanders planned that the enemy would not even reach the target, if he ever discovered where it was. The fight was to be taken to the enemy while he was still over the Channel, on the way in.

"Our black Icarus, Duchamps, meanwhile, had got himself decorated. The first of many to come. Hamilton recommended him for the Distinguished Flying Cross, and gave him permanent command of a four-ship flight. The rank was to go with this not there yet but that too, would follow.

"Our black Icarus was really flying high. God damn him!"

Haines calmed down, and picked up the mobile handset he carried around, to make a call.

"Lowell Johnson," came the ebullient voice.

"Lowell, it's Leroy Haines again."

"Always a pleasure, Senator. Everything okay with..."

"No problems as far as I know," Haines cut in, as if not wanting Johnson to say more. "I'm calling about something else."

"Just say what it is, and we'll handle it."

"Can you find some time to come over?"

Johnson paused, clearly taken by surprise. "Of course. When?"

"How about today? How about right now?"

Johnson paused again. "I'll have to move a meeting, but that's no problem."

"Thanks, Lowell. I appreciate it. It's that time." It was a long prearranged signal.

This time, Johnson's pause was barely noticeable. "I'll be right there." They hung up quickly.

Haines looked at the handset. "Won't have given them enough time to pick up on this."

* * *

Johnson came round the back of the grounds, driving a taxi along the unpaved lane that bordered it. The lane ended at a high, gated entrance to the garden. Martha was waiting to let him in.

She looked at the taxi, which was not new, but in perfect condition. "Still got that old thing?"

"It reminds me of where I come from. If my business ever goes belly up. I can go back to being what I was. I owe the senator plenty."

She told him about the men in the SUV. "Any of their friends around back there?" she asked.

Johnson shook his head. "They haven't gotten round to thinking about it, maybe. They don't expect an old senator to run out on them. I'll go on up."

She nodded. "I've gotten all we need, all ready."

"Ah, Lowell," Haines, dressed to go out, greeted when Johnson entered the study. "Good of you to come."

"It's never a trouble, Senator. The chopper's waiting, and the house up by the lake has always been kept ready for you. So it's happened," Johnson added.

"Had to come one day. And don't you go getting into trouble on my account, y'hear? Just get us up there, and we'll be fine."

"I can arrange some security..."

"That would be like setting off a beacon. The more low-key we keep it, the better. Martha's a damned good shot, and I can still shoot straight. We'll be fine."

"If I didn't know better, I'd say you look...energized."

"Reminds me of the days way back when. Perhaps one last action before I go, might not be a bad thing."

Johnson looked uncertain. "I can still arrange security. But if you're sure..."

"I'm sure. Having a bunch of security men round the place...might as well shout it out loud. No Lowell...but thanks. Now let's get out of here before those idiots out front wake up."

"You got it, senator. I'll have a caretaker company come over and look after the house. It won't be linked to me."

"Good."

Half an hour later the taxi left with the women and Haines, and Johnson at the wheel. There were no men in SUVs to observe their hasty departure. It would take those watching the front a long time to discover what had happened.

Teterboro airport, New York. July, 2006. 1800 local.
 Mary Adams lifted the small jet off the runway as if in a fighter.
 Mike Nolan, in the right-hand seat, glanced at her and said, "Bet you wish this was an F-16."
 "No," she said, "This little bird will do me just fine."
 He grinned at her as she banked onto a course that would take them across the Atlantic.
In the passenger cabin, Ellen and Duchamps were sitting opposite each other. "How does it feel?" she asked.
 "The jet?"
 She shook her head. "Going over to where it all happened."
 He took a while before he answered. "As if I'm following ghosts. You?"
 "Now that we're on the plane, heading there, it...feels as if something's pulling at me. But I don't know what. Or why. It's a weird feeling."
 She looked out of the window as they headed eastwards.
 As with Haines, it would be an even longer time before those who were following them began to realize that their quarry was gone.

LOOKING FOR ACTION & ADVENTURE
AUTHOR ALAN CAILLOU
DELIVERS !

AVAILABLE IN PAPERBACK AND EBOOK

REVISIT THE COLD WAR WITH INTERNATIONAL BESTSELLING AUTHOR
DENNIS JONES

AVAILABLE FROM CALIBER BOOKS IN PAPERBACK AND EBOOK

DON'T MISS ANY OF MICHAEL KASNER'S HARD HITTING MILITARY NOVEL SERIES

BLACK OPS

Formed by an elite cadre of government officials, the Black OPS team goes where the law can't - to seek retribution for acts of terror directed against Americans anywhere in the world.

3 BOOK SERIES

Armed with all the tactical advantages of modern technology, battle hard and ready when the free world is threatened - the Peacekeepers are the baddest grunts on the planet.

4 BOOK SERIES

CHOPPER COPS

America is being torn apart as criminal cartels terrorize our cities, dealing drugs and death wholesale. Local police are outgunned, so the President unleashes the U.S. TACTICAL POLICE FORCE. An elite army of super cops with ammo to burn, they swoop down on the hot spots in sleek high-tech attack choppers to win the dirty war and take back America!

4 BOOK SERIES

FROM CALIBER BOOKS
www.calibercomics.com

FROM FANTASY AND SCIENCE FICTION
AUTHOR ROLAND J. GREEN
THREE EPIC SERIES

FROM CALIBER BOOKS IN PAPERBACK AND EBOOK

CALIBER BOOKS BRINGS HOME MICHAEL KOSSER'S

FIRST FRONTIER ADVENTURE NOVELS

AVAILABLE IN PAPERBACK AND EBOOK

THUNDER IN THE EAST
Beginning of the French and Indian War (1756)
First Frontier Series – Book 1

SILENT DRUMS
Pontiac's Rebellion (1763-1765)
First Frontier Series – Book 2

SHADOWS ON THE LONGHOUSE
The American Revolution (1775-1781)
First Frontier Series – Book 3

MICHAEL KOSSER
writing as Mike Roarke

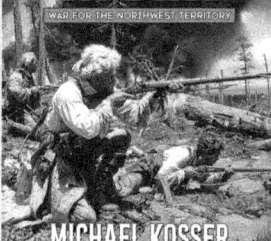

BLOOD RIVER
War for the Northwest Territory
First Frontier Series – Book 4

MICHAEL KOSSER
writing as Mike Roarke

www.ingramcontent.com/pod-product-compliance
Lightning Source LLC
LaVergne TN
LVHW051543070426
835507LV00021B/2370